The Social in the Global

How do influential social ideas contribute to global governance? This book takes an original approach to international relations by looking at the way social ideas help to portray the world in a particular way. Jonathan Joseph begins by analysing the role of important concepts such as globalisation, global civil society, social capital, networks and risk; then examines the role these concepts play in the discourse of international organisations. Using the concept of governmentality, he argues that contemporary social theories help justify contemporary forms of governance. By comparing organisations like the EU and the World Bank, Joseph investigates the extent to which these ideas are influential in theory and in practice.

JONATHAN JOSEPH is Reader in Politics and International Relations at the University of Kent. His areas of research span politics, international relations, social theory and philosophy of social science.

Cambridge Studies in International Relations: 122

The Social in the Global

Cambridge Studies in International Relations is a joint initiative of Cambridge University Press and the British International Studies Association (BISA). The series will include a wide range of material, from undergraduate textbooks and surveys to research-based monographs and collaborative volumes. The aim of the series is to publish the best new scholarship in International Studies from Europe, North America and the rest of the world.

Cambridge Studies in International Relations

121 Brian C. Rathbun
Trust in international cooperation
International security institutions, domestic politics and American multilateralism

120 A. Maurits van der Veen
Ideas, interests and foreign aid

119 Emanuel Adler and Vincent Pouliot
International practices

118 Ayşe Zarakol
After defeat
How the East learned to live with the West

117 Andrew Phillips
War, religion and empire
The transformation of international orders

116 Joshua Busby
Moral movements and foreign policy

115 Séverine Autesserre
The trouble with the Congo
Local violence and the failure of international peacebuilding

114 Deborah D. Avant, Martha Finnemore and Susan K. Sell
Who governs the globe?

113 Vincent Pouliot
International security in practice
The politics of NATO-Russia diplomacy

112 Columba Peoples
Justifying ballistic missile defence
Technology, security and culture

111 Paul Sharp
Diplomatic theory of international relations

110 John A. Vasquez
The war puzzle revisited

Series list continues after index

The Social in the Global

Social Theory, Governmentality and Global Politics

JONATHAN JOSEPH

CAMBRIDGE
UNIVERSITY PRESS

University Printing House, Cambridge CB2 8BS, United Kingdom

Published in the United States of America by Cambridge University Press, New York

Cambridge University Press is part of the University of Cambridge.

It furthers the University's mission by disseminating knowledge in the pursuit of education, learning and research at the highest international levels of excellence.

www.cambridge.org
Information on this title: www.cambridge.org/9781107416703

First published 2012
First paperback edition 2014

A catalogue record for this publication is available from the British Library

Library of Congress Cataloguing in Publication data
Joseph, Jonathan, 1970–
The social in the global : social theory, governmentality and global politics / Jonathan Joseph.
pages cm. – (Cambridge studies in international relations ; 122)
Includes bibliographical references and index.
ISBN 978-1-107-02290-4
1. International relations–Social aspects. 2. International cooperation–Social aspects. 3. Civil society. 4. International agencies. I. Title.
JZ1251.J67 2012
306.2–dc23
2012013661

ISBN 978-1-107-02290-4 Hardback
ISBN 978-1-107-41670-3 Paperback

Contents

Acknowledgements

This book has been a long time in the making. I first thought of the project somewhere on Aberystwyth sea front while on my way to the weekly International Politics research seminar. At that time my interest lay almost entirely with social theory and my concern was with the role that various new social ideas might be playing in undermining, de-motivating or dismissing various forms of collective social action. Over the following ten years, the focus has changed, but the central idea remains the same. International organisations have entered into the picture along with ideas like global governance. Most recently I have benefited from the emergence of a specific IR literature on global governmentality. However, this remains very much a social theory book, albeit one for IR scholars.

A book that has taken this long to figure out obviously incurs debts to a lot of people. After Aberystwyth I took the project briefly to Kobe and then to the University of Kent. I have benefited tremendously from discussions with colleagues and students at each of these places as well as at research seminars, like Sussex and Lancaster that have allowed me to present my ideas. I particularly want to thank Ruth Blakeley and Anna Stavrianakis, who both read almost the entire manuscript and offered numerous helpful comments. Among the many others I should mention are David Chandler, Bob Jessop, Ray Kiely, John Roberts, Justin Rosenberg, Richard Sakwa, Jan Selby, Doug Stokes and Colin Wight.

I also wish to thank the series editors, Christian Reus-Smit and Nicholas Wheeler. Nick has been particularly supportive over the years of my indulgence in social theory. I am especially grateful to the editors for choosing such helpful referees. Although I haven't done full justice to their many comments, this is a much better and more coherent book as a consequence. John Haslam and the staff at Cambridge University Press have been very helpful.

Finally, my thanks to all the family, to my wife Ai and daughter Hannah. Especially for their patience while my thoughts were elsewhere.

PART I

Governmentality and social theory

1 Introduction: social theory, governmentality and global politics

In taking the title *The Social in the Global*, this book attempts to combine social theory with International Relations (IR) theory. However, while the combination of the terms social and global clearly invites a sociological reading of International Relations, this book is also concerned with the relationship in practice – that is to say, how social theory contributes to the practices of global governing. The concept of governmentality is used to explain this latter relationship.

The Cold War prevented IR from finding its sociological feet. It was only with its ending that IR theory was finally able to move away from the asocial and ahistorical accounts of state behaviour and rational self-interest typical of mainstream security concerns. Consequently, the discipline is still some years behind other social sciences in its uptake of 'new' ideas. Such is the case with the theory of governmentality, an argument associated with the French theorist Michel Foucault and developed by governmentality scholars in anglophone sociology to account for the complex techniques used to manage populations and regulate social conduct. Only recently have these arguments started to influence IR theory. Part of the aim of the book is to show the contribution the theory of governmentality can make to an understanding of global politics. Another aim, as the subtitle implies, is to show how a theory of governmentality can help explain rival social theories. Indeed, the book will show the relationship between social theory and global politics as mediated through the role of governmentality.

Governmentality – notwithstanding some of the ambiguities of its meaning to be explored later – is an idea dealing with governance and the 'conduct of conduct' to shape particular dispositions within liberal or even advanced liberal societies. Many governmentality scholars in sociology have gone further and given the concept a specifically neoliberal meaning, looking at its connections to the operations of the market and a rationality of enterprise and risk-taking.[1] As far as the international context is concerned, the question that arises is, to what extent can the international be treated as a liberal or neoliberal domain? In addressing this, the book argues that the international is highly uneven in nature, and that consequently the way that governmentality can be applied – either in theory or in practice – is a matter to be decided in each particular case.

This contribution seeks to stress the positive aspects of applying the concept of governmentality to international relations. It welcomes the new IR literature in this area and tries to engage positively with it. But it also argues that we need to be sensitive to how the concept is applied and to pay close attention to how governmentality works (or does not work) in practice. While this is obviously a call to heed the specificity of international relations, it is also clearly a social theoretical issue. To explain the different workings of governmentality in various parts of the world, it is necessary to take into account the nature of these different societies. What is it about particular social conditions that allows governmentality to work well in some parts of the world but not others?

Simply put, the international comprises many different states and societies and some are more open to the techniques of governmentality than others. Nevertheless, that does not mean that attempts to implement governmentality cannot be made in those parts of the world that are not best characterised as liberal societies. Here lies the particular interest in trying to understand global politics and such ideas as global governance. International organisations like the World Bank and International Monetary Fund, representative as they are of the dominant forms of liberal and neoliberal thinking, do in fact attempt to implement governmentality in places where social conditions are quite different from those in the places where the techniques of governmentality first developed. Thus what is interesting here is the way that a series of practices and techniques that have developed in the advanced liberal societies (to borrow Rose's (1996) term) are being deployed by international organisations that reflect this way of thinking and whose governing structures are dominated by the most powerful states. We nevertheless see these practices and techniques coming up against the

[1] See Burchell (1996); Dean (1999, 2007); Rose (1996). For Foucault's own views on views on neoliberalism see Foucault (2008).

limits of international relations if we understand by the international, a set of different states, societies and geopolitical contexts characterised by different or uneven levels of development. Thanks to these exercises in global governance we find the neoliberal rationality of advanced liberal societies coming up against the stubborn reality of different international situations.

Here, then, the concept of governmentality can most usefully be developed in new directions by examining different international contexts and the extent to which governmentality does or does not apply. But this project remains faithful to a sociological approach in that it tries to give an explanation for the varying levels of applicability of governmentality by looking at its social conditions of possibility. Indeed, this is a social approach that many Foucauldians themselves choose not to take – prone as they are to look at social effects rather than causes (see Rose 1999: 57) – and so the search for the social conditions that make governmentality possible is both a criticism of much of the literature in this field and also a necessary step to take if the differences in applicability are to be properly accounted for. In fact it is a major irony that despite being part of the social turn in IR, the literature on governmentality has thus far not given a sufficiently social account of governmentality – focusing more on the techniques and practices of governmentality than its social basis. Neither has it accounted for the complex social differences across different societies that make the concept's transition from social to global such a difficult one.

Why social theory?

The tardiness of the social turn in IR and the fact that this turn is still criticised by the mainstream 'rationalist' tradition gives a good indication of the problems facing social theorists in IR.[2] Thus we have a situation where the most influential accounts of things like globalisation, governance and risk – issues that one might think would be

[2] The best-known comment comes from Robert Keohane in his presidential address to the International Studies Association, in which he argued that until 'the reflective scholars … have delineated such a research programme and shown in particular studies that it can illuminate important issues in world politics, they will remain on the margins of the field, largely invisible to the preponderance of empirical researchers' (Keohane 2006: 68).

central to an account of contemporary international relations – enter into IR only as borrowings from sociology. In other words, it is not the discipline of IR, but rather social theory, that is providing the most influential accounts of the kind of issues that IR should be leading the way on. This in itself is good justification for starting with an account of contemporary social theory. Another, more provocative reason is to address the fact that many mainstream IR scholars would no doubt not consider these issues to be IR at all.

This must not, however, come across as suggesting that IR ought to take up these concepts and use them in analysis. Indeed, when these ideas have been used in IR, there is often a lack of critical consideration of their meaning (for example, Coker 2002). In contrast, a major aim of this book is to show just how problematic these ideas are. But problematic though they may be, these ideas are influential and have in fact made a significant impact on actual political practice. That many of the ideas discussed in contemporary social theory are both extremely problematic yet also highly influential means they demand both engagement and criticism. The point here, then, is to analyse the ideas rather than use the ideas to analyse. In analysing the ideas and the role that they play in politics, it will be argued that another contemporary theory – governmentality – can play a useful role. Governmentality, rather than just being another such idea, provides an account of the relationship between these ideas and the dominant forms of governance that these ideas more often than not help to reproduce. In this sense, the concept of governmentality is deployed in a manner consistent with the aims of critical theory.

Showing the weakness of these ideas means showing their limits. If one of the limits is social in so far as these ideas provide a misleading account of today's society, it is nevertheless true to say that these ideas play an important role in helping reproduce contemporary forms of governmentality. In this first sense the terms, while misleading, are necessarily misleading, and therefore, as far as governmentality is concerned, play a socially important role. But there is another sense in which these ideas may be limited – not just in theory but also in practice. And it is here that expanding the study to the international dimension is particularly useful. Using the theory of governmentality as a means of critiquing these ideas means looking at governmentality in practice. And if we want to look at the limits of governmentality in practice we need to move outside the confines of the Northern liberal societies in order to examine how governmentality might operate in other parts of the world.

Here the argument of the book is more in keeping with IR. Critics will be quick to complain (e.g. Death 2011: 10; Vrasti 2011) that the argument is based on a fairly mainstream understanding of what IR is because it maintains that states are the most important actors[3] in the international system and that power politics plays an important role in deciding how governance works. The next chapter will defend this focus, arguing that the global governance approach, as well as the critical arguments of many governmentality theorists, too quickly embraces the idea of the global as an alternative to the international. The term global implies an overcoming of difference when we wish to actually examine this. Later we will defend an idea of the international as inter-societal and critique the global politics approach for downplaying inter-societal difference and power inequalities as well as ignoring the crucial role of states in maintaining these. In the next chapter we will examine a range of IR approaches to these issues, ultimately siding more with the arguments of certain neo-Gramscians.

The first part of this book introduces some of the main arguments in contemporary social theory. These ideas are chosen because they go beyond mere 'academic' terms and occur in the wider world of everyday discourse, the media, ministerial speeches and business circles. The best known of these issues is that of globalisation. It is an idea that is hard to escape, yet where its exact meaning never becomes clear. We ask such questions as how it connects to other important issues like risk and awareness, reflexivity and life choices, governance and global civil society. The opening section introduces the reader to a number of these issues. However, it does not try to provide a comprehensive introduction. If anything, far too much has been written on these issues already, and we are still no closer to knowing what globalisation is. More important is to look at some of the connections between these issues in order to explore how social theory relates to global politics and governmentality.

Looking through the documents of international organisations like the European Union (EU) and World Bank, it is clear that any number

[3] This is said on the understanding that states act, but in the next chapter it will be suggested that they are not themselves agents. Rather, their actions are the expressions of agency by various groups.

of terms could have been picked for analysis. Particularly interesting ones might be 'best practice', 'accountability', 'stakeholding', 'responsibility', 'resilience', 'flexibility', 'mobility', 'active citizenship', 'knowledge economy' and 'lifelong learning'. We have chosen to focus on those concepts – such as globalisation, risk and reflexivity – that make the bigger claim about the type of society we are living in. While these theories have become part of mainstream sociology, it is also interesting to note – and question – how they often claim to be critical, radical and progressive in nature. By comparing these theories with that of governmentality this book clearly questions such claims.

In claiming that contemporary social theory supports various forms of governance, this book is suggesting that most social theory has lost its critical edge and instead of analysing the social world, tends merely to reproduce it and to reinforce its dominant ideological forms. Of particular importance is the relationship between contemporary social theory and the project of globalisation. The chapter on globalisation, rather than trying to give a definition of globalisation, emphasises instead how globalisation is a neoliberal project and how contemporary social theory supports the advancement of this project, not least by denying that it is a project. By 'project', what we are suggesting is that the key aspects that define neoliberalism – a rough list of which would include deregulation, privatisation, internationalisation and devolving state activities to market forces – do not happen automatically but have to be actively pursued in the policy realm. We follow Tickell and Peck (2003: 166) in defining neoliberalism as 'the mobilization of state power in the contradictory extension and reproduction of market (-like) rule'. The next chapter argues that many theories associated with globalisation reinforce the dominant neoliberal view that we are rational subjects who should take responsibility for the organisation of our lives through making the right lifestyle choices and reflexively monitoring our behaviour. The idea that we might actually challenge the forces of globalisation at the macro level is never raised – for these, we are told, are conditions we must simply learn to live with.

In the first part of this book, rather than engaging in comprehensive empirical analysis of the world today, the critique is something like a philosophy of social theory. It looks at the role of contemporary social theory. It considers the types of claims social theory makes. It reflects on the picture of the world that it presents and, ultimately, the consequences of this in terms of what social forces or political projects it helps to support – either explicitly or more implicitly. The focus is not so much on what these terms mean, since the many definitions of these terms on offer can be confusing and misleading. Instead we see contemporary social theory as part of a broader social process and as ultimately contributing, as has been suggested, to what Foucault would call a mode of governmentality. By stating this conclusion now, we advance the view that contemporary social theory is largely uncritical of contemporary social processes. It is argued that in the main, the most influential contemporary social theories contribute to the social order rather than criticise it. These ideas may indeed give a very misleading picture of the world. Yet at the same time, and in virtue of this, such theories may actually aid or help the very processes that they fail to adequately explain. To give the obvious example, whether or not theories of globalisation are correct, they become real if enough people believe them and they start to shape actions and policies. But because such theories are so close to the processes they describe or misdescribe that they are unable to account for them, they are consequently unable to account for their own role in contributing to them. In this sense, such theories are closer to being ideologies in the sense that Marx understood the classical political economy of his time as ideology – its closeness to the very economic processes it tried to describe meant it was never able to penetrate surface forms and explain the essential nature of the workings of the capitalist economy (Marx 1956: 104).[4]

Looking at the battle for late modern social theory, it seems that two obvious camps emerge – poststructuralism and critical theory, one based on the legacy of Foucault, the other on the writings of Habermas. One provides a critique of modernity, the other a defence. But things are not so straightforward. Actually many of the heirs of Foucault and Habermas are saying things that reveal more similarity than difference, and even if they have sharp epistemological differences over the claims of knowledge, rationality and whether we can talk of 'the truth', they describe contemporary social life in similar ways.[5] Such theories share a claim that society is becoming increasingly complex, fragmented, uncertain and diverse. They raise familiar questions about the status

[4] Marx argues that the economists explain how production takes place, but not how these relations are themselves produced, hence their categories become fixed, eternal, immutable.

[5] As we go through the different theories we will see that the heirs of Foucault and Habermas include Lash, Urry, Castells, Giddens, Beck, Scholte and Held.

of boundaries and the organisation of time and space. They claim, on the one hand, that politics is becoming more fragmented, diverse and uncertain, that collective agency is undermined and dispersed, and instead politics becomes concerned with the micro level of personal choice, lifestyle, risk-taking and so on. But the recklessness of this position is revealed when we consider that at the same time these theories claim that unstoppable forces are at play that are sweeping away the old world and ushering in the radically new. These macro-level forces are beyond our control, they are described by Giddens as a runaway world that we might be able to help steer, but which we cannot stop.

Fragmentation now appears as a new form of social cohesion and uncertainty as a new form of social consent. In the case of postmodernism, 'reality' becomes a consequence of a plurality of competing discourses. The world is discursively and symbolically 'constructed' so that the boundaries between truth and falsehood, fact and fiction are blurred and destabilised. Postmodernism rejects the Enlightenment project of social development. Society is said to comprise multiple discourses, with no one, single discourse, narrative or tradition. While some of these arguments are useful, the overall effect is to reinforce the fragmentations and divisions within society, celebrating rather than challenging the break-up of unifying discourses and social identities. This undermines progressive attempts to overcome social division and atomisation. In this sense, postmodernism's overemphasis on uncertainty, diversity and social fragmentation reinforces the very society it is describing. Progress and emancipation are regarded as utopian ideals that belong to the past. We must accept that our 'postmodern condition' simply does not allow for such projects, even if they were desirable in the past. More often, such projects are 'radically' critiqued as 'totalitarian' impositions of outdated collective identity. Whether or not postmodernist theorists themselves have a radical intent, the general effect of this stance is to reinforce social divisions and the positions of those who benefit from them. Postmodernism acts to reinforce the individualisation and atomisation of social relations. In this sense, it plays into the hands of those who would want to change our ways of behaving and our social expectations, supporting new forms of social cohesion through the regulation of individual behaviour.

Our examination of those theories inspired by critical theory produces similar conclusions. But because these theories tend to be more positive about society, they better lend themselves to modern forms of social regulation. With postmodernism, writers like Giddens, Held and Beck share the assumption that society is more uncertain and diverse. They also share the attack on tradition and announce the end of class politics and other forms of collective action. But these theorists emphasise the positive aspects of today's societies and the liberating consequences of the break-up of tradition and collective structures. Whereas postmodernists might draw the conclusion that we should turn our back on rational decision-making, the theorists of 'reflexive modernity' argue that social uncertainty leads to a politics of choice, risk-taking and trust. While this does not make Giddens a neoliberal, his theory does lend itself to a neoliberal viewpoint. On the one hand, we are told that there are major forces over which we have little control; on the other, we have the importance of personal decision-making and responsibility which must be adapted to this new social context, and we must make the best out of the opportunities it offers. Because Giddens, Beck, Held and others still draw on the critical theory tradition, they maintain, unlike the postmodernists, a utopian streak to their theorising. Their arguments can be used to legitimate the current social order in the sense that they encourage us to hold out some optimistic hope that global forces (over which we are told we have no real control) are creating the conditions for a better way of life. The more Habermasian version of this in Held goes so far as to posit a better, cosmopolitan world order. In the case of Giddens and Beck, 'reflexive modernity' is said to liberate us from traditional structures and empower us to take personal responsibility for our lives. But this is exactly what neoliberalism wants us to believe, and it fits perfectly with the rationality of contemporary liberal governmentality.

Why governmentality?

Michel Foucault's concept of governmentality would seem to be ideally suited to a project that tries to link contemporary social theory to contemporary forms of governing, or to be more precise, to contemporary rationalities of governance. It also allows for an expanded idea of what is meant by governing so that it is not limited to the role of the government, but involves a variety of different techniques, practices and institutions, while the rationality aspect moves governmentality beyond the traditional confines of understanding power and rule to look at how governing is more deep-rooted in ways of seeing, thinking and acting. This approach to understanding governance has become increasingly significant across the social sciences. In relation to our own project it seems particularly relevant in linking social theory to certain ways of seeing the world, which in turn helps the process of governance. Dean nicely captures this through the idea of an analytics of government whose four dimensions are:

(1) characteristic forms of visibility, ways of seeing and perceiving;
(2) distinctive ways of thinking and questioning, relying on definite vocabularies and procedures for the production of truth (e.g. those derived from the social, human and behavioural sciences);
(3) specific ways of acting, intervening and directing, made up of particular types of practical rationality ('expertise' and 'know-how'), and relying upon definite mechanisms, techniques and technologies;
(4) characteristic ways of forming subjects, selves, persons, actors or agents (Dean 1999: 23).

Foucault advanced the idea of governmentality based on modern society's ability to employ more sophisticated methods of discipline and regulation, using new technologies of observation, calculation and administration. It is connected to Foucault's idea of biopolitics, where population emerges as the new object of government, developing, in particular, the individual's capacity for self-regulation of conduct (2004: 242–3). The focus is now less on the sovereign or the state (although this is still important) and more on the population itself as subject and object of government. The theory of governmentality goes beyond the limits of state power to look at more subtle methods of power exercised through a network of institutions, practices, procedures and techniques which act to regulate social conduct.

We will be particularly concerned with what a governmentality approach can say about neoliberalism as a particular way of limiting state power, governing through a network of institutions and governing individual conduct. Despite setting itself up as a neutral doctrine of non-intervention into market mechanisms, neoliberalism is a political discourse concerned with the governing of individuals from a distance. As Burchell (1996) argues, neoliberalism defines positive tasks for government, constructing the legal, institutional and cultural conditions for an artificial competitive game of entrepreneurial conduct. Burchell notes how this means giving an enterprise form to types of conduct and to institutions (like those of health and welfare) that have hitherto been seen as non-economic, and to the conduct of government and individuals themselves. The governed are encouraged to adopt an entrepreneurial attitude towards themselves. Burchell calls this a new form of 'responsibilisation', where the governed are encouraged, freely and rationally, to conduct themselves in new ways (1996: 29). The subject of government is given new obligations and duties. Government may intervene to help certain targeted groups, but the main emphasis is on the 'rational subject' taking individual responsibility. People are once more told to take charge of their own well-being and take rational decisions to avoid social problems like unemployment and poverty. This is discussed in terms of rights, obligations and moral responsibility, but the economic dimension still seems the dominant one – the shift from state mechanisms to self-regulation follows changes in work relations, while the dominant discourse is of the risks and benefits of rational decision-making.

We have already suggested that the ideologies of neoliberalism and globalisation today act to justify deliberate policies by suggesting that there is no alternative but to follow the flows of capital and the logic of the free market. The argument of this book is that there is little in today's mainstream social theory that challenges such a view. Today's social theorists are the first to criticise approaches such as Marxism for belonging to a certain period of time and having outdated notions of collective action and emancipatory politics, yet they appear uncritical of their own society and the dominant socio-economic processes they claim to be describing. Instead, they focus at the level of individual conduct. In the case of postmodernism, this largely takes a symbolic form. In the case of writers like Giddens, there is less hostility to the advocacy of 'rational conduct'. His ideas, then, are more compatible with the sort of neoliberal framework of governmentality described above. The result is twofold. First, these theories tend to demotivate the sort of (collective) action that might be able to change society and its dominant social structures. Second, having taken the conditions of contemporary society as a given, they switch attention to the conduct of the individual subject, something that plays into the hands of neoliberal forms of governance based on the rational conduct of individualised subjects. Perhaps it is the utopianism in critical theory – in the Habermasian version, certainly – that leads Giddens and others to accentuate the positive aspects of today's society, seeing the unfolding of late capitalist modernity as bringing individual liberation rather than enslavement. By contrast, the poststructural tradition suffers less from this affliction. Ironically, then, despite the problems presented by the postmodern heirs of Foucault, it is Foucault's own work on governmentality that best explains today's condition and indeed the role that today's theory plays in reinforcing this condition. While Foucault's theory on its own will not help us to change society, it is a better heir to the early critical theory and Marxism of the Frankfurt school than is the more Habermasian work of Giddens, Beck and Held. Foucauldian ideas on governmentality and the role of discourse, tied to more Marxist notions of social action, might just help us to better understand contemporary society and maybe to change it.

A strength of the governmentality approach is that it does not buy into the ontological aspects of the things it describes. It sees risk, globalisation, even neoliberalism, as strategies, tactics, techniques and ways of governing rather than as ontological features of late, post- or reflexive modernity. For example, the notion of risk is a strategic intervention that embraces the shift from welfare and social provision to the idea of the rational subject making their own provision. This is a strategy of governmentality wrongly seen by Beck (1992, 1999) and Giddens (1990) as an ontological condition of modernity. The governmentality approach throws such claims into doubt by questioning the naturalness of risk, security, competitiveness and so on. It shows them to be strategic interventions. But this raises a new question: what then is the ontological basis for governmentality itself? Although Foucault hints at developments in the capitalist economy, this issue is not really resolved. To complete the picture, we need to move from strategies and rationalities to conditions of governmentality and to underlying social structures and processes. Although governmentality refers to a set of techniques, practices and institutions that pre-exist and shape agents' behaviour and in this sense can be seen as something underlying, we still need a deeper level that explains the shaping of governmentalities themselves. If governmentality is regarded as a set of techniques and practices, then the issue to address becomes that of how these techniques can best operate – in which societies, which instances and occasions, through which institutions and organisations – and how effective they can be in various different geo-political contexts.

To summarise the strengths and weaknesses of the governmentality approach, first, it introduces a discursive aspect and embraces the idea of rationalities that provides a ground for understanding the role and applicability of various social theories. Foucault's approach is a pluralist one that embraces the diverse nature of contemporary social life and thus captures aspects of advanced liberalism. At the same time, it tries to show how there is actually a unified logic to such societies. Again, this is useful in examining the role of ideas and theories by grounding them in rationalities. They are also related to and sustained by ongoing techniques and procedures. Finally, Foucault's governmentality approach is useful precisely because it sees the things that contemporary social theory highlights – such things as risk, reflexivity, individualisation, competition and even globalisation – as related to these strategies and techniques and thus casts doubt on them as ontological conditions characteristic of late modernity.

The disadvantages and problems with the governmentality approach, which are examined in detail in the next chapter, include the familiar criticism that Foucault explains the how, but not the why. Foucault's account of power looks at its exercise, but there is something of a denial or avoidance of ontological conditions. This is reflected in a weak theorisation of state power and group interests as causes of power. Foucault argues that states and social groups take up existing strategies, tactics and ideas and use them for their own purposes. However, this does not answer the question of why they do this, what it is about them that allows them to do this and why they promote particular interests and ideas. Once we start asking these questions we have arrived at the need for deeper social theory and a broadening out from the governmentality approach to look at things like hegemony, state strategy, capital accumulation and so on. The next chapter will try to situate governmentality in this wider social context and thus better explain the role it plays.

Why global politics?

It is possible to demonstrate how contemporary social theory reproduces governmentality simply by looking at the domestic level. A sociological analysis of this relationship need not engage with IR theory or with global politics. However, an extension of the argument into the global sphere brings about interesting findings in relation to the unevenness of governmentality and the limits of its effectiveness. Indeed, approaching the international in a certain way allows us to examine a fascinating aspect of governmentality in practice. If the exploration of the social basis of governmentality tells us such things as the type of society in which governmentality exists, or the type of governmentality which exists in a particular society, then an investigation of the international aspect of governmentality tells us where governmentality works best and highlights variation in social context in order to explain differences in its operation. Of course this presupposes a certain understanding of international relations that continues to focus on states and power politics, but which unlike the rationalist mainstream IR insists on a more historical, sociological account of the international. For example, the recent arguments of Justin Rosenberg (2006), drawing on Marxism and the historical sociology tradition in IR, argue against the idea that the international is one single domain, seeing instead a relation between many different societies – that is, the international as inter-societal. This relationship is a far from even one, and Rosenberg borrows Trotsky's term 'uneven and combined development' to express the way that these societies coexist. Seeing the international as a series of relations between different societies at different levels of development and with quite different social bases will clearly have a bearing on how governmentality is to be understood. If our first concern is to look at the relationship between contemporary social ideas and forms of governmentality, then the introduction of the international dimension opens up the question of the relevance of these ideas and practices in different places and in different societies. It is here that we have the opportunity to engage with IR by offering a more social understanding of international relations that can help clarify the connections between states, societies and social relations. At the same time, an engagement with international relations is important because it allows us to examine governmentality in different (overdetermined) contexts.

Here it is necessary to be clear exactly what we mean by governmentality, since the concept is notoriously unclear in Foucault's own work. If we define governmentality in the most general possible sense, then it is possible to apply it to almost all situations. But as the next chapter will emphasise, it does seem sensible to define contemporary forms of governmentality as specifically liberal forms of governance that operate through the promotion of freedom, governing from a distance and limitation of government (Foucault 2008: 10). Without placing clear restrictions on what the concept means, it becomes too general to be of much use in political analysis. So if this liberal interpretation of governmentality is to be our working definition, then the immediate question from an IR point of view is the extent to which different (non-liberal) parts of the world have the social conditions necessary to allow such a form of governance to work.

Here lies the importance of looking at forms of global governance. Use of the term global governance is itself extremely problematic, and we will argue in Chapter 3 that it is one of those concepts that lack any clear meaning. However, we use it here to designate an aspect of global politics that is focused on the role of international organisations and their efforts to establish and implement rules of governance. From a governmentality perspective we are concerned with how, despite the uneven terrain of international relations and perhaps the unsuitability of local conditions, global governance brings us face to face with attempts to apply certain ideas outside of the social conditions within which they developed. The second part of this book thus looks at the way international organisations can be seen through the governmentality lens. As an aside, it should be noted here that although a good case can be made for making a distinction,[6] the terms international organisation and international institution will be used interchangeably and that this description will be applied to the EU as well as the IMF and World Bank. The argument will be that while governmentality is something that develops within particular types of advanced liberal society, this does not mean that international organisations like the IMF and World Bank will not try to apply the techniques of governmentality elsewhere, even if there are not the social conditions that would allow these techniques to work properly.

Those IR theorists who use the concept of governmentality need to tread carefully here. Governmentality may be a good way to understand the new language of the IMF and World Bank and the shift in the language of these two institutions from pure free market capitalism to talk of an 'institutionalised' or 'embedded' form of neoliberalism. But it would be mistaken to think that these techniques, developed in the particular social conditions present in the advanced liberal societies,

[6] Oran Young (1986: 108) makes the point that the World Bank and IMF are organisations, that is to say, physical entities with offices, staff and equipment, whereas an institution would refer to something like the Bretton Woods system, or practices comprising rules and conventions governing those in recognised roles.

can be successfully applied to other parts of the world in order to genuinely improve the conditions of local populations or even to effectively govern their behaviour. In this case, the task of governmentality theorists is to explain the difference between the institutional drive towards governmentality and the actual practical consequences of this in particular places. While organisations like the IMF and World Bank may draw up plans for so-called less developed countries based on the promotion of free markets, transparency, accountability, empowerment of civil society and encouragement of entrepreneurial values, the reality is that (neoliberal) ideas and techniques developed in the advanced liberal societies may not necessarily work under different social conditions. What needs describing in these cases is the process by which governmentality is imposed from the outside and how, if judged in terms of its purported aims, it might be considered a failure.

In order to emphasise this point, the second part of the book will compare two different cases. In addition to looking at how the World Bank attempts to implement governmentality outside of its normal social context so, by contrast, we will see how the EU develops forms of governmentality in a region that is more suited to such techniques. Indeed, the chapter on the EU will stress just how suited the ideas of networks, information society, social capital, reflexivity, individualisation, risk and globalisation are to the neoliberal project of reorganising social relations in Europe. A study of recent EU documents and reports will show how ideas like risk, networks and information are being used to justify particular ways of managing populations, defining citizenship and reorganising work and welfare. By comparing the case of the EU with that of the World Bank we get a clear idea of the common ideas these organisations have, but also the very different contexts and consequences of their applications.

However, as we shall explore in the next chapter, the study of governmentality in different contexts leads us to other conclusions. Before considering these, it should be emphasised that this book develops an IR account of governmentality. Thus, while noting how governmentality works differently in different places, this is not an account of how governmentality works at the domestic level. We do not examine how governmentality works in particular countries or places. Rather, we are concerned with how governmentality works at a more transnational level. We are interested in specific conditions in so far as they relate to this transnational governance. Hence we compare the situation inside the EU, where techniques of governmentality find greater resonance with local conditions, and the case of the World Bank, where its techniques have less resonance. But in the case of the latter we go on to suggest that governmentality is operating at a different level and is directed less at local populations and more at their governments. Here we can see, both inside the EU and in relation to the activities of the World Bank, that governmentality is using targets, goals, strategies and techniques to regulate, from a distance, the way that states behave. International organisations use the issues identified by the concept of governmentality – the health, wealth and well-being of populations – as their means of intervention, but the success of these strategies should now be judged not in relation to the effects on the populations themselves, but their effect on the behaviour of governments and state institutions. As the argument develops we will see that this is the basis on which we can understand global governance as a form of governmentality and that the concepts and theories we examine make more sense in this context, rather than in relation to the local conditions across different societies. Thus we will develop a concept of governmentality which can be seen to operate at different, albeit connected and emergent, levels. In this way we can examine how governmentality might have different degrees of success and employability at the local level, while displaying similar ways of operating on a global scale.

The argument of the book

In brief, the main argument of the book centres on a set of social theoretical concepts. Having outlined our conception of governmentality in the next chapter, we go on to examine a range of concepts and argue that these concepts help to form a certain picture of the world that is consistent with contemporary governmentality. It is particularly important to emphasise this in relation to those ideas that portray themselves as somehow radical, liberating or progressive in nature. It is suggested that whatever the conscious intent of the social theorists, their ideas share the same discursive framework as contemporary governmentality.

To reinforce this point, we then go on to look at how these ideas can be found in the statements of international organisations. We compare some statements from the EU with others from the World Bank and other international organisations in order to show their similarity of language. We do not attempt to draw on a large range of documents and statements, or to look in any detail at the implementation of these ideas in practice. But we believe that a glance at some of the most significant statements is enough to confirm this correspondence between contemporary social theory and the main justifications of contemporary forms of governmentality.

As a sub-argument, it is clear that although different international organisations use a similar discourse, the effects of governmentality are different depending on the social context. We have kept this as a secondary argument in order to emphasise the main issue, which is the relationship between contemporary social theory and contemporary governmentality. We also wish to remain focused on transnational or global governance, rather than looking in detail at local forms of implementation. But we do suggest that while governmentality in the EU achieves different effects at different levels, from the transnational to the national to the local and micro levels; this is harder to see in the case of something like the development agenda of international organisations such as the World Bank. In these cases, we suggest that governmentality may not work at the local level, but might have more success as a global form of regulation applied to the behaviour of states and governments. This provides one way of understanding global governance. It also provides the international dimension to our main argument which, to repeat, is the way most contemporary social theory (and thus, by extension, arguments about global politics), reflects, rather than critically analyses, the different forms of governmentality present in the world today.

Finally we might say something about the title of this book. The terms in the subtitle have obviously been covered in this chapter, but what of 'the social in the global'? Has it not just been suggested that when we say global, what we are really referring to is something international, at least in the inter-societal sense discussed above? But if the idea of the global is problematic, then there are such things as global politics and global governance, and these in turn help to construct an image of the global, however misleading this might be. If there were such a thing as the global, then we would have to argue the importance of seeing its social nature, just as constructivists and others have had to challenge rationalist IR about the social nature of the international. By throwing the idea of the global into question, we are left instead with the global politics that constructs the idea of the global. And in studying global politics and global governance, we wish to emphasise to an IR audience the importance of those social theories that inform this global politics and help fabricate the global as an illusion, albeit a very real and powerful one.

2 Putting governmentality in its place

This book is concerned with looking at the contribution a concept of governmentality can make to an understanding of both contemporary social theory and global politics. The first part will explain the concept of governmentality and then use the concept to examine a range of other social theories. It is argued that in comparison to these theories, not only does the governmentality approach provide a more critical account of contemporary society, but in fact it can also explain the *un*critical role these other theories play in reproducing contemporary society's dominant forms of governance. The other theories, by contrast, reproduce the dominant rationality of governance by naturalising the very things that governmentality throws into question. Whereas most contemporary social theory takes certain things like risk, networks and reflexivity for granted (seeing them as conditions of late modernity), governmentality shows these things to be conceptualisations that contribute to (reversible) strategies, technologies and techniques of governance.

This chapter will set out what is meant by governmentality. Although this is a concept that we clearly wish to utilise to maximum effect, it is also our responsibility to show the problems that the concept presents, especially when it is applied to international relations. The first part of this chapter wrestles with the meaning of the concept and tries to ascertain exactly what governmentality refers to. We will see that this is a difficult task given the nature of Foucault's own work on the subject, and our interpretation will try to narrow down the meaning of the concept by looking at its relation to disciplinary power and biopolitics and stressing, above all else, an understanding of the concept in relation to liberalism and neoliberalism. Ultimately it will be this neoliberal version of governmentality that will be of use in trying to understand both the problems raised in contemporary social theory and the role of governmentality in global politics.

After looking at how to define governmentality, this chapter sets about putting governmentality in its place. First, we look at issues concerning the state and the processes of production. Then we move on to look at this in a social and historical context and raise the issue of how governmentality relates to hegemony and state strategies. We next look at governmentality in relation to different literatures, starting with the IR literature on international order, regimes and forms of global governance. A brief exploration of some of the governmentality literature that has emerged recently in IR leads to a clarification of our understanding of how the concept should be used. Finally, the concept of governmentality will be related to other social theories, but this is not addressed at length in this chapter, because it forms the theme for the rest of this first section of the book.

Defining governmentality

It is tempting to see governmentality as a concept that marks a rupture with old ways of thinking, just as it is tempting to view Foucault's work on power generally as a rejection of traditional understandings of power as top-down, hierarchical, centralised, repressive and possessed by a particular group, social body or institution. In contrast to the normal IR conception of power as top-down or, following Weber, as being 'power over' some weaker body, Foucault's work talks of a new type of power that emerges from within the social body rather than above it (1980: 39). In our view it is more fruitful to see Foucault's work as complementing and supplementing, rather than displacing altogether, these conceptions, or as qualifying and giving nuance to our understanding of how power works. To take this issue into IR, a concern with governmentality should not lead us to believe that it displaces sovereign power or the role of the state. We should note that Foucault talks not of the end of sovereignty or state power, but the emergence of the triangle sovereignty–discipline–government. This draws attention to the historical emergence of a new concern for governing the population and the optimisation of health, welfare, happiness and labour productivity. Rather than rejecting the idea of sovereignty (or, to use his expression, cutting off the King's head[1]), Foucault is concerned with

[1] See Neal (2004) for a good discussion of why we should not take Foucault's call to cut off the King's head (Foucault 2001b) as meaning that he is opposed to the sovereignty discourse.

how sovereignty is affected by modern developments in disciplinary and governmental techniques that regulate and order the behaviour of people within a given territory. Although this does not represent a turn away from the question of sovereignty and the state, it does require a shift in focus. As Foucault puts it, 'rather than asking ourselves what the sovereign looks like from on high, we should be trying to discover how multiple bodies, forces, energies, matters, desires, thoughts and so on are gradually, progressively, actually and materially constituted as subjects' (Foucault 2004: 28). This focus on the way that social discourses help in the shaping of these subjects will be at the centre of our study. And it is on this basis that both contemporary social theory (with its focus on the subject) and traditional IR theory (with its focus on sovereignty) will be challenged.

Foucault's work on governmentality does not emerge in any systematic form. Instead, it is developed in a series of lectures given at the Collège de France. In these lectures, Foucault is still clearly thinking through the concept, as reflected in the fact that much of what he says about governmentality is contained in a lecture where his original intention was to talk about biopolitics (Foucault 2008: 317). While these lectures provide a number of general definitions of what governmentality is, the meaning of the term only really emerges through its application to various different contexts and through its use alongside various other concepts and ideas with which it intersects and engages. Even the most general definition of governmentality as the 'conduct of conduct' (*conduire des conduites*)[2] requires considerable investigation. This definition suggests that governance takes place from a distance as the power to influence the actions of others. To understand this further, we have to see how government forms part of a triangle of sovereignty–discipline–government, where its distinctive character derives from having population as its main concern (Foucault 2007: 108).

Looking at how the problem of government starts to emerge in the sixteenth century, Foucault first examines this in terms of disciplinary power – that is, a set of techniques centred on the body. Most famously we find an account of disciplinary power in *Discipline and Punish* (1979), where Foucault traces the shift from very visible forms of punishment like public execution to systems of correction characteristic

[2] Foucault (1994: 237). This term is not translated in this way in English-language editions of Foucault.

of the prison, but also applicable to things like the organisation of the school and the workplace. The body, as the target of power, is placed under constant supervision and surveillance, while space and time are organised such that the body can be better regulated and controlled. As Foucault's lectures develop, he distinguishes between disciplinary power and a form of power called governmentality that works by respecting the 'natural processes' of the economic sphere (Foucault 2007: 353). This is a more liberal form of power that governs from a distance. In contrast to the 'docile bodies' produced by the regulatory techniques of disciplinary power, the focus of governmentality is on the creation of free and active subjects.

Foucault attempts to explain this emergence by focusing on liberalism as a rationality of governance. For liberal governance the idea of governing well is associated with the claim to respect the freedom of the governed and for government to allow things to take their natural course. It works from a distance through the encouragement (or direction) of 'free conduct'. This particular form of power operates through a range of techniques – of observation, calculation and administration – and is expressed itself through an ensemble of 'institutions, procedures, analyses, and reflections, the calculations and tactics that allow the exercise of this very specific, albeit very complex, power' (Foucault 2007: 108).

Consequently, government comes to be understood as respecting the freedom of such processes through the deliberate self-limiting of government – an intrinsic part of governmental rationality (Foucault 2008: 10). *Laissez-faire* governance, based on the liberal principles of political economy, finds its expression in civil society and is legitimated through the liberal concern that one must not 'govern too much' (Foucault 2008: 319). This can be contrasted with sovereign power, with its concern for territory, and disciplinary power, which functions in a more coercive and preventive way (Foucault 2007: 45). However, it is crucial to note how closely this liberal form of governance is connected to apparatuses of security. The idea of freedom for the mass of the population is actually an ideological illusion characteristic of capitalist society. As Neocleous has argued: 'For all the talk of "laissez faire", the "natural" phenomena of labour, wages and profit have to be policed and secured' (Neocleous 2008: 31).

Thus two very important distinctions are required. First, it is necessary to distinguish between disciplinary power as a more direct and sometimes coercive regulation of bodies (perhaps using threat of punishment), and governmentality as governance of populations from a distance (perhaps through encouragement). Second, it is important to distinguish between governmentality in a more generic sense as it relates to the regulation of populations and which the IR literature often equates with biopolitics, and the specific liberal or neoliberal rationalities that lie behind contemporary forms of governance. Foucault's emphasis on the liberal element of rule – governing through the idea of free conduct, self-awareness and self-limitation – distinguishes it from other types of power. This liberalism defines a problem-space of government, its appropriate forms of regulation and its self-imposed limits. It looks to the private sphere and civil society as a way to disguise the imposition of 'market discipline' as somehow an exercise in freedom.

Foucault explains that there is an ambiguity within liberalism between a concept of freedom as human rights, and the idea, which we will concentrate on here, of freedom as the independence of the governed (Foucault 2008: 42). The latter, as Burchell comments, means that the 'objective of a liberal art of government becomes that of securing the conditions for the optimal and, as far as possible, autonomous functioning of economic processes within society or, as Foucault puts it, of enframing natural processes in mechanisms of *security*' (Burchell 1991: 139). Liberal discourse presents this realm as based on the rational and autonomous conduct of individuals free from state interference. However, this freedom and liberty is a construction that is reinforced through a particular set of social practices and a normative discourse. Even Hayek admits that freedom is a cultural conception of something that has evolved over time, establishing a set of rules with their disciplinary effects (Dean 1999: 157). As Dean says, 'in order to act freely, the subject must first be shaped, guided and moulded into one capable of responsibly exercising that freedom' (1999: 165). Individual subjects are constituted as autonomous and rational decision-makers. But the freedom and liberty of the subject is socially constructed through practices that reinforce rational, normalised conduct. Liberalism, Foucault tells us, works not through the imperative of freedom, but through the social production of freedom and the 'management and organization of the conditions in which one can be free' (Foucault 2008: 63–4). The connection between freedom and rationality is noted in Burchell's point that 'an essential and original feature of liberalism as a principle of governmental reason is that it pegs the rationality of government, of the exercise of political power, to the freedom and interested rationality of the governed themselves' (Burchell 1991: 139).

When looking at neoliberalism, the first question to address is what is added by the 'neo' prefix. It certainly raises a question as to the naturalness and purity of liberalism if we have to distinguish between types of liberalism. As noted, pure liberalism is only an ideal type. Neoliberalism distinguishes itself precisely because of social and historical context. This context is provided by the unravelling of the postwar institutional settlement. Neoliberal discourse problematises the national solutions of the postwar states and argues the need to move away from centralised government activity, the welfare state and Keynesian forms of intervention. As Harvey notes, the marked shift under neoliberalism is from government (state power on its own) to governance, defined as 'a broader configuration of state and key elements in civil society', but where the state is still an active player in producing the legislation and regulatory framework (Harvey 2005: 77).

Neoliberalism engages in a process of 'destatification' by introducing the norms and values of the market into different areas of social life through the promotion of competition, initiative and risk-taking. As Foucault says: 'The society regulated by reference to the market that the neo-liberals are thinking about is ... a society subject to the dynamic of competition ... an enterprise society' (2008: 147). Instead of direct governance, the state steps back and encourages people to become more active, enterprising and responsible for their own decisions. They are appealed to as citizens or consumers who are 'free' to take responsibility for their own life choices but who are expected to follow competitive rules of conduct with the logic of enterprise applied to individual acts. Governmentality works by telling us to be enterprising, active and responsible citizens. In Dean's words, this is a cultural form of governance based on ethical orientations, self-responsibility and the moral obligations invoked by notions of freedom and the exercising of agency (Dean 2007: 73).

We will later see this in evidence across a range of documents produced by the EU and World Bank. However, although this discourse invokes moral issues of obligations, rights and responsibilities, ultimately everything is judged against the imperative of economic competitiveness. In doing this, neoliberalism works to define positive tasks for government through constructing the legal, institutional and cultural conditions for an artificial competitive game of entrepreneurial conduct which can be applied to almost all areas of our social lives and which, as Foucault notes (2008: 173), is guaranteed by the state. We will look at how this intervention works to extend the norms and values of the market through applying technologies of competition, initiative and risk-taking across various social domains.

The purpose of the above account of governmentality is to show just how much these ideas are related to the promotion of individualised rational conduct. This in turn helps us to see neoliberalism in a new light. While the discourse of neoliberalism promotes the idea of freedom from regulation, we can see that it is in fact a very specific form of regulation of conduct. This more social understanding of neoliberalism is particularly important given the recent world economic crisis and claims that neoliberalism has been discredited. For neoliberalism is much more than the simple ideology of free-market economics. Neoliberalism is a specific form of social rule that promotes a rationality of individualised responsibility (which we might add is particularly influenced by a critique of postwar welfarism and dependency culture). Clearly these are arguments that match well with developments in today's advanced liberal societies and will continue to be promoted, for example in the development of the EU, irrespective of the economic situation. Although there has been widespread criticism of policies that have allowed banks and other financial institutions to behave in a reckless way, this does not mean that the governmental rationality of neoliberalism itself will be rejected, quite the contrary. This will be used to justify even greater emphasis on the importance of rationalised and responsible self-conduct. In fact the World Bank and IMF had already had these kinds of internal discussions in the 1990s. Recognising the failure of full-scale free-market policies, these organisations took a more institutional approach to development. This led some to form the mistaken view that they had turned away from neoliberalism and developed a new post-Washington consensus. In fact, their development strategies can be seen as moving closer to the type of neoliberal governmentality described above by insisting on greater institutionalisation of economic policies. Instead of insisting on the rolling back of the state, the Second Generation reforms were, to use Graham Harrison's expression, more concerned with the *nature* of state action. This meant an emphasis on institutional capacity-building, finance management, technical assistance and a whole range of policy imperatives (Harrison 2004: 18–20). At no point has the role of the free market been questioned. Instead the new emphasis is on institutions that will help better facilitate market conditions and how to make this more effective through the promotion of greater institutional transparency, financial and civil service reforms, the development of a more dynamic civil society and the empowerment of responsible individuals. As the effects of the financial crisis in the West continue to be felt, it will be this greater emphasis on institutional reform (in the interest of promoting markets), rather than a rejection of the free market, that will drive policy. This institutional reform will be a continuation of what governmentality theorists already understand as neoliberalism.

To summarise the arguments of this section, we have suggested that while different readings of Foucault's arguments are possible, it makes sense to separate his concept of governmentality from the related ideas of disciplinary power and biopower (the latter is much more general in referring to how the basic biological features of human being are objects of a general strategy of power (Foucault 2007: 1)) by emphasising the specific forms that governmentality takes. We have suggested that Foucault's concept is most meaningful when seen in its specifically neoliberal form. This is particularly important when we consider the application of the concept to international relations, because the nature of power relations across the globe means that this neoliberal form of governmentality is the one that is promoted by states, governments and international organisations. The issue, then, is whether it is really possible to implement a distinctively liberal form of governmentality on a global scale, but to do this we need to step back from governmentality itself and look at the wider social context in which governmentality operates.

Encounters between Foucault and Marx

This book does not claim to be Foucauldian. Instead it adopts a historical materialist approach that makes use of Foucault, and reads Foucault in a particular way. It is concerned to makes ideas like governmentality consistent with a broader social context that we will sketch in the next few sections. This approach will be criticised by most Foucauldians and governmentality scholars in IR for being too

'Marxist', but in our view this is the only way to fully understand the social and international dimensions of governmentality.

The usual reading of Foucault is to see him highlighting certain techniques and practices while avoiding bigger ontological questions about social structures, social classes and economic production. This avoidance is best expressed in Nikolas Rose's call for an 'empiricism of the surface' (Rose 1999: 57) and is echoed in IR by Larner and Walters's call to 'bracket' the world of underlying forces and causes (Larner and Walters 2005: 16) and to shift attention away from deep structures and institutional processes in order to focus at the level of mentalities and rationalities of government (Walters 2005: 157). Our argument is that Foucault is absolutely right to highlight these mentalities and rationalities of government and to draw attention to the role of various strategies and techniques of power. But we cannot fully explain how they are constituted and how they work unless we say something about the wider, deeper picture. This is important enough in explaining the social context of governmentality but is doubly so in international relations, where it is also necessary to explain not just how governmentality fits into a particular society but also how it works differently in different places, or indeed how it might fail or prove irrelevant in certain cases.

So what might historical materialism do to explain this wider social context and to what extent might Foucault be compatible with this approach? To answer the first question we might follow Robert Cox in arguing that above all else, historical materialism draws attention to structures of production. A focus on processes of production is critical if we are to explain the specific form taken by the state and wider society. Cox describes his approach as combining a concern with the relation between power in production, power in the state and power in international relations (1996: 96). Another way of putting this is that capitalist production has its own general laws that none the less can be manifested only in specific national and regional forms. While capitalism has its much-discussed global dynamics, these continue to operate within and among national economies and nation states (Wood 2002: 17). This highlights the crucial issue of the relation between the economic and political, a relationship that (contrary to reductionist forms of Marxism) is often conflictual in nature. Cox also argues that, like political realism, historical materialism draws attention to conflict in world politics. It shows the constant remaking of human relations, but it sees this not in the realist manner of reorganising a continuing structure, but as a cause of genuine structural change (1996: 95). Historical materialism also expands the realist approach to look at relations between state and civil society (1996: 96). Having noted these issues, we should also be aware of the serious problems they raise. Although there might be agreement on the importance of productive forces, there is huge controversy within Marxist circles over what weight to give these, and whether to give more weight to forces of production or social relations, a choice that Cox notes can lead either to technological determinism or voluntarism. Another problem area is the state and whether one can avoid an instrumentalist view that sees it as a tool of the ruling class, or a functionalist view that reduces it to a regulator of the capitalist system. Cox's answer to both these problems is to turn to the Italian Marxist Antonio Gramsci. While we are sympathetic to this choice, we will also challenge it to some degree. The rest of this chapter and indeed the rest of this book is as much an engagement with these issues as it is an account of governmentality.

The second question of compatibility can be addressed by looking at some cases where the work of Foucault and Marx has been combined. In the first case we will look at the issue of production, in the second the conceptualisation of the state. In calling for a wider social context we are asking for an account of the social conditions of possibility for governmentality itself. It is clear from Foucault's own work – even if this element is often deliberately downplayed for fear of appearing to be Marxist – that biopolitics, disciplinary techniques and governmentality are seen as emerging alongside the development of capitalist society.[3] In explaining this Foucault himself notes that it is 'impossible at the present time to write history without using a whole range of concepts directly or indirectly linked to Marx's thought and situating oneself within a horizon of thought which has been defined and described by Marx' (Foucault 1980: 53).

Foucault talks about the privatisation of property and the onset of the capitalist mode of production. He links to this the privatisation of power and the development of disciplinary techniques. He thus makes a clear connection between the privatisation of property and the use

[3] When asked about keeping his distance from Marx, Foucault reveals that he plays a game of using phrases from Marx without giving references so that they go unnoticed by those who claim to revere Marx (Foucault 1980: 52).

of disciplinary power both to contain opposition to this and to organise and exploit labour on a new, unprecedented scale (Foucault 1979: 85–7). Elsewhere, Foucault talks of the development of a technology of population as a result of demographic change in Western Europe and the need to integrate the population into apparatuses of production. This requires finer and more accurate mechanisms of control and regulation. He describes issues to do with the labour force as the economico-political effects of the accumulation of men (1980: 171). These linkages are expressed most clearly when he writes that the 'two processes – the accumulation of men and the accumulation of capital – cannot be separated ... the technological mutation of the apparatus of production, the division of labour and the elaboration of the disciplinary techniques sustained an ensemble of very close relations' (Foucault 1979: 221).

So Foucault does clearly make macro claims about wider social developments. However, it is in explaining the micro practices of the labour process that Foucault makes his strongest contribution. So, with 'the emergence of large-scale industry, one finds, beneath the division of the production process, the individualizing fragmentation of labour power' (1979: 145). This process is studied in *Discipline and Punish*, where it is shown how the body is invested with relations of power and domination in order to render it an efficient force of production. Indeed, it is only through being caught up in a system of subjugation that is based on continuous and functional surveillance that the body can be constituted as productive labour power. Foucault himself quotes volume one of Marx's *Capital*, which talks of how the 'work of directing, superintending and adjusting becomes one of the functions of capital' (Marx 1976: 449; Foucault 1979: 175).

According to Alesandro Fontana and Mauro Bertani in their introduction to Foucault's lecture *Society Must Be Defended*, Foucault maintained an 'uninterrupted dialogue' with Marx on relations between power and political economy. They argue the compatibility of Foucault's work on disciplinary power and Marx's analysis of things like the working day, division of labour, machinery and large-scale industry. But they suggest that whereas Marx sees coercion exclusively as a result of relations between capital and labour, Foucault argues that the subjugations, training and surveillance that make this possible are not so much inventions of the capitalist class as inheritances from the disciplinary practices of the seventeenth and eighteenth centuries (Fontana and Bertani 2004: 227; Foucault 1979: 379).

These themes are also developed at length in the work of Richard Marsden. He praises Marx for providing a historical account of how labour is prised off the land and thrown into the labour market, how it is simultaneously empowered and repressed and subjected to the relentless movement of machinery. But when it comes to explaining how labour is organised as a productive power, Marx says very little. He gives no account of how this organisation is achieved, the techniques deployed and the results obtained (Marsden 1999: 132). Foucault, by contrast, gives an account of three methods of disciplinary power that work to train the body: hierarchical observation, normalising judgement, and examination. These combine to 'normalise' the operation of the body, to determine rules of conduct, and control the operation of the body by organising, in fine detail, its movement in space and time (1999: 141). Thus Marx is better at providing the motive for capitalist control, and Foucault better at explaining the means. Summarising the problem in a way that is representative of a more general critique levied against Foucault, Marsden writes:

> Marx explains 'why', that is, he describes the imperative of the social structure that facilitates and constrains social action, but he does not explain 'how', the mechanics of capital's motion. Foucault explains 'how', that is, he describes the mechanism of power, but he does not explain 'why', the motive or purpose of disciplinary power. If Marx's *explicandum* is a cluster of conclusions in search of a premise, then Foucault's *explicans* is a cluster of premises in search of a conclusion. (Marsden 1999: 134)

The issue of the relation between the why and the how can be related to another crucial distinction that Foucault's work raises – that between the macro and the micro. This is evident in debates about Foucault's conception of the state. In a well-known passage Foucault talks of the state as 'superstructural in relation to a whole series of power networks' (Foucault 2001b: 123). While this could be taken as asserting the primacy of micro relations – technologies of the body, for example – Foucault's discussion can also clearly be read as establishing the interplay between networks of power and what he calls a 'metapower'. Rather than undermining the role of the state, Foucault's argument helps to establish the basis of the state in a 'series of multiple and indefinite power relations' that allow this metapower to 'take hold and secure its footing' (2001b: 123). This is a 'conditioning-conditioned relationship' (2001b: 123) and provides the basis for the state to 'codify' a range of power relationships that 'render its functioning possible' (2001b: 123). Elsewhere Foucault talks of the way that micro powers can be 'colonised, used, inflected, transformed, displaced, extended, and so on by increasingly general mechanisms and forms of overall domination' (Foucault 2004: 301). It would seem clear from these paragraphs that while much of Foucault's work is concerned with redressing the balance by emphasising the role of micro powers, he is clearly aware that these powers may be taken up and used by the state, or by ruling groups seeking to use them in particular ways as part of their governing strategy:

> I think we have to analyse the way in which the phenomena, techniques and procedures of power come into play at the lowest levels; we have to show, obviously, how these procedures are displaced, extended, and modified and, above all, how they are invested or annexed by global phenomena. (Foucault 2004: 30–1)

It is this that makes Foucault's arguments compatible with non-reductionist forms of Marxism. This argument has been picked up by those wishing to develop a relational view of the state (as opposed to an instrumental or reductionist one). Indeed Thomas Lemke suggests that Foucault's approach to the state is compatible with that of some of his Marxist contemporaries – notably Poulantzas – suggesting that:

> Foucault expanded his microphysics of power to social macrostructures and the phenomenon of the state ... With this analytics of government, Foucault established a theoretical connection to a tradition within French Marxism that approached the state less as a fixed institutional ensemble or bureaucratic apparatus than as the 'condensation of social relations of power'. (Lemke 2003: 176)

This approach to the state is today best expressed in the work of Bob Jessop. For Jessop, Foucault allows us to see how the state combines, arranges and fixes existing micro relations of power, which are then codified, consolidated and institutionalised (Jessop 2007: 152). This approach views state power as the 'contingent outcome of specific practices' (2007: 66). While many poststructuralists might agree with this view, it is also compatible with arguments within historical materialism – for example the work of Poulantzas, or the Gramscian school – which emphasises the complex interplay of diverse social forces and sees the state as a strategic terrain and the site of the politics of statecraft. Jessop summarises his view of the state in the following way:

> (1) the state is a set of institutions that cannot, *qua* institutional ensemble, exercise power; (2) political forces do not exist independently of the state: they are shaped in part through its forms of representation, its internal structure, and its forms of intervention; (3) state power is a complex social relation that reflects the changing balance of social forces in a determinate conjuncture; and (4) state power is capitalist to the extent that it creates, maintains, or restores the conditions required for capital accumulation in a given situation. (Jessop 2007: 28)

For Jessop, then, we have a paradox where on the one hand 'the state is just one institutional ensemble among others within a social formation; on the other, it is peculiarly charged with overall responsibility for maintaining the cohesion of the social formation' (2007: 79) and, we might add, secures the social conditions for capital accumulation. Such an approach maintains Marxism's focus on the importance of relations of production, but its emphasis on the relational nature of the state's institutional form is also in line with Foucault's critique of essentialist views of the state. As Jessop puts it, Foucault rejects arguments that present the state as a calculating subject, instrument of class rule or product of economic relations of production, but at the same time he 'explored emergent strategies (state projects, governmentalizing projects) that identified the nature and purposes of government (as reflected in alternative forms of *raison d'État*) in different contexts and periods' (Jessop 2007: 37).

This is a good opportunity to raise an issue that affects the argument of this book, namely whether the state should be considered an actor or an agent. What should be clear is that, following Jessop's point, the state should not be considered a rational, calculating subject. This puts us at odds with much of the mainstream IR literature, which even if it does not literally believe this, treats the state *as if* it were a calculating actor. Yet we have also talked of the state as the main actor in IR. Does that mean, therefore, that we have to go as far as Wendt (2004) in giving the state some sort of personhood, treating it as a corporate agent with a collective consciousness? In our view, we should reject Wendt's idea of the state as a person, but not go so far as suggesting that the state does not act. Contrary to what Wendt suggests, the state itself does not possess the qualities of internationality or purposiveness (2004: 291). Instead, states are closer to structures or, more precisely, institutional ensembles. But in our view, it makes sense to say that states can be actors in an emergent sense, just as we would say the same thing of organisations and other collective bodies. Of course social groups do the real acting. More precisely, Jessop argues that we should see this action in terms of struggles to realise contingent state projects (Jessop 1990: 14). The state, therefore, is an institutional ensemble whose structure positions these agents in certain ways, allowing them to exercise power, but also exercising bias in favour of some projects and against others. Strictly speaking, it might be claimed that the state itself is not an actor, but an institution that shapes action. However, it seems sensible to talk of the state as an actor so long as we note that this means it is an actor in an emergent sense, where its actions are technically speaking the actions of state agents, but where these actions are expressed through the state, and therefore subject to its strategic selectivity. We will therefore continue to talk of state action, but with all the above qualifications.[4]

In line with these arguments, the theory of governmentality also rejects a general view of the modern state, and sees it, not as a unified apparatus, but as an ensemble of different institutions and practices. While Foucault is at pains to highlight the micro level, his work on governmentality clearly shows how such practices provide resources for macro strategies to be carried out by dominant social groups or by the government or state. Indeed we could even say that Foucault gives the state a very privileged role in providing 'a schema of intelligibility for a whole set of already established institutions, a whole set of given realities' (Foucault 2007: 286). And although the main aim of Foucault's intervention is to show that 'in order for there to be a movement from above to below there has to be a capillary from below to above at the same time' (2007: 201), we can clearly see that he believes this is a two-way movement in that:

[4] For more on this debate in IR see Wight (2004) and Koivisto (2010).

> the great strategies of power encrust themselves and depend for their conditions of exercise on the level of the micro-relations of power. But there are always also movements in the other direction whereby strategies which co-ordinate relations of power produce new effects and advance into hitherto unaffected domains. (1980: 199–200)

This should do something to allay the concern that Foucault is overly concerned with the micro to the exclusion of the macro. Although these issues have not really been taken up in IR, one exception is Stephen Gill's work. In a brief discussion he raises this familiar problem through an outline of what he calls 'disciplinary neoliberalism'. This term combines the structural power of capital with the micro power and surveillance techniques of Foucault. These techniques, although not universal, are institutionalised (for example across the Bretton Woods institutions) and operate, as we have tried to suggest, unevenly across various fields – public and private, state and civil society, local and transnational (Gill 2003: 130–1). But Gill believes that while Foucault's work is useful in showing the workings of disciplinary techniques like surveillance, as well as the constitution and constraints of various discursive forms, his work is missing the link between micro-level techniques and macro structures. Foucault, it is suggested, fails to adequately explain how the historical emergence of these powers might be linked to the development of capitalism and ignores the struggles that occur over the modalities of power and knowledge (Gill 2003: 121). Our above discussion suggests that this link can be made, and indeed Gill's own account of global governance suggests this. In particular, he gives a convincing account of the disciplinary techniques used by international institutions to advance the structural power of capital. In the next section we outline ways in which this connection between the macro and the micro might be understood through a connection between capitalist regulation, hegemonic projects and governmentality.

These, then, are some of the encounters between Marx and Foucault. We can summarise the main issue as the relation between the macro and the micro and between the why and how. Illustration of the connections should give some legitimacy to our project. The next section will look of the more general contribution historical materialism can make in explaining the context for governmentality. To do this we will return to the issue of economic production, then turn to state strategy and hegemonic projects and finally widen this to look at the international context.

Production, hegemony and social context

We wish to put governmentality in its appropriate social context. As the last section suggests, this should be done by relating it to processes of production and strategies of the state. We have raised the need to study governmentality's conditions of possibility. We have noted that in addressing this even Foucault himself is obliged to talk of the development of capitalism. However, the previous section should have made clear that we wish to avoid a reductive kind of Marxism that sees everything as ultimately reducible to the economic mode of production. Thankfully most contemporary Marxist theory rejects reductionism and economic determinism. Thus Mészáros notes how Marx saw capital as a dynamic moment with a global expansionary logic and a constant drive for self-expansion (Mészáros 2000: 6). But he goes on to note its various structural defects, the contradictions between production and consumption, production and circulation, and most notably the separation of production and control (2000: 57). In contrast to previous modes of production, capitalism separates the political from the economic, yet requires the state to play the role of cohering the social system and providing overall political command. There is no functional guarantee that the state will successfully perform this role. This is doubly so at the international level, where, as Mészáros notes, we find an intensified contradiction between capitalism as global enterprise and its command structure of nationally fractured units (2000: 48).

Our understanding of the relationship between capitalist production and political command can be explained through a theory of economic regulation. The contradictions pointed to by Mészáros are part of the deeper logic of capital, but how they manifest themselves is a social and historical matter, as are attempts to organise and regulate economic relations, to manage these deeper tendencies and try to overcome any emergent crises. Indeed, our starting point should be the inherently problematic nature of capital accumulation. This necessitates a shift of focus to examine how the conditions for stable accumulation have to be socially and institutionally secured. These interventions use a mixture of economic and extra-economic means, and a successful form of regulation depends on the right balance between economy, state and civil society. In contrast to neoclassical economics, this is a conceptual approach that emphasises the institutionalised nature of the economy as well as the importance of social norms and values. We can therefore define a mode of regulation as a complexly structured combination of institutions, norms and values that attempts to offset social and economic antagonisms in order to stabilise the process (or regime) of accumulation.

Those who develop theories of capitalist regulation emphasise its unstable and uncertain nature. One of the best known of the regulation theorists, Alain Lipietz, writes that

> the emergence of a new regime of accumulation is not a pre-ordained part of capitalism's destiny, even though it may correspond to certain identifiable 'tendencies' ... Regimes of accumulation and modes of regulation are *chance discoveries* made in the course of human struggles and if they are for a while successful, it is only because they are able to ensure a certain regularity and a certain permanence in social reproduction. (Lipietz 1987: 15)

While some regulation theorists may take a more functionalist approach in seeing modes of regulation as providing a long-term institutional fix (for an overview see Jessop and Sum 2006), the above quotation should indicate the temporary and historically specific nature of these institutional settlements and the possibility that they may be contested. It is not surprising, therefore, to find comparisons with Gramsci's work on hegemony and historical blocs.[5]

Gramsci's view of the state is consistent with the idea of regulation. While he sometimes talks of the state in a narrower sense by emphasising its coercive function, he also talks of the 'integral state' which combines political society with civil society, or hegemony protected by coercion (Gramsci 1971: 263). Such a notion can be used to show the way that hegemony, coercion and leadership combine as part of specific state projects that must ensure political leadership, social cohesion and economic reproduction. State strategy must project itself across a

[5] As Lipietz says, 'The stabilization of a regime of accumulation or a mode of regulation obviously cannot be analysed in terms of its economic logic alone. Such "discoveries" are the outcome of social and political struggles which stabilize to form *a hegemonic system* in Gramsci's sense of the term' (Lipietz 1987: 20).

wide range of social institutions and practices. While many in IR wish to emphasise the subjective aspect of this process in order to oppose realist understandings of hegemony – Cox, for example, describes hegemony as 'an intersubjective sharing of behavioural expectations' (Cox 1996: 245) – we wish to emphasise, for the moment, the structural nature of this in order to connect hegemony to deeper structures of production. Hegemony is not merely the dominance of the ruling group over subaltern groups. The ruling hegemonic bloc must be maintained through the organising and reorganising of social relations. It needs to respond to deeper-rooted changes in patterns of production and intervene into this process in order to strengthen its own position. For a group to be hegemonic, it must be strongly positioned, not just in relation to other groups, but in relation to the economic, political and cultural conditions that allow it to put itself forward as leading. Gramsci explains that hegemony 'must necessarily be based on the decisive function exercised by the leading group in the decisive nucleus of economic activity' (Gramsci 1971: 161).

Gramsci writes: 'Structures and superstructures form an "historical bloc". That is to say the complex, contradictory and discordant *ensemble* of the superstructures is the reflection of the *ensemble* of the social relations of production' (1971: 366). The best way to explain this is in relation to his account of Fordism. Here Gramsci analyses the introduction of new methods of production, notably the widespread use of machines and production-line techniques, the mass consumption of standardised commodities and new managerial practices concerned with scientific techniques. After Gramsci's death, the processes he identified became more widespread. At the national level this resulted in new collective forms of wage bargaining, monopolistic forms of state regulation of the economy (Keynesianism) and expanded welfare provision. This was matched at the international level by a particular institutional settlement, commonly referred to as the Bretton Woods system, founded around the dominant economic state, the USA, which stabilised the world economy and provided the necessary leadership for a liberal international order. So we see the connection at various different levels between deeper economic structures, the organisation of the labour process, forms of state intervention and the organisation of hegemonic blocs. The postwar order was founded on a combination of changes in production and a reorganisation of the ruling hegemonic bloc, both nationally and internationally.

This system started to break down in the 1970s. The Fordist production process was seen as too rigid and unable to deal with either change in demand or organised class opposition to it. Internationally it was proving difficult to contain trade and capital flows within nationally bounded economic systems. The rate of productivity declined and Keynesian policies caused inflation, a weakening dollar and consequently an international currency crisis. The historical side of this will be dealt with in more detail in the next section. Here we will note the more general aspect of this as a change in forms of regulation and reorganisation of the historical bloc. New information and communications technology was introduced along with the production of more individualised, just-in-time goods, more flexible working practices, flatter and leaner management structures, networked organisational forms and an increased division between highly skilled workers and a disposable non-skilled labour force. While the decline of the Keynesian national-welfare form of state created for many a general impression of state decline, this was far from the case. Instead we saw a changed state strategy and new type of regulation based around an aggressive promotion of the free market and international competitiveness. The reworking of the historical bloc was based on the neoliberal agenda of rolling back state provision of welfare and public services and support for a new legal and institutional framework that promotes open markets and the deregulation of economic activity.

How might governmentality be brought into this picture? Since we take a historical materialist approach, we believe that a theory of hegemony is better at providing an account of the broader institutional context, the role of class forces, how particular interests are represented, how projects are constructed and how deeper structural issues are responded to. As Ngai-Ling Sum notes, Foucault is reluctant to accept the idea of any overall social cohesion other than through the generalisation of specific technologies of power, whereas Gramsci is concerned with precisely this matter of how something inherently unstable and conflict-laden is able to acquire a degree of social coherence (Sum 2004: 5).

But governmentality is better at showing the specific techniques and technologies of power. We will see that the governmentality approach provides a detailed account of the technologies by which neoliberalism works through the governance aspect and its micro-level operation. Hegemony might provide the better link to the social context, but governmentality better shows how this finds its expression in particular forms of governance. It highlights the specific use that can be made of mechanisms of individualisation and normalisation and helps us understand how macro strategies are connected to micro practices that encourage individual self-government. All this gives a new dimension to our understanding of neoliberalism as something not just to do with free markets and privatisation, but the individualisation and responsibilisation of behaviour that is promoted through the idea of the free exercise of conduct.

Governmentality is also better at explaining discursive power and provides an account of the rationalities of governance that is missing from Gramscian approaches. It acts as a counter to the tendency in Gramscian accounts to give an intersubjective view of social activity and to attribute conscious intent to each act. In the previous section we mentioned how Foucault argues that macro powers may colonise already existing micro practices in order to shape them into some kind of project. We applied this to the state, but it applies equally to the process of hegemony formation. So groups do not create hegemony afresh, they take up already existing micro practices, discourses and established patterns of conduct – things that pre-exist the particular project, but which Foucault shows can be colonised and brought together through deploying a macro-level strategy. This explanation has been applied to the way various political projects acquire a neoliberal character. Nikolas Rose mentions that the various tactics that emerged under Thatcher in Britain in the 1980s were 'contingent lash-ups of thought and action' which drew on whatever instruments and procedures happened to be available, but which in the course of the process began to develop a more coherent logic as part of a neoliberal rationality (Rose 1999: 27). The rationality aspect of this is particularly important as it pre-exists and shapes the particular agents who develop particular policies. Through policy we can talk of the use of techniques of governmentality as something intentional, but these policy actions represent conscious action within conditions not of the actors' own choosing. This is not to say that there is some hidden hand of governmentality that does the acting, but it is important to look at what pre-exists those who act and shapes their conduct by providing a background and set of tools and resources that is both enabling and constraining.

Rationalities pre-exist the conscious acts of agents and maybe even particular hegemonic projects. However, there is no clear hierarchical or causal chain, but rather a set of overlapping and co-determining social processes. Types of hegemony and governmentality are emergent aspects of the social whole. That means that they are dependent on underlying conditions of possibility like relations of production, but they are not reducible to such lower levels and have their own emergent properties and characteristics. Having said this, it is our contention that hegemony does help explain something of why governmentality emerges, for example, in its specific neoliberal form, and if governmentality is not wholly caused by, then at least it develops alongside these changes which contribute to the overall conditions of possibility. Governmentality could in turn be described as a condition of intelligibility for hegemony in the sense that it completes hegemony and explains the how without reducing it to the conditions out of which it emerges.

The emergence of particular forms of governmentality is not a 'natural' effect of the mode of production, but is a result of specific historical processes. In particular, the way contemporary governmentality poses alternative modes of governance should be linked to the neoliberal critique of the postwar settlement and a move away from the institutional arrangements of this period. The concept of governmentality on its own can show how this might be expressed, but it cannot explain why it works in the way it does. The wider picture is needed if we are to make sense of variations in governmentality and why current neoliberal forms of governmentality are dominant in the advanced liberal societies and among international organisations. Although dominant, this neoliberal governmentality does not enjoy an equal measure of success wherever it is deployed. It meets different outcomes in different contexts, meets different forms of resistance and comes up against different social systems. By 'bracketing out' the wider social context there is a real danger that governmentality theorists in IR miss out on what is, after all, a fundamental feature of IR, the unevenness of the international (social) terrain. If governmentality is not put in its proper social context, then the danger is that some general notion of global governmentality assumes the role of social ontology and may delude us into thinking that governmentality is now universal and irreversible.

Historical and international context

Taking our study into the international domain means starting with the idea that capitalism as a system is dynamic and expansionary, but that the reproduction of its dynamics comes into conflict with the political command structure. This is especially true of the international system, where the command structure is separated into individual states. Marx and Engels, although perhaps writing about a less global capitalism, themselves noted how the international is the place where 'all contradictions come into play' (Marx 1973: 227) as a result of the 'splitting up of the world market into separate parts, each of which was exploited by a separate nation' (Marx and Engels 1976: 56n). In addition to the problem of the separation of political and economic forms is the fact that the state was not created by capitalism but emerges out of pre-capitalist social relations. The state form then develops alongside the development of capitalism, with sovereign power developing a more and more capitalist form as the state develops the legal and infrastructural requirements for things like property and wage labour. Studying the international requires a subtle analysis that recognises the great influence of capitalism, while not reducing the state to an expression of this. We cannot simply reduce the state to capitalist relations of production, because this cannot explain the territorially fragmented nature of political command. The state system was not created by capitalism, but it is forced to confront capitalism's expansionist logic. Meanwhile the states system has its own structural dynamics, not least the traditional realist concerns of foreign policy and ensuring security in an uncertain world of rival states.

Contrary to the popular belief that capitalism's expansionary logic is eroding these territorial forms, our belief is that power in the international system reflects the dominance of particular states. This might be consistent with a realist view of international relations, but we will go on to insist, first, that the system of power among states can be understood only in relation to the dynamics of capitalism, and, second, that the dominance of particular states in the international system is reflected not just in raw material power, but also in the transposing of features of those states' particular social relations onto the fabric of international relations. This is the case if we examine the dominance of the USA in the early twentieth century, and it is still the case today. Neoliberalism, we will argue, reflects not globalisation, but the dominant social model in the USA today.

We arrive at this position by following historical accounts of US hegemony. The neo-Gramscian accounts of the postwar order provide the best understanding of this. This position builds on a range of critical International Political Economy (IPE) arguments about economic regulation, the role of capital accumulation, production techniques and so on. We saw that Gramsci's own position started from the role of Fordism in US domestic production. Gramsci goes on to use the term 'Americanism' to describe the spreading influence of this system, not just to forms of state intervention, but to worldwide social relations and forms of state action. In other words, Americanism means not just US hegemony among states, but also the influential force of the US production model. This means an intensive regime of accumulation based on mass consumption, a monopolistic mode of regulation, binding collective agreements, regulation of wage relations, extensive welfare provision and social insurance. This was a negotiated compromise between capital and labour, reflected in a new historical bloc that brought together not just different capitalist fractions, but also sections of the working class and labour movement. There were variations in this across different countries. But we can talk of an international consensus based on the interconnection of the historical blocs in different countries through shared ideology and mutual interests (Cox 1987: 7). This allowed the dominant state to fashion a liberal international order based on broad consent and general principles and institutionalised through the role of the Bretton Woods institutions, the dollar system and US military supremacy. We will look at various IR understandings of this system in the next section.

We have already mentioned that the breakdown of this system stemmed from changes at the point of production – a crisis of productivity, difficulties in regulating increasingly global flows and trade, Fordism's lack of flexibility and growing class opposition to the system. Internationally this found its expression in the crisis of the dollar, which both undermined US competitiveness and destabilised the world economy. This leads to a transformation that is again best explained in Gramscian terms. In the most general sense, this entails, in Cox's view, complex changes at different levels – in the powers of the various states, in the balance of social groups, in the uneven development of the productive forces and in the social structure of accumulation (Cox 1987: 209). This meant that a solution to the crisis would require radical changes in the labour process bringing in more flexible forms of production and management. The crisis acted as a spur for radical innovations in information and communications technology – technological innovation was prompted by the drive to reconstitute social relations, yet is presented by the theorists we go on to look at as if technology were the causal power. The state plays the role of encouraging supply-side innovation, promoting partnerships and stressing the need for open, competitive markets. It also leads the way in promoting financialisation, which leads to a whole new situation. The theoretical debates long talked up the idea of post-Fordist production; however, this can be overstated. In fact it might be suggested that the turn to the financial sector represents recognition of the failure to revitalise the US industrial economy (see Gowen 2010: 189–90). Instead, the US economy was restructured around cheap imported commodities and a credit boom. The result has been a huge current-account deficit and the eventual bursting of the credit bubble.

We will argue that at the international level much of this goes under the description of globalisation. The pursuit of policies such as open markets, free movement of capital, restructuring of labour markets and the promotion of international competitiveness gets repackaged as a global phenomenon to which states are forced to respond. The reality of the power inequalities of the international system is that it is the poorer states who are forced to respond, while the richer states are the ones pursuing these policies as an extension of their own domestic strategy of subjecting everyone to market forces. We will argue that it is through international organisations that poorer countries can be subject to the sort of discipline necessary to get them to comply with this agenda. By presenting this process as benign, the globalisation agenda hides the reality of power in the international system and depoliticises the neoliberal policies. We will see that, as with domestic governments, so too international organisations present these policies in technocratic and managerial terms.

The neoliberal agenda can therefore be described as a restructuring project, both national and global in scope, emphasising market rule and the discipline of the economy and spread principally through state power (Tickell and Peck 2003: 165). It presents itself as natural and apolitical and is applied to all the things typical of the field of governmentality – welfare, social insurance, the labour market and workplace relations. Both nationally and internationally we might divide the development of neoliberalism into stages. It first emerges to promote rolling back the postwar institutional settlement, attacking welfare policies, Keynesian state regulation and the labour movement. The coming together of a loose set of ideas is given greater coherence by the actions of think tanks and their influence on the policy agenda. In the 1980s a much more coherent state strategy emerged based on a populist promotion of privatisation, tax cuts, curbing the power of labour and the unions and emphasising strict monetary policy. The 'roll-back' phase of neoliberalism required a certain degree of state aggression. In Britain, for example, this was seen during the miners' strike of 1984–5. In other parts of the world, notably Latin America, the levels of state violence were much higher (see Blakeley 2009: 6–7, 159–61). In other words, before neoliberalism could take the form of governmentality, it required varying degrees of force and coercion in order to establish itself. In the 1990s this aggressive phase gave way to the normalisation of neoliberal modes of regulation and a more technocratic and managerial approach that appeared to depoliticise the strategy. This is what Tickell and Peck call the 'roll-out' phase of institution building (2003: 175). By then the main ideas of neoliberalism were hegemonic and the market logic was largely accepted across the political spectrum. As the governments of Reagan and Thatcher were replaced by those of Clinton and Blair, more emphasis was placed on softer ideas like public–private partnerships, networked governance and an individualised conception of civil society that encourages active citizenship. These ideas were part of a movement that found acceptance not just among many governments, but also among international organisations. This helps explain the shift in the Washington consensus from an aggressive phase of structural adjustment programmes to the new emphasis on the role of the state in building institutions for markets and encouraging a vibrant civil society as a means of empowering local people.

This is how we explain the influence of governmentality, both as a domestic concern in the advanced liberal societies, and in the international organisations as a reflection of the dominant concerns of the powerful states that influence these organisations. While many Foucauldians are keen to emphasise the general character of governmentality as something that arises a few centuries ago and which Foucault (2010) suggests can even be traced back to the concept of self among the ancient Greeks, we are concerned to move from a general concept of conduct to governmentality as a specific social form emergent out of particular social and historical conditions. In today's world, governmentality reflects its conditions of possibility and is thus inextricable from the dominant social, political, economic and global power. It is for this reason that we are concerned to stress the neoliberal variant of governmentality. It reflects the balance of forces in the dominant state – the USA – hence taking an Anglo-Saxon, neoliberal form. The concept of governmentality fits perfectly with ideas like competitiveness (especially emphasising its artificial, constructed nature), the emphasis on individualised, privatised social relations and the stress on flexibilisation, reflexivity and networked forms of governance. It highlights the role given to the market as a tool for shaping social relations, emphasises the importance of innovation and the use of new technology, and shows how market freedoms are combined with state authoritarianism through things like heightened electronic surveillance, databases and various forms of biopower. The only thing missing from the governmentality approach is an adequate account of where it comes from.

We have not tried to engage in a debate about whether there is some sort of generic governmentality that has its basis in the general social condition. Instead, we have emphasised the specific neoliberal form of contemporary governmentality as reflecting, or developing alongside a specific social, historical and institutional context. It is tied to the workings of the capitalist system, but develops in its specific form as a result of the ending of the postwar historical bloc and the transformation of its institutional architecture. Transformed state strategies required the deployment of new techniques of governance that emphasise free conduct and governance from a distance while in actual fact heightening monitoring and scrutiny of behaviour and responsibilising conduct.

There is, though, a clear difference between deploying governmentality in the national and international domains. We believe that because neoliberal governmentality has developed in the United States, and because the USA is the dominant state in the world system, then this governmentality is transferred to those international organisations that the USA influences. But we must distinguish between the influences on these organisations – politics, finance, the education and training of the staff and above all a shared rationality – and the actual efforts to implement this rationality in different parts of the world where social conditions are quite different from those found in the United States. Above all, we are concerned to emphasise that international organisations work across an uneven terrain that is an aggregate of different social systems.

The international is special because it is made up of multiple social contexts. Following Justin Rosenberg we define the international as the domain of inter-societal interaction and coexistence (Rosenberg 2006: 311). Rosenberg goes on to emphasise that this inter-societal coexistence is uneven; indeed, 'the phenomenon of the international arises from the socio-historical unevenness of human existence'; at the same time, the distinctive characteristics of the international must be 'explained by analysis of the resultant condition of 'combined development'' (2006: 313). Hence this concept shows how societies are 'combined' and 'causally integrated with a wider social field of interacting patterns of development' (2006: 321). For Rosenberg the idea of uneven and combined development is characteristic not just of certain countries but also of the very idea of the international itself. It is, he says, 'an intrinsic characteristic of social development as a trans-historical phenomenon – its inner multilinearity and interactivity' (2006: 327).

As we shall see in the next chapter, Rosenberg develops a strong critique of globalisation theory. His argument is that by methodologically foregrounding space and time, globalisation theorists empty social relations of any specific content (Rosenberg 2005: 8). If we now start to raise the question of whether there is such a thing as global governmentality, we are faced with the same need to avoid making claims that overstate the global transformation of social relations without clearly recognising the different social dynamics of various parts of the international system. If, for example, we see governmentality as a product of particular types of society in certain parts of the world, then we should reject arguments that suggest that while governmentality develops as an account of domestic situations, it is relatively easily extended to the international arena.[6]

If we follow our earlier understanding of governmentality in its specifically liberal or neoliberal form, then the uneven nature of the international raises serious issues concerning where this particular

[6] Ronnie Lipschutz writes that: 'Foucault wrote only of national governmentality, with each separate (state) order constituting its own sphere of discipline. As we shall see, the extension of this idea to the international arena is rather straightforward' (Lipschutz 2005: 15).

form of rule can apply. Of course we can always make the case that different types of governmentality operate in different places. Larner and Walters suggest that we can find various forms of governmentality ranging from imperialism through to European integration. They introduce the idea of a new regionalism to describe recent developments in international governmentality that govern from a distance through the active consent of states and populations (2002: 398). But as they themselves note, this particular type of governmentality is far more relevant to something like the EU, whereas 'areas like sub-Saharan Africa are relatively bare spots on the map … [where] networks of capital and information associated with postindustrial progress are sparse and stretched' (2002: 421). We are not concerned in this book with looking at how governmentality works on a country-by-country basis. We could try and make the case, as Bayart does, that there are distinctively African forms of governmentality based on particular local practices and complex 'discursive genres' (Bayart 2009: 271). But we are concerned here with the operation of international organisations and whether they can operate across very different social terrains, raising the issue of whether the types of techniques developed in one place may not necessarily be best suited for somewhere else. While neoliberal forms of governmentality in the advanced liberal societies may not necessarily be desirable, we can at least see how they can operate. When the social conditions for neoliberal governmentality are not present it is more difficult to see how governance might take place from a distance through the exercise of freedom. We have seen throughout the developed economies a process of commodifying more and more areas of social provision. However, this process works alongside and requires liberal forms of state governance. If this is not present in other parts of the world then we have to consider alternative descriptions of what is going on. We could perhaps talk of 'failed governmentality'. Abrahamsen and Williams hint at this:

> The colonial legacy, combined with economic and political factors, have made the production of a 'citizen identity' in many African countries highly problematic, and this lack of social cohesion is arguably a source of many of the continent's security problems. The privatization and globalization of security can potentially exacerbate this situation. (Abrahamsen and Williams 2006: 19)

More often than not, when populations really do have to be controlled, then more coercive forms of power are exercised. This is precisely the point at which governmentality needs to be understood in relation to disciplinary power and the kinds of techniques, institutions and apparatuses described by Foucault in *Discipline and Punish* rather than in his governmentality lectures. While social theorists might talk up the idea of governmentality working effectively in different parts of the world, social reality is always a harsher judge of such exercises.

This is not to suggest that certain parts of the world are not capable of developing their own forms of governmentality. Rather, we are concerned with the way a particular neoliberal form of governmentality gets imposed on other parts of the world by Western states and the international organisations that they dominate. The appropriateness of these methods is highly dubious, certainly if judged in terms of improving people's lives. Indeed, David Roberts goes so far as to contrast biopolitics in the North with what he calls biopoverty in the South. Whereas biopolitics might represent a sort of institutionally secured, physiological security, biopoverty is the antithesis of this – the mismanagement of biopolitical needs and the lack of empathetic or effective government (Roberts 2010: 25–6). In Chapter 7 (on the World Bank) we will argue that although interventions by international organisations have changed since the overtly coercive policies of structural adjustment, such interventions still contribute to biopoverty by privileging support for open markets over effective policies for local populations.

The new approach of 'building institutions for markets' means emphasising good governance, the rule of law, efficient and transparent decision-making, local ownership and effective intervention. But if the state is already weak, and if civil society is quite different from the Bank's 'Western model', it is hard to see how these new programmes can really help to improve most people's lives. Developing countries suffer a modern version of uneven and combined development in so far as they are locked into the social conditions of their own particular development, yet are subject to the strategies and techniques of the advanced liberal countries who dominate the activities of the major development organisations and other forms of global governance. It would take a significant stretch of the imagination to believe that in these cases such organisations succeed in promoting the health, wealth and well-being of populations through advanced liberal techniques of governance.

Looking at the wider picture, critics like Chandler (2006), Cammack (2004) and Kiely (2007a) have noted that what really happens here is that Northern-dominated institutions dictate what counts as good governance while poorer states are forced to take responsibility for implementing these policies, not so much to improve the lives of local people as to improve conditions for the movement of capital by removing potential barriers to accumulation. Chandler argues that states are integrated into networks of external regulation which work by denying ultimate responsibility for the relationship and making the exercise of power appear as empowering rather than dominating (Chandler 2006: 77). We will describe this approach as a form of governmentality applied to states. They are subjected to a normalising discourse that sets standards by which to judge the achievement of certain targets, which can then be used to blame countries when these are seen not to have been achieved. These norms are not imposed as a more direct form of coercive power might be, but are applied using a complex process of assessment of compliance. Indeed, as Cammack notes, an organisation like the World Bank promotes ideas like partnership and ownership because it

> recognises that it lacks the means to enforce the strategy itself, and because the legitimation of its project *vis-à-vis* citizens around the world depends upon its adoption by national governments, which remain indispensable intermediaries in the project. But at the same time it proposes that governments should maintain a policy matrix for external inspection at any time. (Cammack 2004: 204)

This notion of external inspection provides a good way of understanding governance from a distance and subjects states to what Mark Duffield calls 'metropolitan monitoring, intervention and regulation' (Duffield 2002: 1066). We can look at the way international organisations compile data and indexes and use a range of benchmarks and performance indicators to assess compliance with certain rules, norms and performance targets. Various examples of these include the World Bank's World Development Indicators and Global Development Finance databases, the Millennium Development Goals Indicators, the World Economic Forum's Global Competitiveness Report and the OECD's Main Economic Indicators. The guiding criteria are economic ones, an example of what Foucault means when he says that governmentality takes political economy as its method of intervention. In discussing neoliberalism he writes: 'The market economy does not take something away from government. Rather, it indicates, it constitutes the general index in which one must place the rule for defining all governmental action' (Foucault 2008: 121). A number of governmentality theorists have done interesting work on this issue by applying it to the way government action is defined (or appraised) by international organisations. Jacqueline Best sums up this approach in arguing that a governmentality approach 'provides us with some of the tools necessary to understand the ways in which these political economic imperatives have been internationalized and institutionalized in recent years – through the non-juridical logic of international standards, the calculating metric of transparency and the entrepreneurial ethic of self-responsibility' (Best 2007: 102). The issue of transparency is particularly interesting as a way of disciplining states and economies, and international organisations publish a range of indicators to scrutinise whether different countries have managed to meet satisfactory performance targets or to compare how well countries have managed in relation to one another. In other words, neoliberal governmentality constitutes states on the basis of global standards of conduct and competitiveness rather than seeing them as socio-political entities (Fougner 2008b: 118).

We can summarise the last three sections with a question: why is it important to argue that a governmentality approach can fit with a certain form of historical materialism? We will address this as we go through the book. But two crucial points should be highlighted here. First, by setting governmentality within a wider social framework we can better explain how it works. While some poststructuralist approaches to governmentality deliberately remain at the level of strategies, and ignore or reject the idea of underlying capitalist relations, our argument is that by providing this wider context we can better explain what is going on. Not only does this help account for how governmentality works, it also explains how it works differently in different places, or indeed how it might fail or prove irrelevant in certain cases. Second, we can see that this approach not only fits with state theory, but actually requires it. We shall argue that this is especially important in the cases we study because in the application of transnational or global governmentality, we see the state being identified as the main social institution through which these techniques can work. Thus rather than undermining the state, we will see that the techniques of global governmentality are targeted at the state and recognise it to be an essential social institution upon which the success of governmentality depends.

International relations and global order

It is now our task to situate the governmentality approach in relation to IR theory and to show what it can contribute to this body of literature. Like everyone else, we start with realism. Indeed, a serious problem with IR theory is that it has always seemed to be cast under realism's shadow. More specifically, we find most of the interesting approaches to IR and international organisations – liberal institutionalism, constructivism and neo-Gramscianism – continuing to use structural realism as their frame of reference. We then look at the emerging body of literature that draws on governmentality and raise some questions about its assumptions. We will draw on the philosophy of scientific realism to frame some important questions to do with the relationship between the material and ideational and between structure and agency.

It is not really clear where realism starts and ends. Although classical realism has had something of a revival recently, we will assume that we do not wish to define state activity through the lens of human nature, even if the recent revival has sought to draw out the more social and constructivist aspects of this body of work. Neo- or structural realism we have critiqued elsewhere from a scientific realist view (Joseph 2007, 2010). It takes states as its main actors, but assumes them to be unitary, rational and predictable in their actions. The focus on behaviour assumes a billiard-ball model of causation, extrinsic rather than internal, reducible to regular patterns of behaviour and, despite the talk of structure, with no underlying causal mechanism. The concept of structure is quite different from the one we wish to promote in this book. We might say, to paraphrase Morgenthau, that for Waltz and the neorealists structure is Hobbesian man writ large.

Despite all these problems, it is difficult to get away from structural realism. Alternatives are usually built on a challenge to neorealist assumptions that often lead to new errors. Liberal accounts of the world order revived in the 1970s and 1980s, criticising realism's state-centric, security-driven view by bringing in transnational actors and economic analysis. Perhaps the most influential way this was done was through the concept of international regimes. These regimes are defined by Krasner as 'principles, norms, rules, and decision-making procedures around which actor expectations converge in a given issue area' (Krasner 1983: 1). Norms might be considered as standards of behaviour defined in terms of rights and obligation, while rules are specific prescriptions or proscriptions for action. 'Decision-making procedures' means prevailing practices for implementing collective choices. This clearly challenges the narrowness of the realist conception of state behaviour and reflects a belief that the realist approach is too narrow to fully capture an increasingly complex and heterogeneous world (Puchala and Hopkins 1983: 61). Hass goes so far as to argue that under conditions of complex interdependence, states rarely practice self-help, and in the international domain neither hierarchy nor anarchy prevails (1983: 27). Outlining a more subjective view of international regimes, Puchala and Hopkins declare them to be attitudinal and 'embedded in normative superstructures' (1983: 64). They exist through participants' understandings, and expectations.

But Hass, Puchala and Hopkins represent the more subjective side of the argument, following a Grotian belief in international society. A more influential position is advanced by Robert Keohane. Its influence derives from its closeness to realism. For Keohane regimes represent voluntary agreements among actors. Since he assumes conflict to be the rule, institutionalised patterns of cooperation are in need of explanation. He does this by drawing on rational choice and microeconomic theory. Regimes facilitate agreements among rational utility maximisers (1983: 151). Actors enter into institutionalised agreements as part of a bargaining process based on the benefits outweighing the costs. The rise of regimes is linked to increasing interdependence and 'issue density' (1983: 157) causing actors to seek agreements that offer long-term benefits.

There is some debate as to whether regimes depend upon a hegemonic power. Although the rationalist approach to regime theory believes that the main variables are egotistic self-interest and the drive to maximise political power, there is space for the idea that a hegemonic power might step forward to offer leadership and perhaps even provide collective goods. Indeed, in raising the question of whether hegemony is a necessary condition for effective international cooperation Keohane positions his approach close to hegemonic stability theory. Emerging initially in the historical analysis of Kindleberger, this position talks of the need for a country to take the lead in setting standards of conduct for other countries to follow. This means taking on an undue share of the burdens of the system. Kindleberger's assessment in the 1930s was that Britain has the willingness to lead but not the resources, whereas the USA had the economic strength but not the inclination (1973: 28). In Keohane's view, while there was eventually a postwar hegemony based on a stable monetary system, provision of open markets for goods and access to oil, this did not in the long run provide a strong enough resource base for the exercise of US dominance (Keohane 1984: 177). It is this question of whether the USA is able to remain a hegemon that leads Keohane to develop his ideas on regime theory via the view, developed with Joseph Nye, that all states increasingly find themselves in a condition of complex interdependence. This position can be summarised as the belief in (1) multiple channels of a transnational, trans-governmental and inter-state nature; (2) multiple issues with no clear hierarchy; and (3) the increasing difficulty of using military force. Realism is seen as inadequate in explaining a world comprised of different issues, goals, agendas and indeed actors (Keohane and Nye 1989: 25, 114).

Starting with regime theory, our critique would agree with Strange's assessment that these theories often lead to a view of world politics that seeks pervasive patterns of behaviour and is overly concerned with the status quo. They place too much emphasis on the role of governments and elites and assume that order and management is a good thing (Strange 1983: 338, 345). More generally, we can say that most realist and liberal approaches tend to take socio-economic conditions as given and focus instead on the structure of the inter-state system. This often produces a cyclical view of history that sees it in terms of rise and fall of hegemons, who are, in turn, often crudely defined by control over material resources. Underlying this is a certain view of power which rather than being structural (despite the frequent use of the word) might be described as 'power over'. Although they have a more sophisticated approach than most, Keohane and Nye are explicit in defining power as the ability to get an actor to do something they would otherwise not do. Power is defined as control over resources within which lies the potential to affect outcomes (Keohane and Nye 1989: 11). Combined with the rationality assumption, this leads to an ahistorical and asocial view of international relations. Of course it is legitimate to talk of states acting rationally. One does not have to go all the way down the postmodern path of rejecting the whole idea of rationality as merely a discursive construct. But realist and neoliberal approaches make problematic assumptions about the nature of the actors and their contexts, stripping them of their social and historical aspect and seeing rationality in microeconomic terms as preference maximising. Indeed, mainstream approaches reflect a dominant social logic that sees social action in terms of calculation, strategy, decision-making and other forms of instrumental thinking that critical theory regards as characteristic of late capitalist thinking (see Roach 2010: 42). If Foucault is to be useful here, it is not as a means of abandoning the idea of rationality, but in showing it as a social construct and exploring the mechanisms by which it works. The arguments of the rationalists in IR, although telling us very little about the rationality of states, tell us quite a lot, inadvertently, about how capitalist rationality penetrates all areas of thinking, IR theory included.

Having criticised the rationalist approach to international relations, we should note that there is more reflexivity in regime theory than we have given credit for. Keohane and Nye themselves state their dissatisfaction in having only succeeded in moving the neorealist research programme a little further down the path of accounting for political-economic interaction (1989: 254). In *After Hegemony*, Keohane acknowledges that a Gramscian approach better enables us to understand the willingness of partners to defer to the hegemon (1984: 45). John Ruggie discusses how Keohane allows for a limited number of ideational factors like world-views, principled beliefs and causal beliefs. World-views are of most interest to Ruggie – they point, he says, to what exists before the neo-utilitarian model kicks in. Ultimately the difference between the rationalist approach and Ruggie's constructivism lies with intersubjectivity (Ruggie 1998: 19–20). Looking at Bretton Woods, Ruggie argues that this regime produced more than just rules of conduct. Rather, it established an intersubjective framework of meaning, a shared narrative and basis of interpretation (1998: 21). In a well-known argument partly drawn from Karl Polanyi, he claims that the *laissez-faire* liberalism of the nineteenth century was replaced, in the postwar period, with an 'embedded liberalism' that incorporates some of the issues we have been discussing regarding regulation and institutional framework. As we have argued, this means looking not just at relations between states, but the relation between state and society inside the dominant economic powers (1998: 62). The institutionalisation of political relationships and the understandings developed by political actors is addressed through the notion of epistemic communities (1998: 55). Ruggie borrows the idea of episteme from Foucault to describe a particular way of looking at reality based on shared symbols and references and mutual expectations.

While there are things here that are useful – notably the idea of embedded liberalism – Ruggie's argument also shows the problems with a constructivist approach. In trying to develop an alternative to realist accounts of regime change, Ruggie develops the idea of social purpose, which is a useful idea, but places too much emphasis on actors and their intersubjective relations. Explanation of change lies at the level of changes in value commitments, or as Teschke and Heine (2002: 170) put it, regime change is explained through 'epistemic disarray' rather than economic crisis. Ruggie provides an intersubjective account of the re-evaluation of core ideals of the postwar order like welfarism and state intervention. But this focus on value communities lacks an extra-ideational account of why these changes in values occur. There is little account of economic crisis, or problems of productivity and competitiveness. Teschke and Heine's criticism of this work argues that Ruggie tries 'to explain changes in international economic regimes without economics and changes in political regimes without politics' and that his approach ends up obscuring the social processes and political mechanisms 'that generate conflict and compromise, crisis and successful institutionalisation' (2002: 170).

We will continue with this critique of constructivism after looking at a recent book that seems closest to our own project. *Rules for the World* by Michael Barnett and Martha Finnemore takes up the constructivist emphases on how rules shape attitudes, behaviour and expectations and links this to a theory of bureaucratic culture and the institutionalisation of these practices and understandings. This is also an interpretative approach in so far as emphasis is placed on how the rules are understood and interpreted. Consequently Barnett and Finnemore focus on international organisations as examples of bureaucracies that use their expert knowledge to exercise power, tell us what the main problems are and regulate and constitute the world in certain ways (2004: 9). The emphasis on bureaucracy leads to the claim that this is a self-perpetuating system in so far as 'bureaucracies use their rules to help create or constitute the social world and tend to do so in ways that make the world amenable to intervention by bureaucracies themselves' (2004: 18).

This approach tells us how bureaucracies (international organisations) use expert knowledge to classify, constitute and regulate the world. Classification takes place through the creation of categories of problems and the empowerment of particular actors. These organisations fix meanings, establish boundaries and articulate and disperse rules and norms (Barnett and Finnemore 2004: 32). This approach, placing emphasis on rules combined with a theory of bureaucratic organisation, is applied to organisations like the IMF and UNHCR. In the case of the IMF the authors note how it creates rules that determine how best to solve certain problems – such as solving balance-of-payment deficits – which require the sort of economic restructuring that only a strong intervention by the IMF itself can provide (Barnett and Finnemore 2004: 18). This then reinforces an internal culture where international organisations create a shared understanding of their mission and core functions and goals, their symbols and values (2004: 19).

This is an approach to international relations that is well worth engaging with. It ties in with how we would wish to analyse international organisations in so far as the book's analysis emphasises the way the activities of these organisations is an expression of both liberal and rationalist ideas. This is seen in the way that such organisations emphasise the role of the individual and the promotion of democracy and the market. The rationalist nature of bureaucracy means that legitimacy comes from following the proper procedures (Barnett and Finnemore 2004: 166–7). Today this can clearly be seen in the language of an institution like the IMF with its stress on transparency, democratic deliberation and local participation (2004: 170). As with Ruggie's work, there are also some similarities between this constructivist approach and the Foucauldian idea of discourse. Note, for example, the authors' argument that actors 'use frames to situate events and to interpret problems, to fashion a shared understanding of the world, to galvanize sentiment, as a way to mobilize and guide social action' (Barnett and Finnemore 2004: 33). However, as with the Foucauldian literature, this presents the problem (identified earlier by Teschke and Heine) that the desire to emphasise rules and norms (or in the Foucauldian case, strategies and techniques) often leads to an under-emphasis on deeper structures, material conditions and underlying social relations.

Here perhaps is another example of the negative influence of neorealism. The emphasis on rules and norms is seen as a way of challenging neorealism's abstract and ahistorical structuralism, while the emphasis on ideational factors is seen as a corrective to neorealism's reduction of power relations to material capabilities. This takes us to more general problems with constructivism and its equivocation regarding the issue of the material world. Alexander Wendt, in opposing Kenneth Waltz's neorealist view of international structure,[7] argues that we should see the world in social rather than material terms. And because the basis of sociality is shared knowledge, he claims to take an idealist view of structure (Wendt 1999: 1, 20), seeing structure and structural change in cultural rather than material terms.

While there is no doubt that cultural and ideational factors are an important part of the social world – indeed this very book is all about this issue – there must be serious concern about just how this idealist view of structure would deal with the kind of Marxist account of social relations described above. While constructivist arguments are not simply rejected, they need to be put in their proper context. International organisations do not exist in their own world of rules and norms. They cannot be separated from conditions of material production, or the role of states in the international system. However, they can develop their own irreducible properties just as state strategies and hegemonic projects may have their own distinctive characteristics irreducible to the conditions that make them possible.

The constructivist critique of materialism overstates the idea that it leads to a reductionist or mechanical understanding of social relations. This might be the case with versions of neorealism, but few contemporary versions of Marxism can be categorised in this way. Most of today's historical materialism, while starting from the importance of production, challenges a reductionist understanding of this. Indeed as Wendt himself notes, the Marxist notion of production implies relations of production and various ideational aspects (1999: 94–5). Production should be seen as a social, cultural and political process as much as a brute economic relation. Productive forces cannot be considered independently of the social relations that organise them. In the

[7] Where he argues that the structure of the international system (anarchy) compels states to act in a self-interested way and that power in the international system is based on the distribution of material capabilities (Waltz 1979).

broadest sense, capitalism is unimaginable without private property relations, and these in turn are established through a legal framework guaranteed by political sovereignty and an ideational belief in their legitimacy. This already allows for the significance of rules and norms. A Marxist approach that starts from the significance of the mode of production can reject determinism by stressing how the mode of production contains social relations inseparable from political, cultural and ideational factors.

On these matters, it is the neo-Gramscian approach to IR that is closest to our own. Robert Cox, the most influential exponent of this approach in IR, makes a useful contribution in clarifying the role of international institutions and their relationship to underlying power. He argues that institutions can be understood as a means by which world order can be maintained and stabilised, but that at the same time they take on their own life and can become a terrain of struggle (Cox 1996: 99). This link between institutionalisation and hegemony helps close some of the gaps in the constructivist approach. Like Ruggie, Barnett and Finnemore, we find the idea that institutions can develop a life of their own, but there is a stronger notion that these institutions are emergent from an underlying order that partly helps to explain their role (as stabilising world order). This world order, Cox goes on to argue, is not merely an order among states (as realists might argue), but is tied to the world economy, linked to the way the dominant mode of production penetrates other countries and represents a complex of international social relationships, both social, political and economic (1996: 137). This *then* allows for social groups to develop their own (emergent) projects by acting upon an institutional terrain that is conditioned by but irreducible to these underlying conditions. In Cox's view, institutions embody rules that facilitate the expansion of dominant social and economic forces (1996: 138). But we should add that there is no necessary correspondence between dominant social forces and institutional development.

We have already shown how this can be put to work in explaining the institutional arrangements of the postwar order. However, closer examination of Cox's arguments about the nature of social structure reveals some problematic similarities to constructivism.[8] Both

[8] This definition of structure from Cox is indistinguishable from a constructivist position: 'Structures are socially constructed, i.e., they become a part of the objective world by virtue of their existence in the intersubjectivity of relevant groups of people' (1996: 149).

positions start from a concern to correct the errors of the structuralism present in neorealism. Cox compares neorealism to what he considers the abstractness of Marxist structuralism. He therefore argues against those who believe that there is some deeper 'logic' of capital. Rather, structures should be inferred from observable patterns of conduct (1987: 396). The problem with this is that it cannot explain the end of the postwar settlement except in institutional terms. It is true that a meaningful account of this crisis needs to focus on the historical developments described above. But to explain why historical institutions started to fail and why the postwar historical bloc entered crisis, it is necessary to also give an account of the deep-rooted 'logic' of capital and the inherent contradictions (like crises of productivity and the tendency of the rate of profit to fall) that the institutional settlement was trying to overcome through various forms of intervention and regulation. Our criticism of Cox on this issue is therefore very similar to Teschke and Heine's criticism of Ruggie. Cox defines historical structure as a combination of thought patterns, material conditions and human institutions (Cox 1996: 97), but, ironically, it is the material element that we praised in the previous paragraph that is most weakly argued for in his account of structure.

While we have made similar criticisms of Foucault's work, there is an issue relating to intersubjectivity where Foucault offers a useful alternative to constructivist and Gramscian accounts. We saw that Ruggie uses the term epistemic community to describe how a group of political actors are brought together through a particular way of looking at reality based on shared symbols and references and mutual expectations. Cox develops a similar line of argument derived from Gramsci's understanding of world-views and the role of leading groups. At his most subjective, Cox argues that a 'hegemonic order is inscribed in the mind. It is an intersubjective sharing of behavioural expectations' (Cox 1996: 245). He goes on to make the useful point that hegemony at the international level is an expression of hegemony in the dominant countries in the world system. This would certainly help explain how it is that Anglo-Saxon governmentality comes to be so influential today. But he then adds that a hegemonic society is one where the dominant class has made its conception of social order acceptable to subordinate groups (Cox 1996: 246). This raises issues about agency that Foucault helps resolve. His idea of episteme is certainly not as intersubjective as Ruggie suggests. Nor is Ruggie really correct to pick Foucault's term episteme, for this is more like a general rationality of a particular age – for example, Foucault discuses how the Enlightenment replaces medieval ways of thinking that centred on a God-given order (Foucault 1974). Ruggie's concern is more with specific practices of governance or rule and is thus better described using Foucault's term discursive formation. These are indeed ways of looking at reality, but represent an a priori condition of possibility that shapes the way a particular society looks at reality, not the act of looking itself. Thus discursive formation is a prior background or set of resources upon which actors may draw, but which they did not create. It is the basis upon which intersubjectivity might operate, but not intersubjectivity itself. In this sense it works more like the conditioning effect of an underlying structure rather than the intended outcome of conscious acts.

Cox's intersubjectivity suggests that hegemony is a very conscious act. He talks of how, at the very top, consensus formation takes place through prime ministers, presidents, foreign offices, treasuries and so on (1987: 259). This is partly true. But to paraphrase Marx, these actions take place under conditions not of the actors' own choosing. The intersubjectivity present in Gramsci sometimes leads those who take this approach to overemphasise the role of social groups in creating international order even to the point where it is suggested that today's world is governed by a new transnational elite who share similar educational backgrounds and cultural values (Robinson 2004). Other neo-Gramscians in IR are closer to our position. Stephen Gill goes so far as to compare the idea of historical bloc with that of Foucault's discursive formation, the point of similarity being that they represent a set of ideas and practices with particular conditions of existence that have been institutionalised and are only partially understood by participants (Gill 2003: 120). This rightly suggests that actors operate within a pre-existing field, drawing on already existing practices and strategies. This relationship is not as simple as an instrumental one, whereby actors are free to use these strategies for their own purposes. By pre-existing the actors, the strategies and techniques shape the way the actors may behave, exist as part of a broader discursive formation whose rationality shapes the way the actors conceive of the world and form part of a wider ensemble of social relations of which the actors may only be partially aware.

This leads us to a brief account of scientific or critical realism. As an alternative to the philosophy of constructivism, realist philosophy argues that the world cannot be reduced to the actions or practices of conscious agents. There is always some aspect of reality, both natural and social, that we can never fully know or explain. As Gill says of the organisation of production, while this is partly constituted by intersubjective meanings, there is something about the scale and complexity of this process that can be got at only by imperfect abstractions concerning its underlying structural basis (Gill 2003: 21). When it comes to human activity, we likewise develop an understanding of our actions that is often only partially aware of the wider structural context within which they take place. Critical realism argues that while human agency is always conscious, there is a gap between conscious intent and (a) the social conditions necessary for this agency and (b) the reproduced outcome of these actions (see Archer 1995: 106). This contrasts with both constructivism and Cox's neo-Gramscianism, whose arguments suggest there is no gap because structures and agents are mutually constitutive.[9] In our view the deeper structural context is necessary to explain why certain actions have unconscious or unintended consequences and why actors are usually only partially aware of the processes in which they are engaged. It also explains why some agents, thanks to their structural positioning, are able to act in a more influential way, while others will act with less awareness and less ability to change their situation.

It would seem to us that the concept of governmentality is compatible with this view that there is always some pre-existing context that shapes the way we think and act and which often informs us in an unconscious or semi-conscious way. Governmentality itself is not an agent; it does not do this or that. But in existing as a context, it influences those who do act and shapes their conduct. The agents who act do so consciously. But they are usually unaware or only partially aware of the underlying conditions that shape this consciousness. While the underlying conditions include a range of different social structures, governmentality captures a particularly important aspect of

[9] Wendt and other constructivists make this point by drawing on Giddens's structuration theory (Wendt 1987: 339). Cox writes against structuralist theories that 'structures are not in any deeper sense prior to the human drama itself' (1987: 395).

this – the rationality that informs our understanding of conduct. This helps explain something like neoliberalism. While the neo-Gramscian approach tells us a lot about neoliberalism's social and historical context, governmentality tells us more about its rationality. It also tells us that this rationality is not born in the heads of prominent actors, be they politicians, business leaders, World Bank economists or social theorists. It is through the practices these people engage in that this rationality has to be reproduced and developed, but the rationality exists separately from them and shapes and informs their thoughts and actions.

To give an example of how this rationality has its own dynamics we might wonder how it was that international organisations somehow rediscovered the state as the key agent of development, despite the prevailing belief that governance was supposedly now 'beyond the state'? Our answer would be that it was not so much the case that actors in these organisations consciously came to the realisation that they must target states, but that the structural conditions of capital accumulation, global markets, security issues and global unevenness pushed the agenda in this direction. It became impossible to think of creating open markets, removing barriers to trade, flexibilising the supply of labour and of creating secure conditions for investment without somehow subjecting the state to new forms of regulation. The rationality of neoliberalism developed a momentum that was able to colonise more and more institutions, shaping the way people thought about social and global issues. But this rationality itself was shaped and conditioned by a wider structural context – not reducible to this context but not explicable without it, either. From here we can talk of the conscious policy actions of particular people and governments. But policy is shaped by conditions not of its own choosing.

This returns us to our earlier discussion of states as actors. It was argued that states could be considered actors only in an emergent sense and that the real actors are groups of people. But these people are subject to pressures of structural position that enable, constrain and strategically select the projects and activities that emerge. We propose treating international organisations in a similar way. We will see that we talk of the World Bank, for example, acting to do such-and-such or getting states to conform to something. Again, we would emphasise that this is an emergent notion of action based on structurally positioned agents and practices which themselves have been shaped and conditioned by pre-existing conditions like governmentality, other institutions and practices and deeper social structures like the economy. As with states, so with international organisations it is not the case that these are unified, rational actors. Internally there are a range of different positions, as we will see when we examine how the idea of social capital revealed divisions among World Bank staff. But, still, the actions of these organisations are given a strong degree of coherence by the process of strategic selectivity by which the internal structure of the organisation and the external pressures of that organisation's relation to other significant structures, institutions, practices and people – such as economy, state, governmental departments and dominant social groups – end up forming and shaping the type of policies that emerge.

Governmentality is somewhat different from states and international organisations. It does not act. Rather, it pre-exists and shapes the behaviour of those who do. It is an underlying condition. Its rationality informs certain practices while its techniques give expression to these. It shapes the way the world is seen by constructing it in a particular way. However, this can only happen because of the practices that it informs. And it can continue only so long as those actors, engaged in these practices, continue in their activities. Governmentality is both a necessary condition for and a reproduced outcome of human activity. It can only work through its attachment to things like state strategies, hegemonic projects and political actions. It influences these, but they also shape it. Because it relies on these actions for its reproduction, it can always be transformed, albeit within a specific set of conditions. Because it always exists within a particular complex of social relations, this always influences it. We will talk of governmentality as an underlying rationality and set of techniques, but we will also talk of its deployment and exercise by various actors. This is not an instrumental relationship, because it already shapes and influences those who use it. By arguing that governmentality is both a pre-existing condition and an emergent outcome of various projects and strategies we are arguing that it cannot be reduced to its exercise. However, it is nothing unless it is used and deployed, and we will examine how this happens through the activities of states, international organisations and social groups.

From global governance to global governmentality

In *Power in Global Governance* Barnett and Duvall argue that because most definitions of global governance are of a liberal nature, they tend to ignore the presence of power. In arguing the need for a concept of power they make a distinction between structural power and productive power. Structural power relates to the positions that actors occupy and often entails the sorts of relations of domination found in Keohane and Nye's 'power over' approach. Productive power looks at how subjects are constituted within various discursive practices and systems of knowledge. Barnett and Duvall point to Foucault's approach as showing how subjects are both the targets of discourse, but also its effects. Discourse, therefore, is socially productive for all subjects, constituting the subjectivity of all social beings (Barnett and Duvall 2005: 20–1). Our scientific realist approach would disagree with this constructivist move to distinguish between causal (structural) power and constitutive power, believing both understandings to have a structural and causal nature. But this need not concern us here.[10] The important issue is Barnett and Duvall's recognition of the idea of a pre-existing discourse or rationality that is in part constitutive of subjects or agents, both enabling them to act and to address certain problems in particular ways, but also conditioning their behaviour and influencing their outlook. Power in this second, 'constructive' sense recognises the pre-existing rationalities that shape and inform our thoughts and actions.

The emergence of the global-governance approach draws on a number of previously discussed themes like interdependence, the development of supranational regimes and institutions, the globalisation of the economy and the idea of new actors. However, the approach also makes a conscious attempt to break with traditional IR and its concern with power politics and the states system. Having said this, the stress on things like rules, norms and ideas is shared with IR constructivists, while various IR schools, be they neo-Gramscians or the English school, contain wings that support the idea of a transnational or world society. It is also the case that very different meanings are attributed to global governance. As Hewson and Sinclair note, the term could

[10] For a realist critique of the causal–constitutive distinction see Kurki (2008: 180).

refer to developments in the sort of international regimes we have just discussed, the way international organisations address international problems or the political forces shaping political governance (Hewson and Sinclair 1999: 18). Sinclair's own definition refers to the means social forces use to realise a world order made up of global political economy, the states system and the biosphere (Sinclair 1999: 162).

In the next chapter we will concern ourselves less with definitions and more with how the concept works. The development of the idea can be explained in a number of ways – a response to the end of Cold War politics, a belief in globalisation theory, the re-emergence of liberalism or, for James Rosenau, a combination of integration and fragmentation. Writers like Rosenau (2006) and Richard Falk (1995) present a much more progressive version of liberalism. But their arguments still fit with many of the dominant assumptions that we are trying to call into question. Rosenau, in criticising regime theory, calls into question the idea that states are the main actors and argues that more attention should be paid to NGOs, multinationals and social movements. States, he argues, while retaining formal sovereign rights, are able to exercise these in fewer ways as a result of the power of globalisation, increased interdependence, more porous boundaries and a diffusion of authority (Rosenau 2006: 115).

By contrast, we have argued that rather than undermining state power, these are deliberate state strategies. Rosenau talks of influence passing to transnational and supranational organisations above the state, NGOs and social movements alongside it, and subnational groups downwards (2006: 116). Throughout this book we will offer an alternative reading of this as governmentality pushed *by* states, pushed *on* states and pushed *through* states. The integration and fragmentation that Rosenau talks of as a new ontology, is in fact a consequence of this process of governmentalising the state. It is not so much an 'era marked by shifting boundaries, relocated authorities, weakened states and proliferating NGOs' (2006: 111) as a phase marked by reshaped historical blocs and shifting strategies of governance. This reflects the dominant strategies of the dominant powers in the dominant states. Writers like Rosenau talk of a new form of governance that reflects a disaggregated, decentred world with new spheres of authority and no single organising principle, and greater flexibility, innovation and experimentation in use of control mechanisms (2006: 124). We reply that this underplays the idea that these things are strategies, not a deeper social condition, and that they are strategies pursued by the dominant powers both socially and globally.

The criticism of the global governance literature is that it obfuscates the real sources of power in the global system. There are of course far worse accounts of global governance than Rosenau's, which see governance only as a positive thing for coordinating actions, resolving conflicts, finding common purpose and sharing interests. As Barnett and Duvall note, power rarely figures in these liberal accounts, certainly not power as relations of imposition, domination, structural determination or cultural hegemony (Barnett and Duvall 2005: 7). Only a few Gramscians have started to address these issues in terms of continuities of existing power relations. Cox, for example, talks of global governance in terms of a *nébuleuse* of ideological influences grouped around the idea of accountability to the global economy (1996: 298). Rupert argues the need to see how these tendencies are realised in a particular historical context and represent the political project of a USA-led historical bloc that has constructed a new global infrastructure around international trade and finance (2005: 214). At best the global governance literature fails to address these issues; at worst, as we shall see, it provides ideological cover.

The idea of global governance will be examined through the governmentality approach, but what of governmentality theorists themselves? We will end this review of IR theories with a very brief look at some of the governmentality approaches to have emerged recently in IR. It is impossible to cover all angles, because governmentality has been applied to a wide range of different issues. We will start with a sceptical review of some areas of application before concluding with a governmentality approach to global governance.

Our scepticism towards a widespread application of governmentality derives from our expressed view that governmentality is most meaningful when seen in relation to neoliberalism, the end of the postwar settlement and the reorganisation of both domestic and international institutional structures. If neoliberal governmentality is something that emerges in the advanced liberal societies, and the Anglo-Saxon ones in particular, then attempts to apply governmentality to all parts of the globe should be treated with some scepticism. Thus it is difficult to see why we should want to follow Luke (1996) in discussing such things as lawlessness in Sierra Leone and the role of guerrilla movements and village chiefs through the concept of governmentality unless we make the concept so general as to render it virtually meaningless. When he talks of 'contragovernmentality' challenging the state, surely a better term would be counter-hegemony? Likewise, when a recent volume (Perry and Maurer 2003) discusses a whole host of issues from Spanish immigration to South East Asian workers in the Gulf, identity in Hawaii and the global sex industry, why call this governmentality when these can be covered under the broader concept of biopolitics?

The term governmentality is often applied to the operation of private security companies in different parts of the world. Here, perhaps, a more convincing case is given that these companies are operating at a distance from both the local state and foreign powers which no longer hold, or care to hold, a monopoly over the legitimate use of force and so, consequently, security spans both public–private and local–global divides (Abrahamsen and Williams 2007: 132). With multiple actors involved, the provision of security becomes a competitive game governed by market rules. The result, as Leander and van Munster explain, is security governance 'taking place through a set of (quasi-) markets imbued with entrepreneurial values and inspired by a hands-off approach to governance' (Leander and van Munster 2007: 202). This in turn works to 'depoliticise' security and to frame it, like other forms of governmentality, in a technocratic way. Looking at this through the case study of Darfur, Leander and van Munster write that:

> Within the scheme of neo-liberal governmentality the regulation of actors takes place through the employment of private sector technologies of performance such as benchmarking, best practice schemes, codes of conduct, performance indicators and auditing. In line with the view that governing through (quasi-) markets is the most effective way of dealing with problems, the purpose of these technologies is to push control out of the allegedly unaccountable and non-transparent bureaucratic sphere towards the constant scrutinizing gaze of consumers and other stakeholders such as NGOs and other humanitarian organizations. (Leander and van Muster 2007: 209)

Thus far, the idea of governmentality works well in describing the *provision* of security. But this is precisely the problem in so far as the neoliberal discourse of security provision is being imposed in places quite different from those where these discourses and practices first emerged. If neoliberal practices were already contrived in their way of operating, this imposition on very different parts of the globe takes their artificiality to a new level. And in contrast to neoliberalism in advanced liberal societies, the outcome is usually quite different, often disastrously so. The proliferation of private security companies in Africa occurs not because these countries can easily be governmentalised, but usually because of the failings of public provision of security, most notably the lack of a strong and effective state capable of either directly providing security or effectively devolving its provision to others. The absence of these conditions means that governmentality can be imposed, but it cannot develop deep roots and thus fails in its immediate aims.[11] At the very least, the account of governmentality needs to be supplemented with an account of the operation of discipline and the subjection of local populations to coercive power in order to promote security and defend the interests of capital. This need to balance governmentality with disciplinary power equally applies to Ronnie Lipschutz's discussion of the War on Terror. He starts off by posing the issue of how neoliberal governmentality seeks to impose order on 'unruly populations' in both the 'more disciplined industrialized states' and the so-called rogue and failed states (Lipschutz 2005: 13). But he quickly moves on to say that the application to the latter 'involved resort to more direct forms of power in so far as neither self-discipline nor external discipline were considered adequate' (2005: 15). This resort to coercive power rather than governmentality is also clearly evident in state responses to the Arab Spring uprisings. To overplay the hand of governmentality in such cases would be dangerously misleading.

In our view, therefore, the application of governmentality to the field of IR works best when it is attempting to explain the mechanisms of global governance. This means we have less to worry about in terms of whether governmentality actually works on the ground because the primary aim of these interventions, as Merlingen says (2003: 362), is to conduct the conduct of countries. We thus find ourselves closest to IR scholars like Fougner (2008a, 2008b), Merlingen (2003) and Zanotti (2005), who deploy governmentality in relation to the global governance of state behaviour. In Michael Merlingen's view,

[11] For example, a study of private security in Kenya by Abrahamsen and Williams suggests that this is largely a chaotic affair, with little legislation or regulation and no oversight or monitoring of security practices, services and training (2006: 15).

organisations like the World Bank work to bring governments, civil societies and individuals under the 'ordering influence of international governance' (2003: 368). This we will partly agree with, although we will argue that such organisations largely ignore existing civil society and instead fabricate artificial ones that are tied to external intervention. Consequently control of individuals, at least in the governmentality sense, is limited to those officials in positions of governance. They are the ones encouraged to responsibilise their conduct in line with global economic needs, while local populations are subject to more direct forms of coercion. Merlingen recognises this in stating that promoting the 'infrastructure of freedom' often requires the use of illiberal techniques of discipline and policing (2003: 370). We would argue that this requires us to see the flip side of neoliberal freedom not as governmentality, but as coercive and hierarchical disciplinary power.

Merlingen is certainly right, however, to emphasise the governmentality aspect of these interventions in terms of the way they deploy certain types of knowledge that concern themselves with the political, economic and social characteristics of place and population (2003: 368). We would argue that place and people are invoked, not out of a genuine concern for the health, welfare and well-being of populations, but as a means of regulating state behaviour through compiling statistics, monitoring performance and using these to make normalising judgments about states and their forms of governance. Laura Zanotti also hints at this in arguing that interventions target populations in so far as it helps construct modern states (2005: 480). For Zanotti, global governmentality emerges as a new modality for international regimes following the end of the Cold War. Governmentality works at both state and international levels to promote good governance. Like us, she links this to the influence of Anglo-American neoliberalism (2005: 468). Zanotti, Merlingen and others highlight how good governance works through the use of databases, standards and performance indicators. We will examine these in more detail as we go through the book. They work to constitute states in a particular way. Tore Fougner is most explicit in linking this to the competitiveness agenda of neoliberal capitalism, writing that:

[T]he primary concern is not with governmental practices occurring within states, but rather with the rationalities, programs and technologies internal to efforts aimed at governing states from without. While the latter plays

> into the former, the distinction is nonetheless important. To argue that states have increasingly come to be subjected to a form of neoliberal governance implies that there is a growing tendency for them to be constituted and acted upon as flexible and manipulable subjects with a rationality derived from arranged forms of entrepreneurial and competitive behavior. (Fougner 2008b: 108)

Hence Fougner comes closest to our two concerns of linking governmentality to the regulation of states and linking governmentality to neoliberal capitalism. This helps us to understand global governance as a problematising practice that seeks to reconstitute a set of 'global problems' in order to promote free and open markets and a competitiveness agenda. However, we should conclude by re-emphasising what is distinctive about the governmentality approach. For even if we are concerned to emphasise the bigger capitalist picture, we should remember governmentality's specific way of understanding this in terms of strategies and rationalities. While we must draw on a wider range of social theories in order to explain the current reconstitution of capitalism, governmentality allows us to explain the process by which dominant discourses use ideas like global governance to naturalise this process (Fougner 2008b: 118). We will return to ideas like global governance in the following chapters. However, it should now be clear how our project aims to show the way that these ideas function as a part of a dominant rationality, reinforced through a set of strategies and techniques. The chapters that follow will apply the idea of governmentality to an analysis of governance and a range of other social theories in order to show their place in a dominant discourse that is expressed both domestically and also inside international organisations.

Conclusion

The central argument this book makes about governmentality can now be summarised. The governmentality approach is a useful tool in explaining *how* governance works in contemporary societies. However, in order to make the concept work, it has to be properly located by relating it to other social processes. The suggestion here is that it can be put to work within a historical materialist framework that rejects reductionism by developing a more relational and stratified understanding of the social world. Governmentality then comes to explain an important part of this social ontology, but it cannot act as a substitute for a wider and deeper examination of social relations. These are the things that explain *why* governmentality is important.

This wider and deeper examination of social relations, among other things, helps to explain the sort of governmentality we are talking about. As noted, it is hard to pin down a precise meaning of governmentality in Foucault's own work. While it is quite possible to take a general view of governmentality based on Foucault's definition of modern government as 'the conduct of conduct', we soon have to move to something more specific if we want to explain the *how* of contemporary governance. We need to look at the particular conditions that show *why* governmentality takes particular forms. This narrows down the study of governmentality to governance in advanced liberal societies. Here we find such ideas as government through the promotion of freedom, the connection between liberty and security, a continual questioning of the role and limits of government, a responsibilisation of the conduct of subjects, a dispersal of power through the social body and the application of an entrepreneurial logic to social processes.

Governmentality is also defined by its historical context. Thus contemporary forms of governmentality have to be seen in relation to the emergence of neoliberalism and the response to the unravelling of the postwar institutional settlement. This can be seen in relation both to national forms of economic regulation and state intervention, and the international regimes of economic and financial stability associated with the Bretton Woods system. While it is important to look for regional variations, clearly the dominant form of governmentality is this neoliberal version. Among its essential features is a further questioning of the limits of state power and a focus on the market through the introduction of rules of competition and the construction of an entrepreneurial model of conduct. While neoliberalism promotes the freedom of individual conduct, this conduct is 'responsibilised' and urged to be reflexive about its own behaviour. We have seen how national governments have sought to introduce policies through the promotion of strategies and techniques of competition, risk-taking, insurance, benchmarking and best practice. This is combined with more sophisticated techniques of data gathering and surveillance in order to regulate populations from a distance. While this is promoted through the idea of the exercise of freedom and limiting government, we should move beyond this discourse and see these interventions as a particular form of regulation. For Foucault, this 'regulation of society by the market' requires that the mechanisms of competition 'play a regulative role at every moment' (Foucault 2008: 145).

All this can be seen in the advanced liberal countries as well as in the development of regional institutions like the EU. We compare the global governmentality of international organisations like the World Bank with the development of governmentality inside the EU precisely because the latter is a transnational project that would seem to better fit with the idea that populations can be governed from a distance through the idea of free subjects. The European project can be seen to encourage such things as freedom of movement, participation in social networks and active involvement in building new institutions. The governmentalisation of Europe also works through defining subjects in relation to economic markets, promoting responsibility in areas like education and welfare, facilitating innovation and a knowledge society, while also encouraging processes of standardisation and harmonisation of rules and regulations.

Can international organisations export similar techniques to other parts of the world, either directly or as part of some sort of global governance agenda? While some parts of the world may not have the social conditions of possibility necessary for this type of governmentality to organically emerge, international organisations, as reflective of the rationalities present in the advanced liberal societies, may still try to force these techniques on other parts of the world. This turn to governmentality has been encouraged by reflection on the failures of free-market structural adjustment programmes. But is it argued that these types of governmentality, if judged on what they claim to do, are still highly inappropriate to the social conditions in which they are deployed. In so far as the World Bank and IMF are institutions dominated by the advanced liberal countries (in terms of their officials, financial and voting structure, etc.), they attempt to implement the governmentality characteristic of their own societies. This is of course lifting governmentality out of its social context, something that will encounter problems in a different local environment.

To theorise the wider context, and to explain the intersection of the social and the international, we have suggested making use of Rosenberg's approach to uneven and combined development. This approach shows why a set of techniques developed in one part of the world can be imposed on another part of the world. Indeed it allows us to go deeper than the act of imposition, since this itself is a product of the very nature of capitalist development. As Rosenberg puts it: 'This phenomenon – in which the results of one instance of social development enter into the conditions of another – arises directly from the pressures and opportunities of inter-societal coexistence' (Rosenberg 2006: 326). The uneven part of the process indicates how governmentality will have uneven and unpredictable results; the combined part shows that it is the very nature of the international that allows this to occur. The second part of this book develops this point by comparing governmentality in the EU with global governmentality as promoted by the World Bank. As already outlined, our argument is that neoliberal management of populations works – to a certain extent – in European countries because of the nature of their social relations, but that in other parts of the world governmentality struggles to manage populations in such a way. Instead, concern for populations becomes an important pretext for a different sort of governmentality that operates at the level of government and state.

However, the main reason for examining the EU and the World Bank is to highlight the *similarities* of ideas that play such a large part in the neoliberal discourse that both these institutions support. We are particularly concerned with the role played by contemporary social theory in so far as it tends to reinforce new forms of governmentality rather than criticising them. Foremost among these theories, as the next chapter will show, is the idea of globalisation. But even as people start to grow weary of the overstatement of this idea, so a whole range of associated concepts work to construct a particular idea of the global. These include various understandings of governance, networks, flows, social capital, risk, knowledge and reflexivity. Our suggestion is that these ideas reproduce a certain view of the world that reflects its surface appearance, but does not get beneath the surface to look at underlying social relations. Indeed, if we may use Dean's words here, what we have is a world without markings, a 'scratchless' world, a world of surfaces and flows; networks and governance (Dean 2007: 203). In fact Dean is describing neoliberalism, but it can equally be said of the uncritical theories that claim to be analysing the world but instead end up reinforcing the dominant world-view. Our claim, then, is that most contemporary social theories lend their support to contemporary forms of governance and that together with the more practical work of institutions like the EU and the World Bank they contribute to neoliberal governmentality in its various forms across the world. Hence the importance today of criticising these ideas *as* governmentality by giving the concept *of* governmentality a critical and cutting edge.

3 *Globalisation, global governance and global civil society*

The first contemporary social theories to be addressed here are globalisation and the related ideas of global governance and global civil society. It needs to be firmly emphasised that this chapter is not an attempt to explain the 'truth' of globalisation itself, but to cast doubt on the truth of *theories* of globalisation and by doing this to raise questions about what they purport to explain. We cannot even begin to address a question such as whether globalisation is really occurring (Hirst and Thompson 1999) without first raising the question of what it is that these theories think globalisation is. Unfortunately, it is far from clear what 'globalisation' is said to mean, but then it is precisely this lack of clarity that helps the concept create a certain view of the world. We will try to explain this view through the concept of governmentality, explaining the practical effects of the ideas rather than their truthfulness. In this sense we can follow the argument of Larner and Walters, who 'suggest a shift from a concern with the substance of globalization to an account of it in terms of its dispositif. Strangely absent from most answers to the "what is globalization?" question is any reference to these intellectual and epistemological systems that make it visible' (2004: 499). Foucault's concept of dispositif can be taken to mean not only epistemological system or intellectual framework, but also political, administrative and legislative apparatus and set of practices (see Foucault 1981: 84–5). These apparatuses make something visible and also provide the means to act upon something. All this can take place regardless of whether the discourse of globalisation is 'true'. Indeed it is often far more revealing to examine theories of globalisation in their practical context, rather than trying to interrogate these ideas on intellectual grounds. Through the rest of this first section we will also see how the concept of globalisation provides a set of starting assumptions for a range of other contemporary concepts: global governance, global civil society, risk, reflexivity, life choices, complexity, networks and flows. We will see how there is an interweaving of various ontological assumptions that help construct a particular view of the world, the type of actors within it and the types of activities and conduct they engage in. In the second part of this book we will see how these ideas are of practical use to international organisations like the EU and World Bank.

Rather than considering the empirical matter of whether 'globalisation' is happening, the issue to consider is how the question of globalisation is posed. Many of the features described by theorists of globalisation may be true enough, but the causes and consequences, not to mention the explanations, may not be. Of interest to us is how these ideas are bundled together to produce certain political arguments and justifications. As mentioned, Larner and Walters's use of the term dispositif is one way of making this point. However, one should not go to the extreme of arguing that these ideas in effect construct their own reality. They do indeed further a process of social construction of political, economic and cultural objects. But we can follow a philosophical realist path of showing a relation between these constructions and other social processes that produce them.[1] Without a realist element to the argument, it is impossible to say how things might be other than what the globalisation theorists suggest. That realist element relates to our previous discussion of the institutional changes following the crisis of the postwar settlement which in turn requires an examination of the nature of capitalism itself. Thus the critical arguments in this chapter will draw on Marxist critics of globalisation theory like Ellen Meiksins Wood and Justin Rosenberg, who themselves draw on the approaches of Marx, Poulantzas and other more established social theorists to counter current theoretical suggestions.

The aim here is to show how contemporary theories of globalisation provide explanations that are cut off from or mystify these social developments and thus limit our ability to question the basis of the processes they try to describe. In the case of globalisation theory, this usually depends, as Rosenberg notes, on the 'conceptual inflation of space into a "core determinant of social life"' (2000: 39). Explaining globalisation through the concept of spatial transformation turns us

[1] This might be seen as consistent with Foucault's 'archaeology', which, he says, 'also reveals relations between discursive formations and nondiscursive domains (institutions, political events, economic practices and processes)' (1989: 162).

away from the kind of social explanations provided by classical social theorists like Marx or Gramsci. Marx, for example, rather than using space to explain society, would use society to explain the organisation of space, looking at the structural tendencies of the capitalist mode of production to expand outwards and transcend national borders. Gramsci would look at the organisation of space through the geostrategic nature of hegemonic projects. By contrast, today's theories of social change limit the way we can conceive of social processes by taking them for granted, replacing an analysis of specific social forms and their causes with a reliance on spatial transformation as an explanatory category; in effect telling us that today's globalised world has been caused by – globalisation. But before developing this argument, there first follows a presentation of the main issues raised by globalisation theory.

Globalisation: definitions and critique

The notion of globalisation is well known and widely accepted, but theories of globalisation are still hotly contested. There is little point in going into any great detail about such debates in a book of this length. More important is to introduce the concept and then examine some of the implications of these theories for our understanding of the social world, politics and international relations. In particular, we are interested how these theories explain changes in contemporary society as well as changes in governance and new questions about international order. Or perhaps, more to the point, we are interested in how these theories *fail* to explain contemporary developments, and instead provide a description of events that shifts attention away from what might really be causing these changes (note here the philosophically realist argument that there are real processes going on that are irreducible to their discursive articulation).

Justin Rosenberg provides the strongest critique of the usefulness of globalisation theory. In his view the theory fails on three counts. First, because it is unable to provide any clear definition of what globalisation is. Second, because it cannot produce a clear hypothesis about 'the causal significance of its real-world referent'. And third, because it cannot, in its application to concrete historical phenomena, produce anything more meaningful than what is provided by alternative explanations of the same things (Rosenberg 2007b: 417). Nevertheless, it will be argued that despite these failures, or perhaps precisely because of them, theories of globalisation play an important role in constructing a field of action. In keeping with our governmentality approach it is argued that this descriptive (rather than explanatory) role of globalisation theory then becomes the basis for a set of arguments about how we should see contemporary social issues and, consequently, how we should act and behave.

The term globalisation and accompanying notions like global governance and global civil society have only been around since the late 1980s. Yet they have had plenty of time to provide the kind of definition Rosenberg is looking for. The most earnest globalisation theorists would no doubt defend themselves by pointing to the complex processes they are trying to deal with. First, it might be said that globalisation is multi-dimensional, spanning the economic, political and cultural domains. According to Waters, globalisation is most likely to be differentiated, multi-centric and chaotic (Waters 2001: 6), while for Axford, globalisation is not an autonomous system or a single, deep logic, but a 'multi-dimensional process by which the global system is being made' (Axford 1995: 26). Moreover, the consequences are both positive and negative and cannot easily be summarised. Positive consequences might be economic development, improved quality of life, greater diversity of products, cultural benefits, greater understanding and the promotion of new levels of cooperation to solve world problems. Negative consequences might relate to the domination of major interests, increasing inequality, too much homogeneity and the undermining of national sovereignty and identity, although theorists like Giddens would claim that the latter provides new opportunities for us to free ourselves from traditional structures and explore new possibilities.

Jan Aart Scholte perhaps comes closest to providing a set of definitions. To begin with, he provides what he believes are four inadequate definitions of globalisation. The first is internationalisation, by which he means interaction and interdependence between countries and the people within them and a rise in cross-border exchanges. Next he identifies liberalisation, economic integration and the removal of government constraints. Third, he mentions universalisation and the synthesis of cultures. Fourth, Westernisation and the spread of modernity across the world, something that might be seen as a postcolonial form of imperialism. These four definitions, in widespread use, are unexceptional and could easily be accounted for by the mainstream IR literature of the past twenty years. Finally, Scholte mentions deterritorialisation or supraterritoriality. This is the reconfiguration of geography such that social space can no longer be mapped in terms of territorial place (Scholte 2000: 45–6). It is this understanding of globalisation as 'far-reaching change in the nature of social space' (2000: 46) that Scholte believes makes the concept unique. Above all else, then, globalisation should be viewed as a spatial concept. The most common understandings of globalisation are as interconnection and space-time compression. This is conveyed in Anthony Giddens's well-known description of 'the intensification of worldwide social relations which link distinct localities in such a way that local happenings are shaped by events occurring many miles away' (1990: 64). According to Scholte, globalisation should be seen as a transformation of social geography that creates new supraterritorial spaces. Bringing in the temporal, he talks of globalisation's unprecedented speed and its 'juggernaut-like qualities'. It also brings with it new loci of governance beside the state as well as additional forms of community beside the nation (Scholte 2000: 2). The same kind of language can be found in Held and McGrew. For them, 'globalization represents a significant shift in the spatial reach of social relations' (Held and McGrew 2003: 3). By 'eroding the constraints of space and time on patterns of social interaction, globalization, for instance, creates the possibility of new modes of transnational social organization' (2000: 7).

Rosenberg's critique sums up these positions well. What they achieve is the 'methodological foregrounding of space and time' (Rosenberg 2005: 8). Moreover, this foregrounding of space and time is a peculiarly asocial and apolitical form of explanation. As Rosenberg argues, 'the term "globalization" in itself specifies no particular kind of society at all, but simply denotes a process of worldwide spatial expansion and integration *per se*' (2005: 12). Space and time themselves become the 'foundational parameters of social expansion' as this body of theory transfers 'causal agency from the thing that was speeding to the idea of speed itself', resulting in socially empty and reified spatio-temporal measures of 'extensivity', 'intensivity' and 'velocity' (2005: 54). This shows the circularity of the globalisation argument or, in Rosenberg's terms, the fact that globalisation becomes the explanans as well as explanandum, implying 'the claim that the spatio-temporal dimension of human social reproduction is in some way ontologically prior to other dimensions' (2005: 13). Rosenberg gives as an example Giddens's (1990) theory of 'time-space distanciation' that places the weight of causality on time-space compression. Rosenberg contrasts this with a concept like capitalism, which is a distinctively social term implying 'a particular nexus of social relationships' from which spatial and temporal implications follow (Rosenberg 2005: 11).

Marx's work is sensitive to spatial temporal change, the universalising tendencies of capital and the 'annihilation of space by time', but these are seen in relation to specific historical societies. Social change causes spatio-temporal development. By contrast, globalisation theory reverses the direction of explanation so that time and space cause social change. By replacing social explanation with spatio-temporal explanation, recent theories remove any social content and explain change in mechanical terms. As Ellen Meiksins Wood notes, 'Just as in old theories of economic development the ultimate cause of capitalist expansion was an almost natural process of technological progress, now the new information technologies seem to represent not only the necessary conditions of possibility for globalization but its causal *explanation*' (Wood 1997: 553). Wood argues that what gets lost in these narratives is an understanding of the features of capitalist society as specific social forms. Instead, capitalism is taken for granted as the outcome of already existing tendencies, something that has the effect of naturalising it (1997: 543). This leads to a conception of globalisation as a territorial imperative or 'inexorable impulse for liberation from political constraint' driven by natural laws of technological progress. Among other things this denies the importance of the nation state despite the nation state being the main instrument of the processes globalisation theory describes. Wood takes a historical approach to this question in showing how in the past imperialism was able to permeate national boundaries much more easily, whereas today transnational capital relies on the mediation of nation states, local political jurisdictions and local capital (1997: 553). Globalisation, for Wood, is a response to structural changes, not the structural change itself; a response to the universalising tendencies of capitalism, met through specific policy choices that are designed to meet the needs of capital (1997: 558).

Other writers such as David Harvey (2001) develop a social approach to the question by drawing attention to the spatial dimension of Marx's theory of accumulation. Harvey looks at how Marx views technology and innovation and how capitalism develops new equipment and new techniques of production while also developing new wants and needs in the marketplace so that consumption is reorganised in line with production (Harvey 2001: 241). Marx had written that in order for production to keep expanding and for profit to be realised, capitalism requires 'a constantly widening sphere of circulation' (Marx 1973: 407–10). Capitalism creates new room for accumulation by intensifying the social activity of markets and people within a particular spatial structure. While for Marx it is labour that creates value, this is realised through the sphere of circulation. Therefore the kinds of developments highlighted by globalisation theory – advances in transport and communication, for example – are from the outset central to the accumulation process. It is the imperative to accumulate that drives the imperative to overcome spatial barriers (Harvey 2001: 242–3), or as Marx himself writes:

> The more production comes to rest on exchange value, hence on exchange, the more important do the physical conditions of exchange – the means of communication and transport – become for the costs of circulation. Capital by its nature drives beyond every spatial barrier. (Marx 1973: 524)

Harvey goes on to discuss the fact that while more distant markets open up new possibilities, they can also make the circulation process lengthier. Thus the reduction of circulation time through the development of new technology (here we must consider communications, information technology and so on) or speeding up the 'velocity of circulation of capital' enhances the accumulation process and the realisation of surplus value (Harvey 2001: 244). Capital creates its own landscape to advance the accumulation process, but this is tied to particular spatial features that have to be constantly changed and rearranged (2001: 247). It is this changing and rearranging that the globalisation theorists fail to analyse as a social feature of capital, instead focusing their attention on space and time themselves.

The contribution of historical materialism is therefore to put these changes in their appropriate social and historical context, looking at how the development of capitalism, while having a structural basis, is mediated and facilitated by various social institutions, practices and human actions. Theorists like Poulantzas have considered the nature of space not in abstract terms, but through the complex relation between state, nation and capital. He argues that it is the state that plays the decisive role in the unifying, assimilating and demarcating of space. In turn this spatial matrix is rooted in the labour process and social division of labour (Poulantzas 1978: 106). This helps situate processes that globalisation theory takes for granted – the flexibilisation of labour, the globalisation of finance and other restructurings of capitalism in line with the particular needs of the dominant US economy. Unless we focus on processes such as these, we end up with the fetishised view, common at the end of the twentieth century, that the movement of capital is a freestanding, unfettered process that sweeps away all barriers to its development. Such a view was subsequently exposed by the financial crises and the fact that the response to these had to be state-led. For globalisation theory, such political actions were apparently a thing of the past. The power of such states, it was claimed, had been swept away by the global transformation of space. We now see more clearly than ever how wrong this reified, depoliticised view of spatio-temporal change is. The question to address next is why such views became popular in the first place.

The practical consequences of globalisation theory

Having examined the fallacies of globalisation theories, it would be wrong simply to declare globalisation theory an intellectual failure and ignore its practical role in the world. It is not necessarily the best theories that exert most influence, but usually those that best adapt themselves to the current socio-economic climate. In seeming to describe the current period, globalisation theory carries great influence, and in this it has significant practical effects. It may well be that globalisation theory produces a misleading view of the present conjuncture, but in doing so it finds itself, willing or not, contributing to contemporary rationalities of government. As such, it fits practically with the conditions that it seeks to explain even though it dismally fails as an explanatory theory. To explain why this should be so, this section will examine the conjunctural conditions that gave birth to globalisation theory, then look at how this theory acts back upon the conjuncture to justify contemporary governmentality.

The collapse of the Soviet Union and the end of the Cold War are of most significance to IR theorists, many of whom had not expected the postwar set of military and political alliances to come to such an abrupt end. As Rosenberg notes, it is easy to see why the end of the Cold War might lead to the view that the world had suddenly become a single, deterritorialised social space (2005: 4). But consider also the societal effect of the collapse in the East combined with the unravelling of the postwar settlement in the West. If we add into the mix such things as developments in communications technology, the growth of cyberspace and, above all else, the financialisation of capitalism, we end up with an overwhelming sense of spatio-temporal change. While globalisation theory might want to emphasise some positive aspects of this, the general feeling is one of helplessness in the face of unstoppable forces and the feeling of being socially overwhelmed. This feeling of being overwhelmed by social fragmentation on the one hand and unstoppable forces on the other is not something unique to globalisation theory but is characteristic of a more general crisis of confidence in social theory, in particular the petering out of critical theory and postmodernism. Taking the conjuncture as our starting point, we can see that there are problems with theory more generally. The more general problems associated with these different theories include shallowness, overemphasis of social fragmentation, lack of any conception of underlying social processes or structure except in terms of unstoppable forces with near natural powers, a consequent turn to micro politics as if this represents a liberating move or a 'return to politics', an individualisation of political problems that fits well with the neoliberal approach and the reinforcement of the status quo by attacking collective politics, the state and those forces most likely to bring about social change. Thus if the conjuncture has shaped theory and produced a sense of being overwhelmed by change, theory in turn is having an equally negative effect on political discourse.

While developments in the real world were profoundly political, the response of globalisation theory has been to depoliticise them and take them as given. This in turn can be analysed both in terms of ideology and governmentality. The advantage of the governmentality approach is that we do not have to see such theories as consciously advocating the dominant mode of thinking, but as reinforcing this through their assumptions and what they take for granted. In this way globalisation theory should be seen less as theory in the intellectual sense and more as a part of a rationality that is inseparable from the dominant set of social practices and therefore unable to maintain any kind of critical distance. Globalisation theory, in failing to provide an explanation of the wider social causes (reverting instead to spatio-temporal metaphors), might be considered a *reproductive* social theory rather than an *explanatory* one – or, in Robert Cox's terms, a form of problem-solving. By 'solving' problems *within* this framework, it in effect reinforces the framework as something given and turns instead to the micro politics of everyday life. It is because of this that the theory lends itself so readily to forms of social regulation or governmentality. It becomes complicit in the construction of a particular social ontology that articulates human beings and social objects in particular ways. This is well explained by Larner and Walters:

> Globalization can be understood in terms of a historical ontology – a reflexive moment in the discursive construction of ourselves where knowledge of the subject is produced in terms of its interconnectivity, mobility, sovereignty. We are produced as global subjects, emerging from a past of nation-state-focused political struggles. Globalization discourse could thus be seen as a moment of reflexivity, a 'fold' in which another dimension of human existence is opened up. Less a force that impinges upon subjects; more a site in the production of particular kinds of subjectivity and experience: 'be global!'; 'think globally!' Our argument, then, is that globalization is not necessarily global and not simply 'out there' ... We are suggesting that globalization is not so much a new epoch as it is a way of imagining human life. It is a 'world in the making', but this 'making' is being done through very specific imaginaries, processes, and practices. (Larner and Walters 2004: 507)[2]

The discursive aspect of globalisation theory is important because before power can be exercised, its objects need to be defined and boundaries established. To understand Foucault's comments on the discourse of political economy, for instance, we have to see how this relates to particular social problems and the need for government intervention. As he writes, the 'new science called "political economy" arises out of the perception of new networks of continuous and multiple relations between

[2] The phrase 'world in the making' invokes the constructivist ideas of Nicholas Onuf (1989). Against too constructivist an approach to these issues we have to insist that the world is being made in specific ways that interact with the material processes described above, namely economic downturn and the consequent unravelling of the postwar settlement. These are real, structural processes that cannot be reduced to intersubjective practices, language games or rule-following.

population, territory, and wealth; and this is accompanied by the formation of a type of intervention' (Foucault 2001a: 217). We may simply add 'global' in front of political economy to make this statement more relevant to today's discussions. Globalisation theory thus lends itself to a project of social restructuring. As Hay and Marsh have argued, 'the very discourse and rhetoric of globalization may serve to summon precisely the effects that such a discourse attributes to globalization itself' (Hay and Marsh 2000: 9). In this way it supports the regulative processes we described in the previous chapter, using the claims about unstoppable social forces in order to control our expectations of what actions are possible, while legitimating the implementation of neoliberal policies as somehow the only sensible option. Globalisation becomes a strategy designed to support the implementation of a particular set of policies, to legitimate the role of certain institutions and certain forms of intervention and, like neoliberal governmentality, to make political decisions look as if they are non-political. In fact, as Teschke and Heine argue:

> Globalisation refers to a conscious re-structuring of state-society and inter-state relations in response to the onset of the long economic downturn of the 1970s. Globalisation is neither a techno-economically induced, nor a purely politically driven, phenomenon, but the result of private and public strategies of reproduction under conditions of long-term negative growth. (Teschke and Heine 2002: 176)

Arguments like this make the point that globalisation should be seen as a project that responds to the economic crisis of the 1970s and supports institutional restructuring and open markets. In the realm of international relations, it represents the efforts by the dominant state – the USA – to force through market liberalisation and the financialisation of capital (policies that benefit the US domestic economy). What is remarkable is the way that globalisation theory is unable or unwilling to see this and instead promotes a view of the world where states are in decline, collective action is a thing of the past and social life is reorganised according to a new rationality. The ideological effects of this discourse are clearly captured in a passage from Higgins that is worth quoting at length:

> This unchallenged neoliberal ascendancy, I suggest, is the cumulative effect of a number of aspects of neoliberalism's discursive practices of government.

> The most obvious of them is the talking-down of the capacities of nation-states in the putative 'new ballgame' of globalisation. As nation-states remain virtually the only credible sites for programs of social amelioration, writing them off (dogmatically, without evidence) as spent forces strongly discourages the politics of social amelioration as such, to the point of making them discursively unavailable. Secondly, the declining relevance of nation-states becomes a self-fulfilling prophecy once the power to regulate is transferred to transnational organisations divorced from popular sovereignty and political community. These organisations are thus available for regulatory capture, whereby the interests of their most powerful 'stakeholders' mould the regulatory regimes they proliferate. Thirdly, in organisational life as a whole (including the state), the shibboleths of formal rationality (accountability, transparency, value for money and so on), and their enervating rituals of self-presentation and verification, effectively decoy discussion of – and mobilisation around – substantive issues and choices about how we might imagine ourselves living and working together and relating to each other, given the technological means at our disposal and the environmental dangers we face. (Higgins 2006: 25)

So in a perverse way, globalisation theory fits perfectly with current times. But it does so in an unreflective sense as a manifestation of a particular rationality that takes for granted the very things it should be questioning. It deserves to be considered as a form of governmentality because it helps maintain a common set of background assumptions that present the world in a particular way that can then be acted upon in a conscious process of social restructuring. We will look at one way that this articulates itself through theories of global governance.

Governing the global

In an unwittingly Foucauldian manner, global governance is described by Rosenau and Czempiel (1992) as governance without government. This rather vague expression is matched by other definitions, for example Rosenau's argument that '[g]lobal governance is not so much a label for a high degree of integration and order as it is a summary term for highly complex and widely disparate activities that may culminate in a modicum of worldwide coherence' (Rosenau 2006: 116). One of the best-known arguments comes from the Commission on Global Governance's report *Our Global Neighbourhood*, which talks of the 'many ways individuals and institutions, public and private, manage their common affairs' (Commission on Global Governance 1995: 95). As with a whole range of literature covered in this first part of the book, the common themes appear to be the declining power of state governance on the one hand, and complexity of the social or global realm on the other. With global governance there is a sense of worldwide problems and issues that shape the political agenda, but also a vast array of different rule systems that make it impossible to talk of the world in terms of national or international domains, only as a multi-centric globalised space (Rosenau 2006: 163). Indeed Rosenau looks at processes of fragmentation as much as he looks at integration. In these new spaces we find new sources of governance emerging from civil society and micro-level politics. Hence for Rosenau, '[g]lobal governance is the sum of myriad – literally millions – of control mechanisms driven by different histories, goals, structures and processes' (2006: 124).

While some of these issues tie in with some of our arguments about governmentality, this section will build towards two things – a more social conception of these relationships and a stronger explanation of why politics has taken on the global governance theme. Ultimately we can give meaning to the idea of global governance only once we stop treating it as a new global condition and see instead its practical role in shaping particular political projects. These political projects are promoted by international institutions like the UN, World Bank and IMF, which, following widespread questioning of the Washington consensus, realised the need to legitimise their interventions and ground them in a language of good governance and responsible behaviour.

Global governance, we have suggested, is another one of those general terms with no clear meaning. Most notably, it is not clear whether it really does refer to the governance *of* the world on a global scale, or whatever governance there is taking place *in* the world (see Hewson and Sinclair 1999: 6; Rosenau and Czempiel 1992; Whitman 2005: 32). It would appear to be suggesting something going beyond domestic government, but which also reflects the lack of a world state or government. Instead of a world government, there are various systems of rule-making, political coordination and decision-making. The terrain of global governance is multi-layered and pluralistic. The different forms of authority have different, uneven impacts in different parts of the world. While national governments might retain their importance as strategic sites, the new institutional architecture relates to more decentralised decision-making, and delegation of political authority between different layers of governance. At its strongest, the global governance argument suggests that states are now enmeshed in new global networks, and that this global interconnectedness and interdependence means not only that global governance is actually happening, but that it is essential that it should be developed further. One argument for developing global governance is that this is the only way to deal with instability and the risks that affect all of us. As Simai puts it, there are geo-strategic and technical changes affecting the international order and requiring more efficient conflict prevention, multilateral cooperation, collective agreement and risk management (1994: xvi). Others, like Senarclens and Kazancil (2007: 2–3), link these problems to the unregulated nature of neoliberal markets and flows, arguing for a different way of governing globalisation with more participation from citizens and the public sphere, in other words, more regulation and more legitimation.

For writers like Held and McGrew, globalisation has shifted power from the nation state to international regimes, thus raising the importance of a constraining influence like international law in view of the declining security capacity of states (2003: 133). For Scholte, globalisation 'has fostered a dispersal of regulatory competences' (2000: 151) with post-sovereign states sharing the tasks of governance with autonomous regional, local and international agencies. Most of the global governance theorists base their argument on the assumption that globalisation loosens the grip of the state on governance. Scholte argues that it is the case that states continue, but sovereignty ends: 'The resultant post-sovereign state is a major part – but only a part – of a wider, multilayered complex of regulation in which private as well as public agencies play key roles' (Scholte 2000: 157). Here we find two common arguments – either the idea that states are now enmeshed in global networks, or that they are part of a multi-layered system of global governance. In either case, the perception is that sovereignty is now something that must be negotiated and shared, and that political authority is diffused with new bodies existing above, below and alongside the state. For Held and McGrew, new layers of governance have spread across political boundaries, meaning that the 'exclusive link between territory and political power has been broken' (Held and McGrew 2003: 11). The argument of many theorists is that globalisation has brought about a new sort of (extra-territorial) social cohesion by encouraging new transnational networks, cosmopolitan commitments and new types of solidarity. We will tackle some of these arguments in the section on global civil society, as well as in the next chapter on networks and social capital. At the same time, these new types of connections are matched by a new array of problems that a more reflexive or networked state has to deal with. New global problems like transnational terrorism, refugees and criminal gangs reflect, it is claimed, a more uncertain and unruly world. This may require nothing less than the redefinition of the concept of warfare, aided by new technologies that provide new tools like advanced power of surveillance, more sophisticated military equipment and more widespread and efficient data processing. Of course the issue then is whether these new opportunities and threats really do undermine the power of nation states, or whether these states and their governments remain relevant, but are being significantly transformed, leading them to assume new forms and functions. Have these changes strengthened state power by giving states more sophisticated techniques for the management of their populations and territory, or have these changes fragmented the policy-making arena and made the state subservient to more powerful transnational networks and new sites of governance?

Turning to one of the most influential theorists in this area, Ulrich Beck, we find that he rightly identifies, as we highlighted earlier in this chapter, how ideas like globalisation can be used to justify state impotence by telling everyone that nothing can be done to change their situation:

> All around, one hears the assertion that it is not corporate interests but 'globalization' which forces this or that painful break with the past. One of the 'laws' of the global market is that not-A must be done in order to achieve A: for example, that jobs must be axed or relocated in order to keep jobs safe where they are. (Beck 2000: 2)

However, Beck's answer to this problem is also to accept the decline in national forms of state regulation and to concentrate instead on the issue of how to make global governance more effective. In the first step of the argument, Beck accepts the view that traditional issues like the welfare state, pension systems, local government and the labour movement have been dissolved by the globalisation process (2000: 1). However, he goes on to say that globalisation 'also means *no* world state – or to be more precise, world society *without a world state* and *without world government*. A globally *disorganized* capitalism is continually spreading out. There is no hegemonic power and no international regime, either economic or political' (2000: 13). This leads to a discussion of world order and democracy. On the one hand globality is said to be an inescapable aspect of human intercourse at the end of the twentieth century (2000: 15), on the other, we have no world government or order. Putting this within the traditional framework of democratic legitimacy, Beck bemoans the fact that '[w]orld society without a world state means a society that is *not politically organized*, where new opportunities for action and power arise for transnational actors that have no democratic legitimation' (2000: 26). The problem with this argument is the focus at the level of political democracy, when we know that the major economic actors, for example, have never been legitimatised in this political sense of the term. The best we can say is that the actions of corporations, for example, may be regulated by state legislation, something that has recently been loosened. Under a previous form of regulation, corporations and other economic actors had a particular (corporatist) framework within which to act. That framework has now become a neoliberal one. Both models are forms of regulation. Both set down rules of behaviour. Both embody a dominant rationality. And contrary to popular belief, both are global systems. The old system of state regulation, Fordism and Keynesian-welfare politics, although tied to the actions of particular nation states, was as much a *global* form of regulation as today's 'globalised' neoliberalism, while today's neoliberalism is as much a form of *regulation* as the corporatist-welfare model was.[3] And in IR terms we could say

[3] This is obviously a more Marxist argument based on the pre-eminence of capitalism as a system. Within the traditional IR literature, the pre-eminence of the states-system is more significant. For realism, the state and sovereign power remain key to understanding the international system. If there is global governance, this is driven by the influence of one or two states (see Krasner 1983). The argument is that the existence of a liberal world order of trade relations is largely the consequence of US hegemony in agreement with other developed economic powers. Likewise Gilpin (1981) argues that the globalisation of the economy develops best under the guiding influence of a world power or hegemon which provides stability for the international system. Globalisation then presupposes a hegemonic power structure. Neoliberal institutionalism believes that state will continue to play an important role, but through international regimes, rules and institutions. Institutionalists argue that

both forms of global regulation, old and new, reflect or represent the dominant social relations in the dominant state.

Arguments like Beck's create further mystification by claiming to be progressive and taking a stance against neoliberalism. As Beck himself writes, he is opposed to 'globalism' in its neoliberal form, which 'reduces the new complexity of globality and globalization to a single (economic) dimension, which is itself *conceived in linear fashion* as a constant expansion of dependence on the world market' (Beck 2000: 118). In essence, Beck is arguing that global governance is about the intervention of non-economic – social, human, cultural and political – elements to better regulate the bad effects of economic globalisation. How democratic and accountable this really is must be a matter of debate. It creates the impression that this type of regulation is somehow democratic. Others like Held suggest that this sort of good governance stands in contrast to corrupt practices:

> The promotion of good governance at all levels of economic activity – that is, the establishment of transparent public services, the protection of commercial activity from corruption, the rule of law and the maintenance of relevant property rights, alongside accountable and replaceable politicians – needs to be nurtured to ensure that markets eventually work without political, bureaucratic and corrupt impediment. (Held 2004: 61)

One such way of discussing this is through the terminology of good governance. But good governance – which of course implies that it is better than bad governance – is actually exactly what the dominant international powers are now providing. As we shall see in the next section, the 'radical' claims of Beck and Held are actually fully consistent with the interventions of dominant international institutions like

newly emerging institutions will spread the benefits of economic globalisation across the world and that gains are mutual rather than relative. Realists attack the idea that international institutions emerge to deal with universal problems. Thus institutions still reflect the dominance of one or two powers. Institutions emerge if these dominant states want to coordinate their activities with others, not to diminish their power. The operation of these institutions is driven by the underlying aims of states. This way of managing the world economy is in the interest of dominant states. The New Medievalism approach taken from Hedley Bull (2002) sees national sovereignty undermined by economic development and technological innovation and looks at the rise of non-governmental actors, the erosion of hierarchical structures of power, new horizontal networks, different allegiances and responsibilities.

the World Bank, IMF and UN. Despite their progressive claims, these theorists actually provide cover for the actually existing global governance strategies of these organisations.

From global governance to good governance

The new global governance agenda emerges in the 1990s as the so-called Washington consensus starts to shift focus. Institutions like the World Bank and IMF had initially been set up as part of the postwar package designed to regulate the world economy and provide stability. There are various ways of seeing this political order. We broadly agree with the Gramscian development of the idea of historical bloc to argue that order was based on a reconfiguration of the immediate ruling interests, but with substantial concessions granted to a wider layer of social groups. Concessions included welfare systems, incorporation of the leadership of the labour movement into the mechanisms of government, Keynesian state intervention, guarantees of full employment and a stable economic system based on the international leadership of the United States and the regulatory role of the Bretton Woods institutions. In the 1970s this system hit serious difficulties with the abandonment of the fixed exchange rate system and the questioning of state-led economic interventionism. The subsequent rise of neoliberalism can be seen in two ways: as a reconfiguration of the historical bloc and the institutions associated with the postwar consensus but also as a significant shift in the rationality of government. While Gramscians have been keen to highlight the first element of this change, Foucauldian arguments are better at explaining the change of rationality as well as how the different micro techniques of governance might work.

The traditional story that follows is that the period of neoliberal free-market capitalism – here associated with structural adjustment policies and conditional loans that forced poorer countries to liberalise their economies – started to be questioned in the 1990s and that the economic crises of 1997 were the final straw in pushing the World Bank and IMF beyond the Washington consensus of unrestrained free-market capitalism. In this context policy-makers started to turn to the idea of governance. In our view this shift was not a rejection of neoliberalism, but a recognition of the need for a greater institutional embedding of neoliberal rationalities, in particular by paying greater attention to the mechanisms of governance and securing the social conditions by which free markets could better operate. Indeed this is neoliberalism in a deeper sense – a neoliberalism at Foucault's micro level of everyday practices – where the aim, as Duffield remarks, is 'to change indigenous values and modes of organisation and replace them with liberal ones' so that '[i]deas of empowerment and sustainability are largely refracted through a lens of behavioural and attitudinal change' (Duffield 2001: 42). Although these arguments are certainly compatible with the above-mentioned Gramscian arguments about shifting hegemonic blocs, what Foucault adds to this explanation is the idea of a change in the rationality of governance. Or perhaps more precisely, while the 1970s and 1980s represented a more fundamental shift in historical bloc and rationality of governance, the late 1990s were less a rejection of previous neoliberal rationality than a reflexive reaction and modification of forms of governing as institutions and organisations like the World Bank recognised the need to acquire both normative legitimacy and an institutional basis for their interventions.

Recognising the failures of structural adjustment policies, the good-governance argument suggests that these failed because of inadequate local institutions and a lack of legitimacy and local involvement. Good governance requires the accountability of local government, a clear legal framework, support for the rule of law, access to information and transparent, open government. There is something very instrumental about this. As Kiely points out, the World Bank's approach to good governance 'is that it is a means to an end, in which appropriate institutional structures promote the development of an efficient, "free-market" economy' (2005: 88). The 1997 *World Development Report* moves away from the traditional separation of state from economy to talk about the effectiveness of the state (or an 'enabling state') in providing the conditions (rules and institutions) that would allow markets to flourish.

However, what we now find is the recognition that in fact there cannot be such a thing as direct global governance, only 'global' dictates on what 'good governance' should be at a local or regional level. Like other forms of governmentality, the good governance approach is therefore deployed from a distance, asking national governments to implement the right policies and allow their practices to be inspected by outside observers. Loans, aid and technical assistance are tied to practices of good governance in the hope that these practices will then provide the best conditions for markets to flourish and bring economic growth. There is a convergence across all international organisations, not just the IMF and World Bank but in the UN as well. For example, the approach of the Millennium Development Goals is to require states to engage in 'good governance' and open up their policy-making to international scrutiny, as well as promoting local 'ownership'. The term ownership is intended to engage the idea of civil society. As the UN Development Programme puts it: 'The host country should lead and own the effort to design the MDG strategy, drawing in civil society organizations; bilateral donors; the UN specialized agencies, programmes and funds; and the appropriate financial institutions, including the IMF, the World Bank, and the appropriate regional development bank' (UNDP 2005: 53).

Such statements allude to multiple sites of governance, from the local to the global. However, contrary to those who might overstate the power of these different levels of organisation, we should say that global governance exists more as a guiding rationality, rather than as a powerful empirical reality. Or to be more precise, it is a rationality guided by the power of global capitalism that filters down to (or indeed, emerges up from) the micro level of everyday practices. This idea is captured in Sinclair's belief that if we can talk of such a thing as global governance, then it should be in terms of social regulation, so that global governance is the expectation that different societies will adapt themselves to the requirements of global capital and that this is less to do with state-led macro policies and more to do with the micro level of everyday socio-economic experience (Sinclair 1999: 158–9). We can then turn this way of understanding global governance back upon the notion of globalisation so that globalisation, to quote Kiely, 'is less something externally imposed on states and producing uniform convergence, and the end of geography, and more about setting certain global norms and standards that are themselves set by specific localities (and states), and which affect localities and states in an institutionally mediated way' (2007a: 168).

Contrary to those who might see in global governance a chance to reinvigorate political and normative ideals, global governance, in its fragmentary existence, consists precisely in the depoliticisation of government practices and forms of intervention, just as domestic politics in the 1990s (particularly in the Anglo-Saxon world) also took on a more managerial nature. The dry, technical vocabulary of the IMF and

World Bank seeps into the good-governance agenda. This helps in the broader task of neutralising international intervention into domestic governance. As writers like Abrahamsen have noted (2000: 11), development is presented by these institutions as something neutral and humanitarian and without any political or ideological motivations; yet the good-governance agenda pushes a deeply political agenda in raising matters like democracy, legitimacy and accountability. Documents like the World Bank's *Reforming Public Institutions and Structural Governance* talk of state capacity-building, which has the effect of depoliticising the intervention by international organisations into areas previously considered the preserve of domestic government. This at least helps to address the crucial question posed by David Chandler:

> What is it that leads Western states and international institutions to reinterpret economic, social and political problems in other parts of the world as questions which are largely amenable to technical administrative solutions? How can it be that today it seems that the answer to every problem from security threats to human rights to development is now that of global governance and the export of external advisors and capacity builders? (Chandler 2006: 7)

Chandler answers his question with the argument that the language of good governance, capacity-building and empowerment reflects a 'diminished view of the importance of politics, of the importance of self-government and political autonomy' (2006: 7). Labelling this approach 'empire in denial', he claims that the rationality behind it is governance from a distance, aimed at depoliticising intervention while also denying Western power and responsibility. He argues:

> The new administrators of empire talk about developing relations of 'partnership' with subordinate states, or even of African 'leadership', at the same time as instituting new mechanisms of domination and control. Gone is the language of Western dominance and superiority; replaced by the discourses of 'capacity building' and 'empowerment' in the cause of the non-Western other. (Chandler 2006: 9)

While not calling this 'empire', Higgott makes a similar point in suggesting that 'the governance agenda as constructed by the international institutions in the post-Washington consensus era has largely stripped questions of power, domination, resistance and accountability from the debate' (Higgott 2000: 144). Arturo Escobar had earlier talked of the World Bank exercising 'a bureaucratics that ensures the institution against responsibility through a series of practices' (Escobar 1995: 165). As much as anything else, therefore, good governance is about promoting a new kind of discourse and an apolitical way of seeing world problems. Critics of this discourse and its associated practices have suggested that there are two aspects to this process: first, a depoliticisation of activities on the ground by presenting them in technical and managerial terms; second, a denial of Western responsibility for these interventions by the devolution of competences from state to sub-state levels so that 'Western States and international institutions appear less as external or coercive forces and more as facilitators, empowerers and capacity builders' (Chandler 2006: 77).

For Chandler, the consequence of the good-governance agenda is to justify intervention, while at the same time denying Western responsibility. In order to do this, the concept of sovereignty is redefined so that it becomes understood as state capacity rather than sovereign independence or the formal legal right to self-government. Chandler's argument is that once sovereignty is redefined as the capacity for good governance, then there is little wrong with external institutions implementing long-term programmes of engagement since this external regulation is something that is designed to empower and help these states (Chandler 2006: 36). The consequence is an obfuscation of Western power, making the projection of power appear as empowering rather than dominating (2006: 77). The language of empowerment, partnership, ownership and responsibility helps reinforce this strategy. It becomes a means of integrating states into networks of external regulation, while also denying ultimate responsibility for the relationship. The whole idea of ownership, for example, can be used to shift ultimate responsibility to the states themselves; empowerment, meanwhile, shifts responsibility to forces within civil society. Although presented as a partnership, the reality is that it is Western institutions that promote particular policies, and non-Western states that bear responsibility for their implementation. The language of accountability and transparency can always be called upon to shift responsibility away from international institutions and on to corrupt or outdated local practices. The transparency and anti-corruption agenda legitimises international intervention while depoliticising this as upholding technical standards to empower citizens and strengthen democratic institutions (2006: 145). In a similar way, the appeal to the rule of law can be used to render problematic local politics and offers itself as an alternative to popular consent, self-government and other alternative sources of legitimation (2006: 145, 187). A similar point is made by Fraser, who argues that '"bottom up conditionality" thus paradoxically legitimates increasing intervention and implies insulating political processes from the majority of the population' (Fraser 2005: 329).

The question for the rest of this book is how we understand this power as working. For Chandler, the issue is not really that of whether good governance works particularly well, since most states lack the capacity for effective self-government and remain dependent on the West (Chandler 2006: 27). Instead, good governance has more to do with shifting responsibility, rather than achieving effective governance at a local level. This, in his view, rules out the idea of governmentality:

> New practices and forms of international regulation reflect Western economic and social power but it would be wrong to see these practices as a continuation of past forms of empire or of new forms of Foucauldian governmentality. In fact, the drive to extend these forms of regulation stems from the evasiveness brought about by the problems of legitimising power rather than the desire to exercise power more effectively. (Chandler 2006: 191)

By contrast, we have been working towards a position that sees governmentality at different levels of operation. Hence Chandler might be right to wonder whether practices that often prove ineffective should really be described as governmentality – if what he is talking about here relates to the effects of these practices at a local level. This, as we have mentioned, is the problem of trying to apply to one part of the world a set of techniques and practices developed in a quite different context. This does not mean, however, that international organisations do not try to implement such practices, given that they are driven by a particular rationality. While it is true, as Chandler suggests, that governmentality may not be effective at the local level of managing populations, we have suggested, following writers like Merlingen, Zanotti and Fougner (see Chapter 2), that governmentality might also be seen to be operating at a different level relating to the regulation and management of states themselves. This would achieve the legitimising effects that Chandler is keen to emphasise and would allow us to agree with him that governmentality may be ineffective and out of place at a local level, while remaining open to the idea that governmentality is also at work in managing the behaviour of states, something that it is perhaps better at achieving.

Global civil society

We have argued that contrary to the vague rhetoric of progressive change, global governance, in its actual existence through the activities of state foreign policy and international organisations, might be said to represent a particular rationality of government that ultimately acts in the interests of the dominant powers. We moved towards the conclusion that even if these new techniques do not work particularly well in their stated aims – effective local management and the promotion of economic growth – perhaps they work well in fulfilling a different set of understated aims. One does not have to buy into all of Chandler's 'empire in denial' thesis to see what might be going on here with the depoliticisation of problems, denial of responsibility and management of the status quo. But if this represents global politics from the top down, what of a more progressive alternative from the bottom up? Surely there is a positive side to the globalisation process that could be claimed to be transforming global politics? Even if our view of actually existing global governance is correct, is there not also some sort of opposition to this, a globalisation from below or at the grassroots level? Is there not also a movement to democratise globalisation, build genuine consensus and legitimacy, involve local communities in global networks and promote a new cosmopolitanism?

For IR theorists like Richard Falk and Mary Kaldor, the answer to these questions is global civil society. The end of the Cold War, it is argued, brought about a reconfiguration of global politics and new opportunities for global citizens to engage with one another in a truly transnational sphere. Theorists of global civil society also draw on the normative turn in IR theory to make their case for a concept that, as Keane suggests, is something of an ideal type, namely, a dynamic non-governmental realm of various networks, organisations, institutions and actors that bring the world together in different ways (Keane 2003: 8). By making it a normative issue, civil society becomes, as Kaldor puts it, 'a way of understanding the process of globalisation in terms of subjective human agency instead of a disembodied deterministic process of interconnectedness' (Kaldor 2003: 142). Falk, meanwhile, looks at the way the concept expresses 'an overriding commitment to join the struggle to shape emergent geogovernance structures in more satisfying directions' (Falk 1995: 35).

But global civil society is not just a normative ideal. According to these theorists, it exists in the here and now as what Keane calls 'a vast, sprawling non-governmental constellation of many institutionalised structures, associations and networks within which individual and group actors are interrelated and functionally interdependent' (Keane 2003: 11). And according to Kaldor, there is a correspondence between the 'degree of globalisation (the extent of the interconnection of trade, capital, people and organisations), multilateralism (signing and ratifying treaties, respecting international rules, joining international organisations) and the density of global civil society (membership in INGOs, hosting parallel summits, tolerating strangers)' (Kaldor 2003: 138). This growing space, dense with new organisations offers great potential. For globalisation theorists like Scholte, it is the place where civil society associations can develop new rules and norms (2005: 88). Scholte and his colleagues have made a notable contribution to the debate by looking at what they see as progressive new forms of multilateralism based on organisations that are independent of the state and operating with new methods of organising from the bottom up. This even prompts them to quote Robert Cox:

> The 'old' or existing dominant form of multilateralism is a top down affair where state dominated institutions are taken as given ... The 'new' or emerging multilateralism is an attempt to 'reconstitute civil societies and political authorities on a global scale, building a system of global governance from the bottom up'. (O'Brien *et al.* 2000: 3, quoting Cox 1997: xxvii)

In particular, O'Brien *et al.* are keen to emphasise the growing role of NGOs and social movements. These large and diverse networks have no central core, but have organisational nodes, the most significant of which are the NGOs that have the ability to develop global networks, participate in multilateral arenas and facilitate interstate cooperation (O'Brien *et al.* 2000: 16). They are able to do this because globalisation is undermining the role of the state and creating new means of bringing about change through the impact of communications technology, the liberalisation of economies and changes in ideology. The authors argue that a new, complex multilateralism now exists and that the pressure of social movements, NGOs and business actors can work to modify and change international public institutions and to broaden the policy agenda to include new social issues. However, the diversity of these different actors with their conflicting aims and goals means that they produce very different impacts and outcomes (2000: 6). It is most important, therefore, to look at the impact these movements can have on the major international institutions such as the World Bank and IMF. It is argued that these movements and NGOs can exert significant pressure, and that because of public opinion, and the constant changes in the structures of governance and the global economy, they can influence the agenda of these organisations. There is certainly evidence of this. For example, it could be said that pressure from NGOs forced something of a change in World Bank policy towards the idea of environmental sustainability (see Wade 2004). On the other hand, as others have argued (Bøas and Vevatne 2004: 99), international organisations like the WTO are so wedded to a neoliberal framework that concepts like sustainable development can make headway only if they can be adapted to meet the parameters of liberal trade theory.

It is the latter that reflects the real issue of where power lies in global governance. The danger of the global civil society approach is that it loses sight of the neoliberal nature of globalisation, global governance and the wider issue of power in the global order. The promotion of NGOs and local groups is an important part of the post-Washington consensus with its talk of pluralism, networks and partnerships. To turn this into the view that global civil society offers a new progressive politics shows a naivety about the nature of actually existing global governance and evades the question of where power actually lies in the international system. It is more meaningful to look at this relationship the other way around and see how the arguments and activities of civil society movements can be co-opted into the global governance agenda. As far as governance is concerned, the involvement of civil society organisations is useful for local legitimation, and better allows international bodies to claim that their policies have a local consensus. For these reasons the IMF and World Bank have turned to NGOs over issues of legitimacy and 'ownership', with the World Bank setting up an NGO Working Group in 1984. Through NGOs international institutions can claim that there is local control over their projects and that their good-governance agenda encourages local participation and empowerment through the mobilisation of civil society. The strengthening of civil society, it is argued, improves the quality of governance and is helpful in tackling corruption and ensuring efficiency and accountability. But we are entitled to wonder about the accountability of the NGOs and civil society groups themselves. And at a global level, just how accountable are these interventions, given that it is overwhelmingly Northern NGOs who enjoy most regular contacts with the Western international institutions (see Nelson 2001: 71)? Again, the question to pose is whether this is really about effective governmentality – that is, efficient local management of populations from a distance – or more an exercise in legitimising the power of international institutions through various regulatory practices?

The two can, perhaps, be seen as working together to a limited degree. Even if local participation is limited, appeals to the idea of civil society can help influence local populations' belief in the values of liberal democracy and promote acceptance of the rules of the game. In a case study of South Africa Julie Hearn talks of how support for procedural democracy helps remove possible challenges to the system and ensures that democracy in the new South Africa is geared to system maintenance rather than genuine social transformation (Hearn 2000: 828). This strategy draws on the discourse of democracy and civil society to control the governance agenda and the expectations of the local population. Hearn writes that the new approach to South African democracy recognised the important role played by civil society in opposition to the apartheid regime, making it all the more important to penetrate civil society and gain control over popular mobilisations. Hearn notes how aid is strategically targeted at the country's most influential advocacy-orientated groups such as women's organisations, youth and student movements, human rights groups, professional media associations, private policy institutes and business associations (2000: 818).

The so-called bottom-up approach is therefore more top-down than it first seems. It works through targeting and promoting specific groups, intervening and restructuring civil society, pressuring and legitimating specific groups in order to achieve certain aims. It can be described as governmentality in so far as it uses indirect means to manage the aims and expectations of local populations, although the success of this will vary from country to country. We therefore need to look at what concepts like civil society and global civil society mean in the here and now, rather than adopt the Kantian view that ponders what global civil society *might* become. In the actual interventions of international organisations we find the promotion of certain ideas like civil society, empowerment, accountability, networked relations and, as we shall later see, social capital as part of a new rationality of governance that selectively promotes certain micro-level practices as part of a top-down strategy of management and control. To understand why this is going on, we need a macro-level picture – for example Chandler's argument about empire in denial or a Gramscian argument about hegemonic reconfiguration as well as an account of the specific rationalities that inform these interventions and construct particular targets of intervention.

While Gramscian and historical materialist accounts might help explain the top-down, hierarchical nature of international order and the link between these interventions and matters of securing order, legitimacy and the free movement of capital, Foucauldian approaches help explain how the ideas themselves lend themselves to particular deployments. The benefit of a governmentality approach is that it helps explain how concepts that may not have much explanatory value from a social theory point of view still play a significant role in supporting dominant forms of governance. In the case of the concept of global civil society, rather than dismissing the concept, we should look at how it works in practice. Here the arguments of Jens Bartelson are particularly useful. He writes:

> Rather than asking what the concept of global civil society might mean and what kind of institutions and practices it might refer to, we should ask what is *done* by means of it – what kind of world is constituted, and what kind of beliefs, institutions and practices can be justified, through the usage of this concept? (Bartelson 2006: 372)

Thus the concept of global civil society provides a kind of conceptual raw material from which legitimacy can be managed through the selective involvement of particular groups that meet the requirements of specific institutions. This chapter has argued that the process that leads to global civil society is itself underpinned by general claims about globalisation, new global problems, new forms of governance and new social actors. Together these form a new rationality of global governance that is then taken by Western-dominated international organisations to specific places around the world, where it seeks to construct a bottom-up sense of partnership, ownership and engagement as part of the institutional embedding of neoliberal practices.

However, we should end with caution. Bartelson argues that '[t]heories of governmentality focus on the role of the concept of civil society in creating and sustaining a distinct governmentality, by providing a new set of answers to the perennial question of how to govern effectively' (Bartelson 2006: 381). In fact, the jury is still out on this issue. If one looks at whether the actual practices of international institutions bring effective governance to particular areas, then we may well question this claim. As we have stated before, the ideas that dominate international organisations derive from the rationalities dominant in the advanced liberal societies. Whether these ideas really do produce effective governance when deployed in less developed countries is a moot point. While the governmentality approach is good at explaining the rationality of governance, it has less to say about how this rationality relates to different social conditions. But if, at a different level, we extend the concept of governmentality and move from governance on the ground to the governance of states themselves, then we have to conclude that concepts like global governance and civil society, by promoting ideas like partnership and legitimacy, can play an effective role in maintaining global order and stability.

Conclusion

This chapter has made a broad sweep of a vast literature on globalisation and the related ideas of global governance and global civil society. It is impossible to cover all aspects of these theories in a single chapter like this. Instead, we have concentrated on some of the arguments advanced by those claiming to offer a new, radical and progressive form of politics, and have attempted to show that not only do their arguments turn out to be less radical than claimed, but that, in fact, they often tend to support dominant forms of governance. In particular, we looked at how this relates to the practice of international organisations like the IMF and World Bank. This is something we will need to develop further in later chapters. This chapter will conclude by drawing more links between some theoretical arguments and contemporary neoliberal governmentality.

Our concern with the idea of globalisation focused on the ontological implications of the various positions and their assumptions about the nature of the social world and the actors within it. Our argument was that ultimately most theories of globalisation end up accepting a certain view of the world that matches with a particular social conjuncture and the influence of the neoliberal project in organising many aspects of social life. Instead of questioning the various social processes that seem to be occurring, these processes are seen as things in themselves, separate from underlying causes. Perhaps the biggest problem with globalisation theory is that it is unable or unwilling to provide a causal account of the processes it describes and in so doing (or not doing) it accepts the world as it appears in its surface forms of networks, flows and spatio-temporal change, without ever discussing what the underlying structure or causal mechanisms might be. This both depoliticises the various actions, projects and strategies that are promoting and facilitating these changes (often the actors themselves – states, classes, social groups – are declared to be losing power), but also denies or hides the structural changes that are both producing and being produced by these projects, while reifying the processes of globalisation itself as both the cause and outcome of these changes.

The idea of mentality is important because it does help explain how it is that certain actions come to be rationalised in particular ways. While one might question Robertson's well-known argument that the concept of globalisation 'refers to both the compression of the world and the intensification of consciousness of the world as a whole' (Robertson 1992: 4), it does at least point to the importance of consciousness and the idea that even if many of the claims of globalisation theory are wrong, if enough people believe these ideas, they start to become real in their effects. Unfortunately the main effects that are reinforced by globalisation theorists are negative ones. In particular, as mentioned, they depoliticise the changes that are occurring, reify or mystify their effects and generally accept, rather than challenge, the processes they are claiming to explain. The most important effect is to promote the view that there is no alternative to the developments being described as globalisation and that these global flows are so powerful they render powerless other political forms of organisation. One has no choice but to accept a certain globalising logic or, as Axford says: 'The idea of a global system suggests that this interconnectedness and interdependence is making it increasingly difficult for social units like nation-states, localities and even individuals to sustain identity without reference to more encompassing structures and flows' (Axford 1995: 27). In fact there is nothing new about these global flows themselves since this has always been the logic of the capitalist system. What is new is the acceptance of a specifically neoliberal view of the world that naturalises these flows, while ignoring the political strategies that lie behind the regulation of social life.

Some writers (for example, Held and Koenig-Archibugi 2005; Senarclens and Kazancil 2007) have argued that the problems of neoliberal globalisation can be overcome by good global governance and that this can be done by addressing issues like distributive justice and social protection. David Held (2004: 16) sets out an agenda that he calls global social democracy, but on examination this means pretty much the same as what the World Bank considers to be good governance – the rule of law, transparency, accountability – plus social justice and a better distribution of life chances. He also talks of regulating global flows and stakeholding. He believes this sets his vision apart from neoliberalism and the Washington consensus. But it is difficult to see much in this that is different from the post-Washington consensus arguments of the World Bank and IMF, while the issue of regulation and making global flows accountable will surely become a big issue in the post-economic-crisis version of neoliberal governance, with its greater emphasis on institutionally embedded governance. This argument is not helped by the way theorists of global accountability refer to the affected parties as 'stakeholders' (Held and Koenig-Archibugi 2005: 3), believing that somehow this difficult-to-define group of people will hold decision-makers accountable for their actions.

Theorising civil society is another area where existing order is reinforced rather than challenged. According to Scholte (2005: 88) it is a political space where civil society associations can develop rules and norms. Usually, however, the concept of civil society is reduced to the activities of NGOs, which are themselves being increasingly integrated into the development programmes of international organisations, while the rules and norms come from above rather than from below. Nevertheless, some constructivists in IR have seized on the idea of global civil society to promote a less instrumental view of politics. But actually, their arguments often support neoliberalism's (instrumental) turn to institution-building and embeddedness. Higgott notes evidence of this in the UN's 'Global Compact', writing:

> While it fits firmly within a neoliberal discourse for developing an interaction between the international institutions and the corporate world, it is an important recognition of the need to globalize some important common values. In this regard, it has strong constructivist overtones too. This should perhaps not be a surprise when one considers its intellectual driving force. That the 'global compact' reads like an attempt to globalize embedded liberalism is perhaps to be expected. The intellectual architect of this agenda was John Ruggie in his capacity as Chief Adviser for Strategic Planning to UN Secretary General Kofi Annan (1997–2000). (Higgott 2000: 140)

Despite the high level of Kantian idealism in their arguments, theorists of global civil society often end up supporting actually existing civil society, something quite different from the ideals they claim to support. In fact, their arguments could be used to support an *alternative* to global civil society, that is to say, a combination of the *ideal* of global civil society combined with the *actuality* of neoliberal practices of global governance. As Bartelson suggests, 'the concept of global civil society can be used to justify the exercise of governmental authority within an emergent world polity to the extent that it provides a substitute for a truly transnational demos' (Bartelson 2006: 373–4). Bartelson's harsh conclusion is that:

> [W]hen people are using the concept of global civil society in order to justify their resistance to what appears to be illegitimate power and unbridled global capitalism, they are in fact contributing to the reproduction of a social reality very different from that actually described by that concept. According to the logic of governmentality, the belief in the social reality of global civil society and its relative autonomy from governments and markets is a necessary condition for the smooth functioning of both. Thus, the real hopes of resistance and emancipation might reside somewhere else, outside global civil society and its institutions and practices. (Bartelson 2006: 374)

An equally harsh judgment is made by David Chandler and those who believe that advocates of global civil society are part of a process of depoliticisation, accepting the neoliberal view that the old politics is over and the new must accept the dominance of the market (Chandler 2005: 11). In our view, even the more progressive literature on global civil society accepts the main body of neoliberal assumptions and sees the globalisation project as an enabling framework for action. Inadvertently, then, this theorisation of the practices of NGOs is locked within the rationality of neoliberal governmentality, even if the theorists themselves often create a Kantian vision to justify their faith in civil society.

In actuality, organisations like the World Bank work with an Anglo-Saxon notion of civil society based on individual self-interest rather than any notion of public good or collective rights (Tussie and Tuozzo 2001: 112). Despite their Kantian rhetorical flourishes, many theorists of global civil society reinforce this individualistic image of social interaction. For example, Held writes that 'global citizenship underwrites the autonomy of each and every human being, and recognizes their capacity for self-governance at all levels of human affairs' (Held 2005: 263). Kaldor likewise believes that a normative project that challenges the undemocratic structures of global governance should demand 'autonomy, self-organization or control over life' (Kaldor 2003: 76). She defines civil society 'as the medium through which social contracts or bargains are negotiated between the individual and the centres of political and economic authority' (2003: 142), while Keane sees global civil society as 'a vast, interconnected and multi-layered non-governmental space that comprises many hundreds of thousands of more-or-less self-directing ways of life' (Keane 2003: 9).

We need to go back to classical social theory for a proper causal account of both civil society and the consciousness it creates. The following extract from Marx's *On the Jewish Question* explains both the basis of civil society and also the individualistic consciousness it creates not only in its members but those who theorise it today:

> [T]he member of civil society, is now the foundation, the presupposition of the political state. In the rights of man the state acknowledges him as such ... The constitution of the political state and the dissolution of civil society into independent individuals – who are related by law just as men in the estate and guilds were related by privilege – are achieved in one and the same act. But man, as member of civil society, inevitably appears as unpolitical man, as natural man. The rights of man appear as natural rights, for self-conscious activity is concentrated upon the political act. (Marx 1992: 233–4)

In other words, Marx's account is both an explanation and a critique of civil society. By contrast, contemporary accounts of civil society and global civil society reproduce the apolitical ideology of it as an individualistic domain of interaction. Although we have said that the theories covered in this chapter take for granted the processes they are supposed to explain – globalisation, global governance and global civil society – what they really take for granted is ultimately the nature of capitalist society itself and the various surface forms of knowledge and practice that it generates. These theories give an account of the world as it appears to be, or as it is experienced, rather than as it actually is. And in remaining at this level, they reinforce such surface forms and the dominant rationality that is at work there.

4 *Networks, governance and social capital*

Having seen how the discourse of globalisation constructs a particular picture of the world that makes it amenable to particular political projects, this chapter sees the same thing in the latest arguments about social structure and organisation. Here we will be revisiting some previous issues, especially in relation to theories of governance. But this will be approached through criticism of the idea that the structure of society has fundamentally changed as new, dynamic, flexible, non-hierarchical, reciprocal, fluid and contingent forms of social organisation replace the old, top-down, hierarchical social order.

While the theorising of networks is now extremely popular, in IR and across the social sciences, this chapter argues that most network *theories* give a misleading picture of the changes they claim to describe. As with globalisation theory, a major problem is the way that network theories actually limit the ways we can think of these changes by denying the possibility of causal explanation and promoting a shallow social ontology that concentrates on surface forms and modes of experiencing the world, while at the same time either denying that society has a deeper structure or presenting structural changes in the same kind of deterministic way that leads some theorists of globalisation to talk of it as an unstoppable process. As with the previous chapter and its approach to globalisation theory, the aim here is not to provide a comprehensive account of the different types of network theory, but to sketch a general outline of the kind of world-view network theory promotes and then to look at the role these ideas play in actual political processes. One way this might be done would be to look at a range of social practices to do with work, business and management in order to see the effects of networks at the micro level. However, this chapter will be more concerned with the way network theories contribute to the political discourse of governance. We have already covered some of this in the last chapter through discussions of good governance and the World Bank. This chapter will spend more time looking at some of these arguments in relation to the EU. Finally, the chapter moves on to discuss the concept of social capital, since this is important in relating networks to norms and trust while maintaining a social ontology based on the rational individual. All these cases, it is argued, lend themselves to contemporary forms of governmentality in so far as they construct a picture of the social world that naturalises the role of markets, introduces the ideas of competition and performance into social relations, mystifies the role of states and state strategies and promotes liberal governance through the free conduct of the individual subject.

The discourse of networks and flows

Network theories are not as new as their advocates might claim. Rather than representing the latest social developments, these theories can be traced back to perceived social changes in the 1970s and 1980s. In those days, such theories talked about the coming of post-industrial society (Bell 1973). Later theories talked of post-Fordism, the end of organised capitalism, flexible production, the information age and, finally, the network society. What unites these theories of social change is the view that capitalist society – its forms of production, modes of consumption and use of technology and communication – has been undergoing some sort of profound reorganisation. It should be remembered that these new ideas emerged in a profoundly political period when the postwar settlement entered crisis and new thinking emerged on how best to deal with developing social and economic problems. We have suggested that whereas historical materialists might refer to the underlying basis of this crisis as a crisis of accumulation and its associated social forms, linked to a hegemonic crisis and the break-up of the postwar historical bloc, much of the new thinking has downplayed this political and institutional context. This was certainly the case once these arguments came to be combined with globalisation theory. Then, as we have seen, such changes tend to be regarded as inevitable and unstoppable. Changes in the postwar institutional arrangements are often presented as deeper-seated changes in modernity itself rather than as specific political strategies related to the reordering of the institutional arrangements of postwar capitalist societies. We have argued this in relation to globalisation theory and we will continue to argue this in relation to other contemporary theories such as Beck's claim that we are living in a risk society, Giddens's argument that we have entered a new (reflexive) stage of modernity and, in relation to the focus of this chapter, Castells's claim that we now live in a network society. Arguments about the new significance of networks and flows started to fit very well with the type of capitalist reorganisation necessitated by the social and economic crisis of the postwar project. The problem with these theories is that they naturalise these changes by presenting them as deep-seated changes in the nature of modernity rather than as the product of a particular social and historical context. The consequence is ultimately to lend further legitimacy (or to rationalise) the very social and political changes they are trying to describe, and it is for this reason that we might try to understand these theories through Foucault's concept of governmentality.

Networks are open structures that develop through the addition of new nodes. They tend to have a more informal nature in comparison with the hierarchical and ordered nature of traditional forms of social relations. Networks are horizontal and reciprocal, more open and flexible, although ultimately they form some more or less stable pattern of social relations (Klijn 2005: 329). In a perceived contrast with previous forms of social organisation, 'a single central authority, a hierarchical ordering and a single organisational goal do not exist ... None of the actors has enough steering capacity unilaterally to control other actors' (Klijn 2005: 330). Some of the more postmodern theorists of networks like Bruno Latour and Arturo Escobar are inclined to make more explicitly anti-realist claims that conflate the existence of networks with epistemological issues, arguing that networks are 'not epistemological centres and peripheries but a decentralized network of nodes in and through which theorists, theories, and multiple users move and meet' (Escobar 1995: 224).

Problems arise as soon as these ideas start to be seen as the main category of understanding for contemporary societies. Van Dijk, for example, starts off talking about the role of new media, the significance of high-speed communication and the huge storage potential new technology provides (1999: 17) but soon turns to claims about a new information age where the dominant functions and processes become organised around networks related to production, experience, power and culture. He goes on to claim that the network society has replaced the mass society of industrialisation, cities and nations. Of particular significance is the way that transnational companies have started to spread to more and more areas and to subcontract their operations. It is claimed that large companies have decentralised executive power, a process that can now be seen not only in corporations but also with governments. This has a spatial effect in so far as the geography of places is being replaced with a geography of flows. Van Dijk argues that this 'flow economy' is the most obvious solution to the economic crisis of productivity of the 1970s (1999: 61). This argument sounds as if it is moving towards the kind of institutional analysis we have suggested is necessary to look at changes in postwar capitalist societies. But we are not told how widespread this process is, whether it affects some sectors more than others or, most of all, whether this is a reversible strategy or an inevitable process? Unfortunately it seems more like the latter when in a sweeping statement characteristic of much of this literature van Dijk argues that twentieth-century history is that of the dissolution of families, neighbourhoods and workers, privatisation and individualisation (1999: 159). The consequence of these sorts of remarks is to turn this into a natural process rather than a consequence of recent strategies and techniques of governance.

However, it is the work of Castells that is best known for its bold claim for a new type of society, a network society, based on a 'historical linkage between the knowledge–information base of the economy, its global reach, its network-based organizational form, and the information technology revolution that has given birth to a new, distinctive economic system' (Castells 2009: 77). The network society takes the form of 'a social structure based on networks operated by information and communication technologies based in microelectronics and digital computer networks that generate, process, and distribute information on the basis of the knowledge accumulated in the nodes of networks' (Castells 2006: 7). Many critics have noted the economic and technological determinism present in Castells's arguments, something he almost seems to enjoy embracing when sarcastically commenting that: 'We are witnessing an increasing contradiction between current social relationships of production and the potential expansion of formidable productive forces. This may be the only lasting contribution from the classical Marxist theory' (2006: 20).

What distinguishes the new society is the diffusion of information technology in all spheres of social and economic activity. In particular the IT networks allow for the development of social and economic flows, reducing the significance of particular places. Society comes under the influence of finance capital, which in turn relies on the knowledge and information generated by information technology. This, it is claimed, subsumes the logic of the old industrial society, embodying knowledge and production in processes of material production. Indeed it is claimed that the material foundations of society, space and time are being transformed and reorganised around the space of flows. It is claimed that the new economy is informational, global and networked with the productivity and competitiveness of units dependent on knowledge-based information, production, consumption and circulation and organised on a global scale (Castells 2009: 77).

Castells's claim is that there has been a transformation in relations of production leading to a new form of capitalism called informational capitalism. The productivity and competitiveness of the global economy comes from innovation, flexibility and network enterprise. Two processes, the inexorable development of information and technology and the organisational logic of networks, drive Castells's model. The latter argument is developed through arguments about management and labour. On the management side, flexibility and innovation are the key words. On the labour side, individualisation and fragmentation are emphasised. The effect of information and technology is the restructuring of firms and the redefinition of the role of labour. The work process is increasingly individualised, labour is disaggregated in its performance and reintegrated in its outcome through multiple tasks and interconnections. The workforce is fragmented between skilled informational producers and replaceable generic labour. The general effect of information and technology on the work process is the individualisation of labour and work, the decentralisation of management, customisation of markets and the segmenting and fragmenting of societies (Castells 2009: 282).

What is troubling about the argument is not so much the claim that individualisation is taking place, but the absence of a social explanation of the causes of this. Instead, individualisation is presented as an inevitable consequence of technological development that we can do nothing about. It is we who have to change our behaviour and learn to live in a new type of society. As with Giddens, we see the two main arguments of contemporary governance appearing: unstoppable macro forces on the one hand, individualised self-conduct on the other. A similar theme is expressed by Bauman: 'Ours is, as a result, an individualized, privatised version of modernity, with the burden of pattern-weaving and the responsibility for failure falling primarily on the individual's shoulders' (Bauman 2000: 7–8). Here we have another example of naturalising recent neoliberal strategies by claiming their effects to be a general condition of modernity.

Flows are seen as an alternative to organised forms. For Urry they are waves made up of individual particles (Urry 2003: 41). Lash sees flow as a quality of information alongside some of the other ideas we have seen in Giddens and globalisation theory – 'disembeddedness, spatial compression, temporal compression, real-time relations' (Lash 2002: 2). Urry sees examples of these in the globally integrated networks of enterprises like McDonald's, Microsoft and Sony. These transnational corporations, it is claimed, have a minimum of central organisation. It is interesting to note how often such commentators use the example of corporations when discussing the network form, something we might call a fetishism of the firm. These globally integrated networks then contribute to what Urry calls global fluids. These deterritorialised particles of people, objects, money and images 'move within and across diverse regions forming heterogeneous, uneven, unpredictable and often unplanned waves' (Urry 2003: 60). They create their own context, have no clear end or point of departure, and represent unpredictable, deterritorialised movement (2003: 60). Again, as in many of the theories of networks, the ideological effect of such statements is to claim that fluids create their own reality, that they have no social cause or context, they cannot be controlled, they cannot be contained and their flow cannot be stopped. In light of the recent crisis of financial capitalism this has been shown up as a fetishism of movement at the expense of the actual social nature of capital.

Urry is best known for his work with Scott Lash, and in their book *Economies of Signs and Space* they emphasise the importance of flows of capital, labour and commodities, but in particular, information and images. These 'structured flows and accumulations of information are the basis of cognitive reflexivity' (Lash and Urry 1994: 7), and again there seems to be the view that they create their own reality: 'there is indeed a structural basis for today's reflexive individuals. And that this is not social structures, but increasingly the pervasion of *information and communication structures*' (1994: 6). This is another example of technological determinism, in that it reifies communication and technology by suggesting that they are somehow not social. Lash and Urry write that whereas their book *The End of Organized Capitalism*

(1987) argued for vertical disintegration, flexible specialisation and post-Fordism, their next book argues that flexible specialisation means informationalisation or the flexible economy based on information. This is organised through collective, practical and discursive forms of reflexive modernisation (Lash and Urry 1994: 109). There is a shift from the modernist space and time of the workplace (Taylorist and Fordist systems) to late or postmodern subjectivisation of workplace time and space in flexibly specialised systems, while cultural capital or information-processing capacities can be accumulated through training and education. Now it becomes access to communication and information that is the major determinant of class position (actually an updating of a traditional Weberian view). And since the core of the new economy is said to be advanced business and communications services, what tends to be produced are post-industrial informational goods or else aesthetic products. The latter in particular mark the transition from use value to exchange value to what they call sign value or the 'simulacrum of a simulacrum'. Increasingly what are produced are not material objects but signs. The most notable example of sign value is the brand. These signs and images best exemplify the space-time compression of the globalised world, and the brand is the ultimate example of a product that is constantly flowing in and out of different cultures. It is claimed that in this new economy of signs, 'Pleasure seeking is a duty since the consumption of goods and services becomes *the* structural basis of Western societies' (1994: 296). This is just one of many statements to be found attacking, undermining or confusing the idea of structure.

What we find here is the argument that the material foundations of society, space and time are being transformed and reorganised around a space of flows. Economic relations are no longer organised around the production of material goods, but instead are ordered around information and knowledge. This argument allows for a focus on the surface level of movement – people, the Internet, money, brands and logos – rather than on the social structures that produce them and facilitate their movement. There is little hope for organised opposition to this process. According to contemporary theorists the transformation of economic relations is accompanied by the declining significance of political practices, social groups and the role of the state. These ideas will be examined in more detail when we turn to theories of governance.

So finally we will turn to Boltanski and Chiapello for a more nuanced view of networks. What is more encouraging in Boltanski and Chiapello is the way that the idea of networks relates not so much to a new condition of modernity, as might be found in all the previous theorists, but to what they call a 'new spirit of capitalism', a view that is closer to Foucauldian ideas on rationality, discourse and strategy. In particular, they are interested in the ideas behind the reorganisation of capitalist social relations. In contrast to the deterministic and teleological views of other network theorists, this recognises that capitalist social relations require institutional organisation and structuring and that ideas and strategies play an important role in this process. The fact that this restructuring has been based on the role of financial markets and a flexibilisation of the labour process, especially in the Anglo-Saxon model, inevitably leads to a stress on the ideas of networks and flows as legitimating features of a new political ideology. The difference between Boltanski and Chiapello's approach and that of the other network theorists considered here is that they recognise this as an ideology and relate it to the deeper structure of capitalist social relations. The other theorists, by contrast, reinforce the ideology by claiming it as a deeper social condition in its own right.

Boltanski and Chiapello's approach therefore looks at the reorganisation of capitalism by focusing on management texts and their advocacy of more flexible, networked forms of organisation:

> [I]t was by opposing a social capitalism planned and supervised by the state – treated as obsolete, cramped and constraining – and leaning on the artistic critique (autonomy and creativity) that the new spirit of capitalism gradually took shape at the end of the crisis of the 1960s and 1970s, and undertook to restore the prestige of capitalism. Turning its back on the social demands that had dominated the first half of the 1970s, the new spirit was receptive to the critiques of the period that denounced the mechanization of the world (post-industrial society against industrial society) – the destruction of forms of life conducive to the fulfilment of specifically human potential and, in particular, creativity – and stressed the intolerable character of the modes of oppression which, without necessarily deriving directly from historical capitalism, had been exploited by capitalist mechanisms for organizing work. (Boltanski and Chiapello 2005: 201)

New themes in this discourse included a rejection of hierarchy, promotion of competition and technological change, the transformation of the manager into a network figure who relies on social and spatial mobility and the importance of trust and flexibility (Boltanski and Chiapello 2005: 70–1, 79). The new discourse of the network world opposes itself to the industrial world where people have certain fixed duties and responsibilities and occupy particular positions and posts: 'In a connexionist world, people are called upon to move around, to forge the links they use in their work themselves – links that cannot, by definition, be pre-established in advance ... Their flexibility, their ability to adapt and learn continuously, become major advantages, which take precedence over their technical expertise' (2005: 135). The network organisation of work bases itself on lean firms, subcontractors and a malleable labour force. It portrays these changes in positive terms as involving people more in their work and taking responsibility for their actions. This reminds us of trends noted by Foucault and theorists of neoliberal governmentality, as does the idea that '[f]unctioning in networks also satisfies the highly human characteristic of wanting to be simultaneously free and engaged' (2005: 127).

The development of new ideas on networks is described by Boltanski and Chiapello as contributing to a network paradigm. They argue that the formation of this new paradigm 'was bound up in a very general way with a growing interest in *relational properties* (and relational ontologies), as opposed to properties substantially attached to entities they supposedly defined in themselves' (2005: 143). As we move on to the next section we can see the similarities, not between Boltanski and Chiapello and other network theorists, but between these other network theorists and the management discourse that represents the 'new spirit of capitalism'. In terms of philosophical commitments there is a startling parallel: 'Rather than assuming a world organized according to basic structures ... it [the network paradigm] presents a world where everything potentially reflects everything else: a world, often conceived as "fluid, continuous, chaotic", where anything can be connected with anything else, which must be tackled without any reductionist apriorism' (2005: 144). Except that these arguments are based on the a priori assumption that the rise of networks is an inevitable process lodged in the very nature of the unfolding of modernity. Whereas one should be careful with Boltanski and Chiapello's arguments and recognise that they apply to management discourse and practice, but not necessarily to all aspects of the capitalist system, in the case of other work on networks it does not so much describe the new spirit of capitalism as uncritically embrace it. We might tentatively claim that most network theory, for all its philosophical grandeur, is a part of the very same paradigm it claims to be analysing.

Networks and international relations

If we look at the influence of network theories in analysing international relations we can see similar issues to those raised in the previous chapter. As we have seen, globalisation theory puts forward the argument that radical changes in the organisation of time and space have produced radically new roles for the state and civil society and new forms of power and modes of governance. For Held *et al.*, globalisation is a process 'which embodies a transformation in the spatial organization of social relations and transactions – assessed in terms of their extensivity, velocity and impact – generating transcontinental or interregional flows and networks of activity, interaction and the exercise of power' (Held *et al.* 1999: 16). Globalisation, viewed as multiple flows operating across territorial borders, is believed to lead to the undermining of state power and the replacement of old social relations with new, more dynamic and adaptable networks. The power of global flows – of things like capital, goods, and information – requires the development of new institutions and the need for old ones to become part of new networks. This forms the basis for arguments for new forms of governance – networked governance – based on the coming together of governments, civil society and transnational policy networks, to shape government policy and public opinion. This, it is argued, leads to a new type of governance that is more informal in nature, requires greater cooperation and trust among network partners and stakeholders and leads to changing fortunes for the powers of the state and civil society.

For Held, Scholte, Rosenau and many other theorists of globalisation and global governance, power has shifted from the state to international organisations, regimes and networks as well as to civil society, NGOs, social movements and global civil society. States have a reduced capacity to deal with central issues and problems and must share their governance responsibilities with other bodies and agencies. As we have noted, this is conceived of either in terms of the state being enmeshed in new global networks, or else that they are part of a multilayered system of global governance. Sovereignty becomes something that has to be shared and negotiated, political authority is diffused to new bodies existing above, below and alongside the state. In the previous chapter we argued that if these developments are understood through the concept of governmentality, then it is not so much a question of new forms of power overwhelming the state as of the state consciously engaging in this reorganisation of institutional relations in order to reflexively fine-tune its own powers and responsibilities. Rather than taking the accepted view that these developments have made the state subservient to more powerful transnational networks and new sites of governance, we argue that embracing this new rationality of governance has given the state more subtle and sophisticated techniques for the management of their populations and territory, and has led to states supporting and encouraging the very changes that the governmentality literature claims are threatening their existence.

The problem with many of the network theorists – certainly those keen to make grand sociological claims – is that they reify this process by ignoring the proactive role of the state and fetishise networks and flows by giving them a life of their own. Featherstone and Lash, for example, talk of the

> sociocultural processes and forms of life which are emerging as the global begins to replace the nation-state as the decisive framework for social-life. This is a framework in which global *flows* – in mediascapes, ethnoscapes, financescapes and technoscapes – are coming to assume as much, or greater, centrality than *national institutions*. (Featherstone and Lash 1995: 2)[1]

This depends on a particular view of national institutions, long held by IR realists if not by historical materialists and other sociological accounts of state power. This one-sided view is nicely expressed in Luke's belief that: 'As containers of modernity, modern realist states presume the existence and acceptance of elaborate discourses of instrumental action, rational reflection, linear causality, natural objectivity, complex hierarchy, inert matter, universal materialism and human subjectivity' (Luke 1995: 93). As we have seen when examining the work of Lash and Urry, such attributions are common among those wishing

[1] Or even more outrageously, they claim that a 'central implication of the concept of globalisation is that we must now embark on the project of understanding social life without the comforting term "society"' (Featherstone and Lash 1995: 2).

to set up their own position as somehow more sophisticated and better able to deal with things like complexity. When they are set up in such a way, it is hard not to be swayed by the persuasive power of flows:

> Flows, then, are decentring, despatializing and dematerializing forces, but they work alongside and against the geopolitical codes of spatial sovereignty. The local and the global are commingling in new 'glocal' modes of production across and outside of national boundaries. Within the flow, there are new universals and new particulars being created by the networks of transnational exchange as fresh identities, unities and values emerge from sharing access to the same symbols, markets and commodities in a new pattern of 'glocalization'. (Luke 1995: 101)

In looking for alternatives to state power, some network theorists claim there has been a shift in power towards global civil society. We have seen how theorists like Keane use the idea of global civil society as an ideal type of a dynamic non-governmental realm where various networks, organisations, institutions and actors come together in different ways (Keane 2003: 8). While the promotion of global civil society as an alternative to the power of the state may be far from the truth – in fact, as writers from Marx (1992: 233) to Foucault (2004: 350) have argued, civil society is the necessary correlate of the state – we have suggested, following Bartelson (2006), that the idea of global civil society can play an important role in enhancing the dominant forms of governmentality as implemented by both state and non-state actors. It allows international organisations like the UN, for example, to promote the development of global public policy networks to deliver or regulate global public goods, build bridges between different actors, develop knowledge and engage stakeholders (Reinicke *et al.* 2000). These networks, as Stone (2005: 90) notes, can bring together and institutionalise relations between international organisations, government agencies, corporations and civil society. But while this may potentially give a greater role to civil society, this does not necessarily democratise global policy-making: 'The global agora is not a level playing field for networks. It is characterised by an uneven distribution of resources and a hierarchy of discourses in which relatively few can be public actors' (2005: 89). For some critics like Stone, therefore, even if there is a perceived empowerment of new global networks, it is more likely that these represent 'new constellations of privatised power' rather than the dispersal of power and the breaking down of hierarchies. For Stone, there is no 'bottom-up' democratic governance, but instead a form of governance implicated in the affairs of states and international organisations (2005: 90).

Yet the networks *discourse* functions effectively in creating the impression that new forms of governmentality in fact offer great opportunities to a variety of different actors. We have already seen how states and international organisations have been able to use the discourse of stakeholding, empowerment, ownership and inclusiveness to encourage us to see new forms of governance in a positive light despite their obvious lack of democracy, lack of inclusiveness and conscious depoliticisation (or managerialisation) of social issues. This governance *rationality* is supported by those social theorists seeking to cast global governance in a positive light by claiming it has a radical and progressive nature, for example Held's (2004) agenda for global social democracy, Kaldor's (2003) advocacy of global civil society or Scholte's work on globalisation and his contribution to O'Brien *et al.* (2000). Here it is argued that there now exists a new, complex multilateralism and that the pressure of social movements, NGOs and business actors can help modify and change international public institutions and broaden the policy agenda to include new social issues. Networks bring together NGOs and activists whose principles and beliefs are supported by information exchanges. As with most theorists of global civil society, there is a strong normative basis to these arguments, even if there is sometimes recognition that the ideas of these new actors have yet to be well integrated into actual policy-making.[2]

This normative approach carries over into the arguments about transnational advocacy networks. The belief here is that networks of activists can put pressure on global institutions as well as states, either to change their policies or adopt new ideas. The networks multiply the voices of activists, provide alternative channels of communication and allow flows of alternative views and information (Keck and Sikkink 1998: x). The networks are guided by values rather than material

[2] We noted this in the previous chapter when discussing the limited impact NGOs and social movements have had in bringing new social issues to international organisations like the IMF, World Bank and WTO. There has been some progress on gender and environmental issues, particularly with the World Bank, but the normal pattern is the co-opting of these groups into the global governance agenda.

interests or professional motivations; their aim is to help to frame debates, get commitments, influence behaviour and persuade and pressure for change (1998: 2, 201). As with the sociological literature, these networks are defined by Keck and Sikkink 'as forms of organization characterized by voluntary, reciprocal, and horizontal patterns of communication and exchange' (1998: 8). Other ways of describing these sorts of networks of actors and activists include knowledge networks, epistemic communities, transnational discourse communities and disembedded knowledge networks (Stone 2005: 95–6). The common feature of these networks is that they provide a means for sharing knowledge, rationalising action, generating ideas and establishing goals. The theorists themselves often rely on a constructivist approach, emphasising the role of rules and norms and intersubjective understandings (Keck and Sikkink 1998: 8; Stone 2005: 96; see also Riles 2001). They rely on symbols and language as sources of power, with intersubjective criteria for establishing the truth or validity of their claims (Stone 2005: 95–6). However, Stone notes that these can equally become tools of power for dominant interests, part of the micro politics of the dominant hegemony or neoliberal order by reproducing ideas supportive of it (2005: 96). Or as Rai puts it, these networks can be both democratic and exclusionary, expansive and integratory. The issue then is expansion to and for what? Integration with and into what (Rai 2005: 126)?

The World Bank, for example, now uses the discourse of knowledge-sharing in its development programmes, arguing that through the sharing of knowledge and information, it can achieve 'best practice' in areas like the environment, sustainability and corporate citizenship (Stone 2005: 93). The World Bank's Global Development Network[3] operates a knowledge bank that works through the integration of local and global networks. As critics have noted, in doing so it imposes a rationality that gives precedence to the 'conception of knowledge rather than the ideals of community', integrating these networks into the dominant development policy framework, thus legitimising it and ensuring the communicative codes against challenge (Rai 2005: 126). As we have already noted, the World Bank operates through a discourse of good governance, establishing conditions for the receipt of loans, grants and technical advice. While now recognising the role of states as necessary

[3] www.gdnet.org.

for the promotion of effective markets, these states need to be subject to monitoring and surveillance. The Global Development Network can play an effective role in establishing a discourse that supports the Bank sending out supervising missions to examine public management, accountability, information availability and transparency.

In conclusion, we should note the appeal of networks in offering a politics of action and intervention, but it is precisely this that renders them important tools of governmentality by international organisations intent on regulating the behaviour of states, governments and populations. Networks, Rai argues, are no different from other structures and agents in our society – they are implicated in dominant power relations, but '[t]he seduction of networks is providing a sense of agency against all odds, at times emphasising the process over outcome, at other times through emphasising "empowerment" without the transfer of resources that denotes changes in power relations' (Rai 2005: 136). This is precisely the attraction of networks – their surface-level appeal – which leaves intact the deeper social relations that ultimately influence them. Networks are not as pluralistic and open-ended as their theorists like to claim. It is precisely because they do not replace existing social relations, as is often claimed, but operate within these social relations and the hierarchies of power that flow from them that networks can be used to reinforce these relations while at the same time denying or downplaying their existence. Networks, Stone notes, can be used to systematise knowledge and impose a rationality that gives precedence to a particular conception of the world that is consistent with contemporary governance. Participation in these networks is informally restricted and regulated through boundary drawing, while decision-making is put in the hands of private stakeholders or dominant epistemic communities (Stone 2005: 100). Ultimately networks reflect the dominant forms of governance with their emphasis on private interests, market mechanisms, public administration, neoliberal ideas of accountability, reflexivity and risk management, usually – if they are influential – reflecting private-sector ideas that foreground organisational techniques like competition, performance and cost efficiency.

Governance

The concept of governance has already been discussed in relation to global governance and good governance. Now we will examine governance in relation to networks or network governance. We will then move to a more general discussion of governance as a new form of power, looking at its specific function in relation to things like information, technology and benchmarking. In particular, this will be developed in relation to debates about governance in the EU, although comparisons will be drawn with the OECD and World Economic Forum. We end with a comparison with the concept of governmentality and ask whether governance can be seen as a neoliberal technique or rationality that promotes the conduct of conduct. Indeed this is also our starting point in so far as it provides our first definition of governance as a networked form of power that regulates behaviour through the promotion of self-steering capacities. As Triantafillou's admittedly over-general definition puts it: 'we could broadly characterize *network governance* as the diverse governmental rationalities, technologies and norms that seek to govern by promoting the self-steering capacities of individuals and organizations' (Triantafillou 2004: 498).

New approaches that focus on governance are particularly concerned with the idea that this governance is different from the old hierarchical forms of power associated with the political authority of the nation state. As Pierre and Peters (2000: 16) suggest, new forms of governance entail a critique of hierarchy by promoting the theme of horizontal networked power involving multiple actors and a globalised social context, and thus a weakening of national state power. The idea of networks plays a useful role here in arguing that hierarchical state authority has given way to a dehierarchised self-reflexive form of politics based on multiple actors operating at many different levels. The most influential approach here, certainly to EU studies, is called precisely this – multi-level governance – and emphasises the importance of reflexivity and self-reflection among different actors operating across different levels, pooling their sovereignty and sharing resources and objectives. Other approaches to network governance go still further in emphasising the way that different actors stand in mutual relation to one another, with shared identities and understandings emerging out of this interaction. For Rhodes, '*governance refers to self-organizing, interorganizing networks* characterized by interdependence, resource exchange, rules of the game and significant autonomy from the state' (Rhodes 1997: 15). This leads to a constructed environment, which Hajer and Versteeg believe emerges because governance first has to develop a shared discourse, set the stage and develop its logic of appropriateness (Hajer and Versteeg 2005: 346). Governance networks are seen as the arenas where actors engage with one another, argue, interpret, explain and justify themselves. They work on the basis of shared knowledge, trust and a mutual understanding of potentially unstable conditions (2005: 342).

Governance theorists recognise that because networks formulate rules and standards in such ways, they encounter problems of accountability (King 2007: 142). Some, like Chhotray and Stoker (2009), attribute this to wider changes like globalisation and democratisation. We prefer Hirst's view that most understandings of governance suggest that the issue is not one of democracy, but a post-political search for effective regulation and accountability (Hirst 2000: 13). This is the case precisely because governance is a move away from government, or as Stoker puts it: 'The essence of governance is its focus on governing mechanisms which do not rest on recourse to the authority and sanctions of government' (Stoker 2002: 17).

It is easier to define governance in terms of what it is not,[4] and so the network metaphor is important in stressing the move away from both hierarchical state authority and the blurring of public and private (socio-political), and the crossing of territorial boundaries (global). This then gives us a definition of governance based on the recognition of the multi-layered nature of decision-making, changes in state, structures and institutions and the development of a complex range of institutions and networks operating at the international and supranational level (Chhotray and Stoker 2009: 216). To start with two very general definitions, we have, first, Chhotray and Stoker's claim that governance represents 'the rules of collective decision-making in settings where there are a plurality of actors or organisations and where no formal control system can dictate the terms of the relationship between these actors and organisations' (2009: 3). Second, Stoker provides a useful set of governance bullet points:

[4] Hirst gives a list of five different ways that the term governance is used: (1) as economic development, as in the World Bank's use of 'good governance' to make markets work better; (2) as international institutions and regimes, the realm of governance without government; (3) as corporate governance focusing on accountability and transparency of management; (4) as New Public Management; (5) as networks, partnerships and collaborative forums as opposed to more hierarchical corporatist representation (Hirst 2000: 14–19).

(1) Governance refers to a set of institutions and actors that are drawn from but also beyond government.
(2) Governance identifies the blurring of boundaries and responsibilities for tackling social and economic issues.
(3) Governance identifies the power dependence involved in the relationships between institutions involved in collective action.
(4) Governance is about autonomous self-governing networks of actors.
(5) Governance recognizes the capacity to get things done which does not rest on the power of government to command or use its authority. It sees government as able to use new tools and techniques to steer and guide. (Stoker 2002: 18)

We have seen how many globalisation theorists are prepared to argue that these new forms of governance are part of a general decline in the power of the state. But this idea of the nation state as the main regulatory body within a given territorial space has to be seen in its appropriate historical context. As Hirst (2000: 22) argues, the idea of national democratic control is something of an illusion caused by the particular form of macroeconomic management and public-service provision established in the postwar period. As a result, changes in the prevailing ideology create the equally illusory impression that economic liberalisation is the same thing as the globalisation of political power. A more historical account of these changes would instead link changes in forms of governance to deeper socio-economic relations and the institutional crisis of the postwar system of national state regulation. Jessop calls this eventual failure to mobilise ideological support for accumulation strategies, state projects and hegemonic visions an '*internal disarticulation*' or institutional crisis at the level of state apparatuses. This was seen in a declining effectiveness of state apparatuses 'in terms of their vertical coherence across different organizational levels and their capacity to engage in horizontal coordination of different domains of activity' (Jessop 2002: 177). To take up Jessop's term 'hegemonic vision', we might also introduce here the crisis of the prevailing ideology and an emerging crisis of political representation, two trends which further encouraged the depoliticisation and managerialisation of governance.

This is the context by which we should understand the changing nature of the state and forms of governance. Not the decline of the state or the replacement of the state, but a change in the nature of the state, at least at the level of *state strategy*, if not in terms of its fundamental social functions such as securing the conditions for capital accumulation, maintaining the rule of law and guaranteeing social cohesion. We can talk of the 'hollowing out' of the state only in so far as the means of achieving some of these functions have been transferred or devolved to other bodies above, below or alongside the state. This is less a move away from the state than a 'governmentalisation' of the state (Foucault 2004: 109). This helps us understand the relationship between state and civil society, as well as why globalisation theory mystifies this process. For example, when Scholte writes that the 'contemporary expansion of civil society has been a response to altered contours of governance in the wake of globalisation' (Scholte 2002: 150), we can see that this places the burden of explanation on an unspecified notion of globalisation as an external actor, rather than highlighting the institutional changes going on within states as a result of changes in the relationships between states and deeper socio-economic relations. It should also make us wary of claims that governance blurs the distinction between state and civil society to the point where there is no longer any sovereign actor to steer or regulate (Rhodes 1997: 56). This use of governance is precisely the means by which new strategies of regulation take place, encouraged by governments deliberately dispersing the state's regulatory powers, deliberately engaging new actors and activating new sites of governance. It is with this in mind that one needs to critically interpret comments by governance scholars like Stoker when he writes that the governance perspective embodies two aspects – increasingly complex systems of government, and the stepping back of the state with responsibility being given to the private sector and civil society (Stoker 2002: 21).

The subtle difference that must be insisted upon here is that the state is – paradoxically – at the heart of this transformation. Thus when Sørensen argues, in a rather Foucauldian manner, that 'the state has become a differentiated, fragmented, and multicentred institutional complex that is held together by more or less formalized networks' (Sørensen 2006: 100), we should note that this is a process of self-transformation. This is well captured in King's emphasis on steering networks. We have noted that use of the term 'steering' often requires us to see the state as having lost absolute control, as in Giddens's well-known claim that globalisation is like a juggernaut that can be steered but not stopped. But King's comment suggests that it is precisely through steering techniques that the state supplements its control and renders it more effective:

> Governance refers to the process of steering networks by the state rather than it commanding, controlling, producing and delivering. It describes the changing role of the state ... above all in which formal state regulatory authority is supplemented by the informal authority of networks. In this view, networks are a distinctive coordinating mechanism separate from markets and hierarchies, and the regulatory state rules through the regulatory activities of other groups rather than by direct bureaucratic hierarchy. (King 2007: 19)

We would argue, though, that this approach does not replace hierarchical state power, but supplements it and offers new, subtler techniques that regulate from a distance. If we move into the area of EU governance, then we certainly find these techniques playing a significant role. Here we certainly find hierarchy, but we also have a complex of overlapping powers, a wide variety of actors and decision-making processes, various external actors, and perhaps most importantly, indirect market-led steering mechanisms and suggestive forms of decision-making.

This development of the EU system matches exactly with the type of neoliberal governmentality sketched previously. First, there are the directly economic initiatives concerned with the European market. The institutional process by which this market is 'constructed' relies on the liberal self-limitation of government or the idea that the state itself always governs too much. Thus, the Maastricht Treaty, the basis on which the euro was launched, imposes strict economic conditions that restrict public spending and welfare provision. It deliberately limits the funds available so that the EU cannot but be a regulatory body rather than a more strongly interventionist institution. We can extend this economic limitation into the political sphere if we consider things like qualified majority voting, which restricts the capacities of national governments and makes it difficult for them to control EU policy-making. Meanwhile, this process of policy-making is limited by the particular way that the EU has developed in so far as its development is a result of a series of treaties – that is, agreements to achieve certain ends through particular institutions. The effect of this is an emphasis on soft power and use of influence rather than stronger sanction or compulsion. The aim is to build consensus among institutions and governments through a common framework of action. However, the consequence of this is not weak government but the particular way of 'steering' already noted above. All this is neatly summarised by Sbragia, particularly in relation to the role the economy plays in this process:

> Thus, governance within the European Union – however defined – takes place within an institutionalised policy framework which structurally privileges certain policy content or at least policy norms. The fact the Union is based on treaties – which are about policy choices – rather than a constitution is fundamental to understanding why the Union can steer in areas where national governments find it difficult ... they also favour certain policy positions ... in a way that constitutions do not. While the unconventional way in which the Union is governed and the complexity of its decision rules is due to the power that the treaty-making process gives to national governments, that same process allows the norm of economic liberalization to be privileged in ways difficult to imitate in a constitution-writing process. (Sbragia 2000: 223)

This norm of economic liberalisation can be seen as the basis on which the objects of governance are constructed. For Foucault, what is characteristic of neoliberal governmentality is the way the market economy 'constitutes the general index in which one must place the rule for defining all government action' (Foucault 2008: 121). The EU project is simultaneously creating new markets, while also developing a regulatory framework in order to channel these into new areas like health and safety, the environment and consumer protection (Sbragia 2000: 225).

Neoliberal governance establishes market-led performance criteria in order to assess the functioning of public institutions and actors and encourages cooperation between public, private and non-state actors (Tömmel 1998: 56). These non-governmental agencies are encouraged to deliver public services and assist in policy-making, and in the EU this is particularly important, as Tömmel notes (1998: 65), so as to circumvent any obstructive behaviour, inefficient practices and unwieldy procedures of the different Member States. As well as involving private companies, the EU seeks to engage different interest groups and NGOs as can be seen in the EU's 2001 White Paper on European Governance. This shows how the EU Commission is actively building itself as a decision-making centre at the heart of a set of informal networks. It establishes the basis on which different civil society groups have access to this decision-making centre and to EU policy-makers as well as the huge web of information at whose centre it has put itself. These information flows can be redirected by the Commission and allows it to set the agenda itself. Since the EU is a regulator rather than an enforcer, this can be seen more as a form of networked power, less hierarchical in its nature, but highly institutionalised and requiring continuous negotiation (see Christiansen *et al.* 2003: 2–9).

These different processes are described within the EU literature as multi-level governance. This term brings together the diffusion of decision-making to different levels and multiple centres, the use of new forms of public administration and the less hierarchical, more apolitical move towards public–private networks and quasi-autonomous bodies. However, there are reasons for preferring a theory of governmentality to explain these changes. As Jessop notes, there are serious problems with the way that multi-level governance conflates three different things – the denationalisation (or hollowing out) of the state, the move from government to governance (the destatisation of politics and governmentalisation of the state), and the rearticulation of territorial and functional powers (in this case, across the EU) (Jessop 2007: 207). The governmentality approach also allows us to better explore the paradox whereby processes of denationalisation, destatisation and internationalisation represent advanced liberal forms of state power, however ineffective and imperfect aspects of European governance may be.

Those like Jessop and Hay who develop what they call a strategic relational approach challenge the idea that governance takes place through non-hierarchical networks by emphasising the strategic selectivity of institutional arrangements and the complexity of various horizons, interests, strategies, tactics, alliances and modalities (Hay 1998: 43; Jessop 2007: 223). Action takes place in a strategically selective context that depends on specific institutional, organisational and practical contexts. This context requires awareness of the constraints and opportunities imposed by social structures. In this way we have to situate changes in the EU's political forms in the wider context of the reregulation of global capitalism (Jessop 2007: 223). This reregulation requires the active intervention of the state. But, as mentioned earlier, this is in the paradoxical sense of Foucault's account of neoliberal governmentality. Certainly the EU starts to assume various state-like characteristics, but not necessarily in the way the state is normally understood. Just as Foucault understands the state as a principle of intelligibility, a regulatory idea of governmental reason, a rationality of an art of government, so the development of the EU represents the application of a schema of intelligibility for a set of emerging institutions and practices (Foucault 2004: 286).

Governmentality through benchmarking and indicators

This section starts with the EU and the Lisbon Agenda, which uses the Open Method of Coordination (OMC) as a key regulatory tool that works through benchmarking and measuring performance. A main goal agreed at the Lisbon summit was to make the European economy more dynamic and competitive through encouraging the development of a knowledge society based on highly skilled jobs and innovation in research and development. This in turn requires EU discourse to talk up the idea of a more flexible and participatory form of governance that emphasises how it will support these developments. Sometimes the neoliberal agenda is blatantly obvious, as in the statement by Luc Soete that Europe needs an environment of innovation and entrepreneurship where emphasis is placed on risk-taking rather than on security and employment protection. He asks 'how much of the social achievements of the European model is Europe prepared to give up to keep up with the United States' and suggests, as is implicit in most of the sociological work on networks and information, that 'the social security model developed at the time of the industrial society is ... increasingly inappropriate for the large majority of what should be best described as "knowledge workers"' (Soete 2006: 145). But if some experts like Soete are more blatant about their neoliberal agenda, it is more usual to see neoliberalism taking the form of softer, performance-related initiatives designed to regulate the conduct of conduct. Here the goals of competitiveness and dynamism are reflected in the Lisbon summit's fixing of guidelines and timetables to achieve a range of goals and benchmarks and quantitative and qualitative indicators to measure performance. This encouragement of good performance is also a form of monitoring. States share information and best practices, engage in evaluation and peer review, yet at the same time are judged and evaluated. The idea is to both mobilize and at the same time discipline, with the Commission playing the central role as performance assessor.

This is neoliberalism in the governmentality sense of the term. Not necessarily pure free market capitalism, but governance from a distance through encouraging a particular type of conduct of the self. As Haahr (2004: 215) notes, this is a structured and conditioned freedom that works through the manipulation of techniques and mechanisms. It requires reflexive government whereby states consider their practices and compare them with other states, with the Commission playing the central role of encouraging states to develop their policies in line with certain guidelines and agreements. There is, however, one problem with this line of analysis. As we noted previously, governmentality has population as its object. In this case it is not populations but states that are being treated as liberal subjects.

The danger of applying governmentality to things like OMC is the anthropomorphic one of treating states as if they were like people. There are a number of ways to try and resolve this problem. First, we can follow Haahr in noting that OMC is attempting to change the behaviour of states by changing the behaviour of members of state bureaucracies through influencing their knowledge domains and frames of reference. This then 'transforms its participants [i.e. the state bureaucrats] into "calculative individuals" within a specific "calculative space", namely the notion of a European economy' (Haahr 2004: 220). OMC therefore acts on states, but it does so by acting on the knowledge and behaviour of their officials and bureaucrats. Second, we can call OMC a system of neoliberal governmentality in so far as it does indeed target the wealth, health and well-being of populations, but does so indirectly by issuing performance instructions to states that they will then pass these on to their citizens. Or to put it a different way around, OMC is aimed at states, not populations or individuals, but it targets these states on the basis of their performance in relation to their populations. This then allows us to return to Haahr's assessment of OMC as governmentality:

The OMC thus embodies a vision of society as a *machinery of performance*. It is an economic machine, in so far as an economic rationality and economic notions of efficiency, wealth and competitiveness occupy an important place. But it is also a biological machine, in so far as the active management of populations, of their education, their entry into and exit from labour markets, etc., occupies an equally important place. Finally, it is an advanced liberal machine, for it is a machine which seeks to work mainly through freedom, through establishing and securing mechanisms which can effectively unleash the energies of society. (Haahr 2004: 225)

The question now is whether, having covered governmentality in relation to the performance of EU states, this can be applied more generally. Haahr clearly thinks it can, seeing OMC in relation to the broader issue of governance from a distance by means of manipulating techniques and mechanisms. He also talks about it as a supervised form of freedom and a mentality that works through knowledge of populations (Haahr 2004: 227). We also saw in the last chapter that the World Bank and IMF do this through the 'good-governance' agenda. Two other international bodies can briefly be mentioned. The World Economic Forum (WEF), while not in a position to force states to comply, plays an important role in discursively constituting a global arena within which states and other stakeholders agree to engage in responsible behaviour as measured by 'best practice' and willingness to conform to certain standards of conduct. The WEF publishes a Global Competitiveness Report that requires states to reflexively assess their competitive performance, helping to constitute states on the basis of global standards of economic competitiveness (Fougner 2008b: 113). The OECD is another organisation that can be said to conduct this sort of neoliberal peer review of states. Its report *The New Economy: Beyond the Hype* makes the case that economic growth requires developments in ICT, human capital, innovation and entrepreneurship, themselves requiring governments to follow policies of macroeconomic stability, openness and competition (OECD 2001: 8). The OECD document goes on to link the promotion of new technology to the reorganisation of work, encouraging the introduction of new work practices like teamworking and employee involvement. It says:

[It] is essential here to give workers greater voice in the process of change and institutions of labour-management cooperation should be strengthened in certain countries. This calls for modernisation of traditional systems of collective bargaining and wage formation. In addition, regulations should provide for more flexibility in working hours, allowing new forms of work to flourish. (OECD 2001: 15)

Governmentality theorists interested in these issues are thus concerned with the way that states themselves are constituted in a particular way and then assessed in terms of their performance in meeting a set of key targets or, in the last case, encouraging new practices (in relation to labour flexibility). This can be considered neoliberal in two senses – first by constituting states as competitive entities that must meet performance targets in relation to one another, and second by constituting states in relation to the competitiveness of the global economy. The benchmarking process and use of indicators help in constructing a particular reality to which states must conform. This renders states as calculative agencies, in constant reflection on their performance and driven by global standards of conduct (Fougner 2008a: 319).

Social capital

We turn briefly to the concept of social capital as an extension of our discussion of networks. The concept is explicitly connected to networks in so far as its main argument is that people gain through their connections to others because of the goods and resources inherent in these relationships. The concept is also relevant to our study of governmentality because of its emphasis on rational, individualistic behaviour, its asocial character, its link with liberalism and its appeal to a technical, scientific rationality. We also briefly look at the way the concept relates to debates on development, with a later chapter looking at this in relation to the World Bank.

There are no straightforward definitions of social capital, for it is one of the most amorphous concepts to be covered here. But there is general agreement, even in the sociological work of Bourdieu, that social capital refers to the relationship between networks, social values, norms and expectations. However, the earlier work of Bourdieu was concerned with the production of structural inequalities in power relations,[5] whereas the Anglo-Saxon literature dropped this concern

[5] Bourdieu and Wacquant (1992: 119): 'Social capital is the sum of resources, actual or virtual, that accrue to an individual or group by virtue of possessing a durable network of more or less institutionalised relationships of mutual acquaintance and recognition.' Their main aim is to understand social hierarchy and why some people are better placed than others. This is based on a study of the production and reproduction of capital.

and gave the concept a more individualist, rational-choice character. Another way of putting this is that as the concept developed, a greater emphasis was placed on the idea of social capital as a form of capital – that is to say, as a type of investment in resources that is expected to bring about significant returns. In comparison to other types of capital like physical capital (manufactured resources) and human capital (knowledge and skills), social capital is understood to relate to shared knowledge, norms, rules and expectations about patterns of interactions (Ostrom 2000: 174–6).

People engage in social networks because they recognise that these networks contain social resources that enhance the outcome of their actions. Networks can be seen as reinforcing an individual's social credentials, identity and their social recognition (Lin 2001: 20). Social capital, like physical capital, accumulates as a stock, which produces a stream of benefits. This requires investment and regular maintenance and crucially is something that cannot be built individually. Being a node in a network allows people to connect to others and thereby access resources and capital. Networks allow cooperation for mutual advantage while reducing opportunistic behaviour. They also facilitate the flow of information and therefore make it easier to get collective decisions and action. By emphasising networks, the concept provides a picture of capitalist relations that can be focused on positive tasks for developing the economy, enhancing government and building social cohesion. For these reasons the concept has been promoted by the World Bank as an important tool in the new approach to development. Two of its economists provide a useful summary of the concept as 'the institutions, relationships, attitudes, and values that govern interactions among people and contribute to economic and social development' (Grootaert and van Bastelaer 2002: 2).

The two best-known writers on social capital are Robert Putnam and James Coleman. Putnam's *Bowling Alone* brought the concept into the public domain by raising the problem of political and civic disengagement among Americans. Putnam emphasises the importance of networks of community engagement in the face of what he sees as the weakening of social capital through pressures of time and money, suburbanisation and commuting, electronic entertainment and generational change (Putnam 2000: 283). This emphasis on the importance of vibrant communities was first developed in his earlier work, *Making Democracy Work*, where Putnam considers the importance of networks of civil engagement and links this to the performance of political institutions. Cooperative horizontal networks based on norms of reciprocity are said to foster the best forms of civil engagement. Here social capital 'refers to features of social organization, such as trust, norms, and networks, that can improve the efficiency of society by facilitating coordinated actions' (Putnam *et al.* 1993: 167). The idea of trust is particularly important here and is defined as 'an emergent property of the social system, as much as a personal attribute ... Individuals are able to be trusting ... because of the social norms and networks within which their actions are embedded' (1993: 177). This emphasises the point that self-interest must be related to broader public needs, civil virtue and an awareness of the interests of others. Trust, norms and networks mean that social capital, unlike private capital, is ordinarily a public good (1993: 170).

Coleman's work also stresses the themes of reciprocity, trust and shared values. He perhaps pushes further with the economic nature of the concept and its link to theories of rational conduct. Social capital is considered a form of capital in the sense that it gives rise to resources that actors can draw upon and enables them to pursue their goals more effectively. Actors aim to maximise their utility within an environment that shapes their actions.

> I have attempted to introduce into social theory a concept, 'social capital,' paralleling the concepts of financial capital, physical capital, and human capital – but embodied in relations among persons. This is part of a theoretical strategy that involves use of the paradigm of rational action but without the assumption of atomistic elements stripped of social relationships. (Coleman 2000: 36)

This raises the first of our points to consider – the asocial aspect of the concept. The quotation above reveals that Coleman's starting point is not society, but the rational behaviour of individuals. Critics like Ben Fine attack Coleman's work for its universal, asocial, ahistorical concepts like resources, power, interests, externalities and public goods – concepts that reflect the colonisation of social theory by economic terms (Fine 2001: 75). Indeed Fine argues that the very term social capital invites an asocial or ahistorical reading. In suggesting that the social is being brought back in, it gives the misleading impression that other forms of capital are not social in nature. The concept therefore presupposes an initial false separation of the social and the economic (Fine 2001: 25–6). This contrasts with arguments by Marx that emphasise that capital is a social relation (1976: 932) and that seeing it in isolation from its social context represents a form of reification. Many economists tend to embrace this reified view of the world by starting from non-social assumptions about individual behaviour as purposive and rational. This should not be unfamiliar to IR scholars, given the way that rationalists like the neorealists and neoliberal institutionalists often model their approach on microeconomic theory (see Waltz 1979: 91). But ahistorical and reified though this may be, it has an undeniable scientific appeal.

This scientific appeal is enhanced by the fact that social capital appears to be dealing with social and normative issues that would normally be difficult to grasp or measure. The concept appears to build bridges between individual action and social context, and between rational action and normative ideas. It allows Putnam and others to claim that they reject those economic approaches that focus exclusively on individual rational conduct. Walters, who looks at how social capital corresponds to governmentality, writes that the concept seems to bring a scientific approach to a broader range of social issues:

> The appeal of social capital to policymakers and public debate resides perhaps in the fact that it marries the ethical appeal of other discourses of community, civility and civil society, with the prestige of social scientific rigour and operationalizability. Social capital brings the ambition of positivity and calculability to ethopolitical discourses. Unlike these other discourses, it offers a quantitative rendering of the ethical field, all the better to enhance its governability. It purports to make trust and civility measurable. (Walters 2002: 390)

Despite claims that social capital takes a more social approach, its 'scientific rigour' is based on its rational-choice method, its neoclassical orthodoxy and its openness to mathematical modelling and statistical methods. Of course this is going to leave the arguments open to many sociological and methodological criticisms, among which are reductionism, methodological individualism and an asocial account of human behaviour. Nevertheless, it can be argued that the social-capital approach is flexible enough to maintain the rational-choice focus on self-interested and competitive individuals while correcting its overly atomised social ontology. It shows, for example, that cooperation and association are not things that can be taken for granted, but are complex affairs. It contains a cognitive aspect that considers how mental processes are influenced by norms and values, as well as a structural aspect that focuses on forms of social organisation and networks with their rules, procedures and roles. This structural aspect is, however, very limited and reproduces the type of social ontology associated with network analysis. We have already noted how the dominant approach to social capital ignores Bourdieu's concern with the structural inequalities of power relations and other forms of hierarchical power. But then ignoring such matters makes the social-capital approach more suitable as a policy tool in today's economic environment. For if we are to explain why the idea of social capital has proved so influential we must ultimately consider how well it fits with prevailing social conditions and dominant rationalities, which, put in terms of this study, means how well the concept lends itself to contemporary forms of governmentality.

The final way in which social capital lends itself to governmentality relates to its liberalism. Francis Fukuyama, high priest of the neoliberal condition, goes so far as to claim that:

> Social capital is important to the efficient functioning of modern economies, and is the *sine qua non* of stable liberal democracy. It constitutes the cultural component of modern societies, which in other respects have been organized since the Enlightenment on the basis of formal institutions, the rule of law and rationality. (Fukuyama 2001: 7)

This perhaps best expresses the world-view behind social capital and why it fits so well with a large range of other contemporary ideas. However, these liberal notions are rather vague. In keeping with our governmentality approach, it is more meaningful to look at what the concept might be able to offer in a practical sense. Diana Coole makes the useful suggestion that we see social capital as a policy initiative that helps to repair the ideological resources of contemporary liberal states (Coole 2009: 374). In particular, she is concerned with the role social capital might play in the context of the way states deal with global changes like deregulated markets and deterritorialised flows of capital (2009: 374), or as we would put it, how states transform themselves through their support for an agenda of deregulation and devolution of powers. In the face of global change – or we might say, as part of a strategy by which states 'globalise' and turn themselves outwards – state strategies use the idea of social capital as a way of managing individuals and groups through a process of 'recoding'. This takes place at the micro level as states experiment with new forms of governmentality and governance (2009: 376, 378). Policy-makers have been quick to see the bridging role social capital can play in recoding problems of social cohesion, urban regeneration and social and ethnic divisions that result from these wider social changes.[6] Local spaces are reorganised as sites of communal activity and interaction, as social capital engages in community building while also allowing the management of populations through surveillance and other disciplinary techniques (2009: 393).

If the concept of social capital can be used as a means to governmentalise local issues in advanced liberal societies, what of its application to other parts of the world? A later chapter will look in more detail at how the concept became important to the World Bank's development strategies in the post-Washington consensus phase. The World Bank sees the concept as providing the 'missing link' between the tough economic policies associated with free markets and consciousness of a social agenda. It can also bring together neoliberals who are sceptical about the role of the state and grassroots activists who are interested in local forms of participation (Harriss and De Renzio 1997: 920). We saw in the last chapter how the World Bank seeks to use ideas of empowerment and local ownership to engage civil society groups, private entrepreneurs and NGOs as well as national governments, and the idea of social capital is one important way in which the development agenda can be articulated. Social capital therefore provides an analytical framework by which the World Bank can encourage national development alongside private-sector entrepreneurial activity, without having to be seen to be taking an exclusively economic approach of the sort discredited during the era of neoliberal adjustment policies. This fits well with the post-Washington consensus approach and the World Bank's recognition of the folly of trying to separate out states and markets. Some have argued this from an institutional perspective, suggesting that this opens up a more progressive approach that better engages with local people and institutions. Some see this as a result

[6] See for example the approach taken by New Labour (Performance and Innovation Unit 2002) and the work of David Halpern, a policy adviser to the Forward Strategies Unit in the Cabinet Office.

of pressure within the World Bank from staff wishing to challenge the ideological hegemony of the neoclassical economist alongside a separate process of networking and lobbying, supported by NGOs, in favour of 'participatory' projects (see, for example, Fox 1997: 964).

Others have argued that the social-capital approach is too vague to be of much use, even as a tool of governmentality; in effect, it lacks precision and can mean all things to all people. The need to bring the 'social' back in can be posed in negative terms in so far as orthodox economic theory failed to account for differences in the countries where the standard package of adjustment policies was applied. Social capital comes in to deal with 'market imperfections' and to account for different internal social and cultural conditions and the importance of norms and values in governing the interactions of people. But this is such a general argument that it is far from clear what role civil society or social networks can really play in helping development. Ultimately, the World Bank is only really interested in institutional and organisational networks that can promote market efficiency, and the social is only brought back as the means of addressing market imperfections. This reflects the nature of the concept itself. As noted, it starts from a pre-social understanding of capital in relation to the self-interested behaviour of rational individuals. The social can be brought back only if it has first been stripped away, just as the state and civil society can only be brought back in once neoclassical economics has first tried to ignore them.

As with many of the other ideas examined in this book, it is therefore more meaningful to look at how the concept is used, and how it relates to a particular rationality of governance. In that sense, we have suggested that social capital shares with the other concepts covered in this book various assumptions about human behaviour, the separation of the economic and the social, a networked view of social interaction, an instrumental view of why people engage in these social networks, a view of the social that concentrates on micro- or meso-level practices and an essentially liberal view of social life. On the latter point, we could say, more specifically, that the term finds its usefulness in relation to neoliberalism, if we understand by this term a specific social project founded on the reordering of social relations and the construction of social order. We suggested that this could be understood, for example, in relation to processes of deregulation and devolution of state powers. This fits with development strategies that now recognise the importance of the state, but want the state to operate through the activation of civil society associations. For these reasons we find that social capital fits with our understanding of governmentality, with the deployment of particular strategies at the micro level that support the macro-level drive to enhance economic performance and competitiveness. One such approach that also sees the concept in these terms argues that the concept works as a capitalisation of the social (Walters 2002: 392) and that social values and practices like civility, association and cooperation are affirmed, not on their own merits, but because, as Putnam says, 'Social capital enhances the benefits of investment in physical and human capital' (Putnam *et al.* 1993: 1). Social capital seeks an engagement with social norms and values while translating these into a discourse of performativity. In practical terms, the concept helps play an ordering role in social life. As we have suggested, neoliberalism is not simply a return to a liberal economic view, but a new way of coding social relations through extending the ideas of 'competitiveness' and 'enterprise' into new areas of social life. Yet the strategic aspect of this is hidden from view behind the ideological façade of social capital being 'out there' in real social relations, communities, networks and civic associations. Social capital has its own governable space. The theory of social capital is given the task of quantifying this and measuring it, rendering the social and the individual calculable in terms of their associativeness and civility (see Walters 2002: 394).

Conclusion

Instead of asking how social capital explains society, we should ask what role social capital plays in constructing a governable space. A governmentality approach would ask how social capital contributes to new modes of governance and what assumptions it makes about things 'out there' like networks and civic associations. How do these help construct something considered to be a self-governable space, or a space free from, or with only very limited, government interference? One important aspect of social capital is the way it encourages the idea of free association and civic involvement, the very basis on which contemporary forms of governmentality operate, while supported by the equally illusionary notion of the rational, reflexive, decision-making individual. Contemporary governmentality tries to recreate the subject as an active citizen who, among other things, takes responsibility for dealing with social problems. This, we believe, fits closely with the reflexive approach discussed in the next chapter as well as with the idea that governmentality moralises the population and responsibilises their conduct.

The social-capital approach starts from the classical economic assumptions of the rational individual, but brings the social back in by looking at how these individuals perform better when engaged in networks of association. The concept of networks functions here to link these individuals together, giving social relations an enduring nature but not so much that we might think of these relations as somehow deeper than this. For liberalism cannot afford to conceive of deeper social structures in the Marxist or scientific realist sense that might somehow impede the rational individual's right to be a free actor. Instead, what new forms of liberalism do is to give these relations a more contrived entrepreneurial form that emphasises the self as a more productive, flexible, innovative and reflexive actor. Lest this become too self-serving, social capital supplements these virtues with 'soft' virtues – the sentiments, beliefs and values that build trust and civic responsibility within communities (see Roberts 2004: 484).

Yet the irony in all this is that the main initiatives to encourage the building of social capital come not from the 'autonomous space' of civil society, but from the policy initiatives of government and the state. In an age of increasing global volatility, when capital and population flows might put at risk social stability and cohesion, it is the state that intervenes to 'resocialise' subjectivities and to reconstitute people's daily interactions, health and well-being (Coole 2009: 393). The state, then, is at the heart of governmentality in codifying, consolidating and institutionalising the emergent strategies and techniques associated with the micro-level politics where the idea of social capital is at work (Foucault 2007: 287; Jessop 2007: 152). Indeed, as Coole notes, even if strategies and techniques emerge first of all at the level of micro practices, these are then colonised by the state and administered in a top-down fashion, being then re-embedded at local and neighbourhood levels as part of government strategies for local regeneration (Coole 2009: 385).

If governments like New Labour in Britain deliberately use social capital as a tool for regional interventions, then governance strategies in general should also be seen in such ways. The fact that governance is somehow seen as distinct from state strategies is the ideological effect of postwar history and the unravelling of the national-welfare policies with their view of society as a unitary domain. If postwar governance worked by suggesting that the state should play an interventionist role by providing security, economic regulation, welfare provision and social insurance through a national framework, then it is easy to see how contemporary forms of governance give the impression that the state's power has declined. The reality is somewhat different, explained through the ideas of changing hegemonic blocs, altering state strategies and the promotion of a more neoliberal form of governmentality that combines self-imposed limits on government with a shift of attention to micro practices of governance. Governmentality suggests both a change in methods of governance and a change in the dominant rationality that informs these methods.

The governmentality approach captures the shift to the individual that is characteristic of neoliberal forms of governance. We can see this at different levels ranging from the local interventions just discussed, to new types of regional and transnational governance such as that characteristic of the EU. New bodies above, below and alongside the state are charged with performing different governmental functions and tasks. This gives the impression of a less hierarchical form of governance based on public–private cooperation, less formal networks, consultative processes and cooperative relationships. These bodies act to coordinate and regulate governance within their specific region. At the European level we have seen this taking place through new institutions, agencies and commissions. These bodies claim legitimacy on the basis of their technical expertise in the face of increasingly complex issues of regulation, competition and performance. At the international level we find bodies like the World Bank, IMF and OECD using similar ideas either to support the idea of global governance, or as the basis for development strategies. Again, the irony here is that while the ideas of social capital, networks and governance seek to question the role of the state, the post-Washington consensus is actually a recognition that states play an indispensable role in mobilising civil society, supporting markets and ensuring effective governance.

The wider context might be reasserted through a critique of the claims of network theory. What is being argued for in this chapter is not a rejection of the idea of networks, but a critique of the overextension of the concept in the sociological literature and the claim that this is a new condition of modernity. The consequence of this is to cut off these networks from their social and political context. In the IR and governance literature, the exaggeration of the influence of networks, combined with the idea that the role of the state is diminishing, means a failure to see networks in relation to state strategies. The overstatement of changes like globalisation and the emphasis placed on networks and flows is part of a general theoretical trend that at the same time questions such things as underlying social structures and causal mechanisms, states, class relations, political parties and various forms of collective action. Meanwhile things like the role of the market or the monitoring of our behaviour are taken as normal, and arguments that question processes of marketisation, privatisation, individualisation, responsibilisation and so on are ruled invalid or outdated. By contrast, the work of Boltanski and Chiapello is distinctive in emphasising the strategic nature of networks and networks discourse in reshaping capitalist social relations. They argue that what is new about networks is the 'societal project', the way that networks involve an ideology and a normative basis (2005: xxii). Here the concern is with the ideological or discursive changes that accompany transformations in capitalism.

To bring in the bigger picture is to look at the transformations taking place in the organisation of capitalism. In reality, networks can operate effectively only with the support of state and hierarchical institutions of governance (Thompson 2003: 222). By downgrading the role of the state, contemporary approaches end up naturalising markets (and information and technology), thereby denying the necessary role of the state in guaranteeing the required legal arrangements. In other words, the state supports the very things (like networks, information, technological development) that it is claimed are making it obsolete (May 2002: 128). Internationally, the literature claims that 'traditional' forms of organisation are being swept away by unstoppable global flows when in fact the intensification of these flows results from state strategies of deregulation, financialisation, commodification and encouragement of competitiveness in the global economy. The fact that states are subjected to these pressures should not hide the fact that the dominant states, led by the USA, are the ones pushing this neoliberal global agenda. Most of the new literature ignores this by presenting social, political and economic change as natural, or grounded so deep in modernity that it is irreversible, while actually ignoring, rejecting or downplaying discussion of actual social and economic structures, causal mechanisms and the strategic responses to them. These ideas reproduce contemporary governmentality by taking at face value a whole range of new social practices related to the reorganising of capitalism and its associated political and institutional forms (the things considered to be governance) without critical analysis of their causal basis. And in reproducing this governmentality and its associated practices, the result is to support the deeper social structures that these practices sustain, but which this literature usually denies.

5 *Reflexivity, knowledge and risk*

This chapter concludes the study of influential social theories by focusing on theories of reflexivity and risk. The best-known approach to risk is outlined in Ulrich Beck's *The Risk Society*, a sociological work that gained huge influence in the 1990s. Beck's work also provides a strong sense of a persistent theme among a range of different contemporary theories, that is, the overstatement of a particular idea. For Beck's argument is not just that risk becomes increasingly important, but that it becomes the central defining feature of our society. Thus we can see parallels with the way globalisation theory takes one apparent aspect of society and turns it into the main feature of contemporary modernity, or how Castells insists not only on networks, but also on network society. This sense that we are being overwhelmed by change is expressed in Beck's view that:

> A characteristic of the global risk society is a metamorphosis of danger which is difficult to delineate or monitor: markets collapse and there is shortage in the midst of surplus. Medical treatments fail. Constructs of economic rationality wobble. Governments are forced to resign. The taken for granted rules of everyday life are turned upside down. (Beck 1999: 143)

We have noted in relation to other contemporary theories that such statements tend to be empty in so far as they pin everything on one central feature of modern societies, as if networks, globalisation or, in this case, risk, were determinant of all else when in actuality all the things Beck mentions have more precise causes. The danger of pinning it all on risk is to mystify these processes and deny a proper causal explanation. We know that Beck is not alone in making these kinds of arguments. More specifically, Beck's work on risk has developed alongside the approach of British sociologist Anthony Giddens. Their work, while promoting the idea of risk, also goes one stage back to ask what it is about contemporary society that makes risk such a dominant feature. Thus we start with their arguments concerning reflexive modernity in order to see how again these theorists are making fundamental claims about the social conditions of modernity and how ultimately these theorists have mistaken the effects of recent social and political changes for some deeper social condition of modernity. We will then explain how the idea of risk is better understood in relation to governmentality so that risk is considered in a strategic way as an organising principle of modern social life.

Reflexive modernity

To understand theories of risk, we have to see how they interact with a sociology of reflexive modernity. Giddens and Beck start to make arguments about the reflexive nature of modernity at about the same time. Giddens comes to this position through a critique of more structural approaches to sociology, but also because of a reluctance to embrace the idea of postmodernity. He characterises history as passing through the stages of pre-modernity, simple modernity (industrialisation) and then (post-industrial) reflexive modernity. He also continues the argument of his earlier work, where he develops the idea of the double hermeneutic which claims that the social sciences themselves contribute to modernity's reflexivity and that modernity itself is deeply and intrinsically sociological (Giddens 1990: 43). Reflexive modernity for Giddens refers to the reflexive appropriation of knowledge or the constant examination and re-examination of social practices in the light of new information (1990: 38). Giddens takes an institutional approach to this matter; modernity, or more precisely, modern institutions, come to be constituted through this reapplied knowledge (1990: 39; 1991: 20). This institutional reflexivity may be summarised as 'the regularised use of knowledge about circumstances of social life as a constitutive element in its organisation and transformation' (1991: 20).

Giddens sets up reflexive modernity as the radical outcome of the consequences of modernity as opposed to the idea that we have passed beyond modernity into postmodernity. There are obvious similarities with postmodernity in so far as both approaches emphasise uncertainty about who we are and our place in society. Giddens writes that postmodernism captures something about a situation we find ourselves in where things appear to be beyond our control. But rather than being postmodern, this is a period where the consequences of modernity are more radical and universal (1990: 2–3). This new period is called late or high modernity because modernity has not yet run its course; indeed the present period could even be seen as a second coming, where the first (industrial) phase of modernity is being swept away by a second wave that continues the attack on traditional forms of social life in an even more radical and universal way. Tradition – for example in the form of class affiliation, local identity or family life – sustained modernity through its industrial phase, but now these forms are being undermined as we enter a period 'cut loose from its moorings in the reassurance of tradition and in what was for a long while an anchored "vantage point"' (1990: 176). Modernity, for Giddens, continues to radically alter social life and sweep away all traditional types of social order (1990: 4). Giddens can argue this because for him social development can be understood not in terms of social structure, mode of production or social class, but ultimately in terms of changes in time and space. One way of understanding this is through the idea of extensionality: 'On the extensional plane they have served to establish forms of social interconnection which span the globe; in extensional terms they have come to alter some of the most intimate and personal features of our day-to-day existence' (1990: 4). Another way Giddens expresses this is through the idea of space–time distanciation (traditional societies having a lower level, modern societies a high level). Modernity increasingly separates space from place and lifts out social relations from their local context, restructuring them across space and time.

The separation of time and space and its recombination in various forms is seen as the fundamental dynamic of modernity. This is also Giddens's way of understanding globalisation as an expression of fundamental aspects of time–space distanciation (1991: 21). Globalisation is like a 'stretching process' where 'the modes of connection between different social contexts or regions become networked across the earth's surface as a whole' (1990: 64). This process is both one of stretching of social relations and also an intensification of them, something indicated by the use of the network concept to show increasing linkages whereby events in one place affect ever greater numbers over ever greater distances. This furthers the disembedding process (the lifting of social relations out of their specifically local context) so that more and more people live in circumstances where disembedded institutions link local practices with globalised social relations.

Summarising all these ideas Giddens writes that modern social life is characterised by institutional reflexivity, the profound reorganisation of space and time and the expansion of disembedding mechanisms that lift social relations out of their specific locales (1991: 2).

Modernity is said to be torn away from its traditional order, undermining our ontological security, which had based itself on routinised social practices (Giddens 1990: 105). Giddens uses the concept of trust to convey our confidence in a person or system, particularly expert systems that perform complicated tasks for us. We put our trust in these and rely on them to provide expected outcomes. But this becomes more and more uncertain and impersonal, forcing us to become more reflexive. Trust is a good example of how the reflexivity of modern life is founded on two extremes of 'extensionality' and 'intentionality', that is to say, the influence of globalisation on the one hand and personal dispositions on the other (Giddens 1991: 1). Beck expresses similar feelings, arguing that we are caught between two epochal processes, individualisation and globalisation, and that this is changing the foundations of our social life (Beck 1992: 169). The process of individualisation is given prominent emphasis in Beck's work and links with Giddens's views on socio-institutional change. He defines individualisation as 'a concept which describes a structural, sociological transformation of social institutions and the relationship of the individual to society' (1992: 202) and examines how this leads to changes in identity and consciousness and how people change their life patterns and personal biography. This leads to a reflexive conduct of personal life in relation to our own lives and the social relations we are engaged in. Indeed part of this dynamic, as we have also seen in Giddens, is the belief that people are set free from the traditional forms of these social relations as we leave behind the certainties of industrial society and enter a new reflexive age. Compare these similar statements from Giddens and Beck. As Giddens puts it: 'The more tradition loses its hold, and the more daily life is reconstituted in terms of the dialectical interplay of the local and the global, the more individuals are forced to negotiate lifestyle choices among a diversity of options' (Giddens 1991: 5). For Beck: 'Individuals are released from structures, and they must redefine their context of action under conditions of constructed insecurity in forms and strategies of "reflected" modernization' (Beck 1999: 110).

In Beck's case, however, we find a little more pessimism. He talks, for example of how the new reflexivity of our social relations also creates new forms of insecurity (Beck 1992: 98). Indeed, he distinguishes his approach from that of Giddens in one important sense, in that for him, reflexive modernisation is not so much knowledge in the sense of awareness, but rather, it is reflexive unawareness (Beck 1999: 119). This type of reflexivity is more like self-confrontation, where we have to deal with the *unintended* consequences of modernity. The more modernity develops, the more unintended consequences are produced and so the more we must reflect on the foundations of modernisation. The development of modernity should not, however, be seen as a linear unfolding. He argues that 'in equating reflexive and *expert-determined* modernization, Giddens underestimates the *pluralization* of rationalities and agents of knowledge and the key role of known and repressed types of *un*awareness, which establish the discontinuity of "reflexive" modernization in the first place' (1999: 130–1). In criticising linear modernisation, Beck is not criticising Giddens, but rather, the belief in tradition and safe forms of expert knowledge that block out awareness of our inability to know. As Beck puts it: 'The crucial issue of reflexive modernization, however, is this: how do "we" (experts, social movements, ordinary people, politicians, not to forget sociologists) deal with our unawareness (or inability to know)? How do we *decide* in and between manufactured uncertainties?' (1999: 132).

Beck's more pessimistic view leads him to argue that new forms of inequality develop on the basis of the distribution of the unawareness of unintended consequences. What is interesting – and this matches with a range of theories of networks, information and knowledge – is that inequality and social status are being redefined away from 'traditional' social structures. It is notable how strongly Beck criticises the idea of class, claiming that people no longer seem to understand or experience class society. It is not that class disappears, but it is superseded by new sources of social bonds, private relations, identities and social lifestyles. In particular, we shall see that Beck thinks a process of individualisation deprives class of its social identity. Inequalities do not disappear, but there occurs an individualisation of social risk. Beck would seem to give theoretical support to contemporary institutional trends, for example arguing that individualisation 'is conceptualised theoretically as the product of reflexivity, in which the process of modernization as protected by the welfare state *detraditionalizes* the ways of living built into industrial society' (Beck 1992: 153). As well as taking for granted the demise of the postwar welfare state, he supports the view that reflexivity can be a source of productivity through knowledge-based innovation, flexibilisation of work and ongoing rationalisation (1992: 114). From a political point of view this is interesting in so far as Beck's (and Giddens's) arguments support those who are critical of class, welfare systems and labour relations, while taking for granted the inevitability of new, individualised, fragmented, pluralistic and flexibilised social relations. It is deeply ironic that Beck claims that he is theorising reflexivity as dealing with the unintended consequences of modernity when his own theory is (perhaps) unintentionally the *un*reflexive acceptance of particular social and institutional changes in claiming that they are deep-rooted and irreversible.

This inevitability is accompanied by a positive assessment of such changes. Although Beck is more pessimistic than Giddens, we still find him describing how individualisation frees us from traditional roles and constraints (Beck and Beck-Gernsheim 2001: 202) Changes in work patterns, leisure activities, trade union and club membership, voting patterns and so on are presented in positive terms. Elsewhere he writes of how 'people will be *set free* from the social forms of industrial society – class, stratification, family, gender status of men and women' (Beck 1992: 87). Beck appears to welcome the fact that we increasingly confront capitalism without classes and in a more individualised way (1992: 88). As with network theory this argument flips between the idea that structures are actually becoming things of the past, and the view that individualisation 'is becoming *the social structure of second modern society itself*' (Beck and Beck-Gernsheim 2001: xxii). This means Beck offers both a strong confirmation of what he believes is the deep-rooted, structural nature of recent changes, and a positive evaluation of the consequences for individual self-expression. He naturalises the process of individualisation by claiming that:

> [R]eflexive modernization dissolves the traditional parameters of industrial society: class culture and consciousness, gender and family roles. It dissolves these forms of the conscience collective, on which depend and to which refer the social and political organizations and institutions in industrial society. These detraditionalizations happen in a *social surge of individualization*. (Beck 1992: 87)

The consequence is to deny that collective struggle has any continuing relevance in reflexive modernity; instead we must accept our individualised existence and maximise the opportunities it offers us. Both Giddens and Beck attribute this individualising process to late modernity and make it an ontological condition of the contemporary era. This denies us any possibility of seeing individualisation as a governmentalising strategy that is therefore potentially reversible.

Reflexivity is seen as our main response to ontological insecurity and uncertainty. It is presented positively as a freeing up of individuals to make their own choices and decisions. Indeed, Giddens goes so far as to call this new situation emancipatory. Three processes – individualisation, detraditionalisation and globalisation – coincide in our contemporary age to offer us a new 'life political programme' (Giddens 1991: 9). But behind the idealised talk lies not a new second modernity, but the political reality of neoliberal governmentality with its emphasis on individual responsibility, consumer choice, flexibility and self-interest. Arguments such as those of Giddens reflect what Dean (1999: 147) calls technologies of citizenship, based on positive claims to be encouraging self-esteem, empowerment, consultation and negotiation, seeking to render us active and engaged citizens, productive workers and eager consumers. This is the new politics of choice based squarely on the rules of the market, reconfiguring our expectations of the state and making us more dependent on our own ability to negotiate the risks and hazards of our social existence.

Risk, individualisation and globalisation

The context in which Beck introduces the idea of risk is one of increasing complexity and uncertainty. This is linked to the idea that modernity is continuing to erode our old systems of reassurance. Indeed the new modernity is brought into being by the erosion of the classical industrial society just as modernity eroded the feudal society before it (Beck 1992: 9, 10). Beck goes so far as to claim that industrial society is replaced by a new type of society, the risk society, where the social production of wealth is accompanied by the social production of risk and where techno-economic progress is accompanied by the production and distribution of risks. To put this slightly differently, the risk society produces new antagonisms and sources of conflict where the 'place of *eliminating scarcity* is taken by *eliminating risk*' (1992: 47).

Beck's justification of the idea of risk society is a familiar one. Just like globalisation theory and the theory of the network society he relies on technological determinism to make his case. As he writes: risk society 'describes a phase of development of modern society in which the social, political, ecological and individual risks created by the momentum of innovation increasingly elude the control and protective institutions of industrial society' (Beck 1999: 72). In other words, technological innovation creates new risks that old institutions cannot cope with. Even when Beck diversifies to talk of five interlinked processes of globalisation, individualisation, gender revolution, underemployment and global risk (1999: 2), we are left wondering where these processes themselves have come from. Of course Beck will argue that risk is a social construction and that it is produced by institutional change. As we have already noted: 'Risk society begins where tradition ends, when, in all spheres of life, we can no longer take traditional certainties for granted ... The less we can rely on traditional securities, the more risks we have to negotiate' (Beck 1998: 10). But what has undermined these traditional certainties? The argument is cyclical. Beck's concern is to show how the controllability present in the first modernity collapses, but he does not provide a convincing explanation of why it has done so. Instead we are simply informed:

> A new kind of capitalism, a new kind of economy, a new kind of global order, a new kind of society and a new kind of personal life are coming into being, all of which differ from earlier phases of social development. Thus, sociologically and politically, we need a paradigm-shift, a new frame of reference. This is not 'postmodernity' but a second modernity. (Beck 1999: 2)

In contrast to Giddens, Beck often defines these developments in negative, almost fatalistic terms. He talks, for example, of 'manufactured uncertainty' becoming an 'inescapable part of our lives' with everyone facing 'unknown and barely calculable risks' (1998: 12). He talks of complexity, disorder, distrust of traditional knowledge expertise, institutions and authority and a breaking apart of scientific and social rationality. While there is greater risk awareness, this is often expressed as something irrational, as disorientation or a malaise. We experience the world with a greater degree of anxiety. But within this negative approach is a positive dynamic in so far as risk acts as a political motor. As Beck argues:

In contrast to all earlier epochs (including industrial society), the risk society is characterized essentially by a *lack*: the impossibility of an *external* attribution of hazards. In other words, risks depend on *decisions*; they are industrially produced and in this sense *politically reflexive* ... risks become the motor of the *self-politicization* of modernity in industrial society. (1992: 183)

At this point, however, the focus on the process of individualisation becomes clear. For this politicisation is focused on the individual as the new unit of social activity. Individuals are understood as self-motivated, calculating actors responsible for their own life decisions. We are back to some of the issues discussed in previous chapters, although Beck is keen to emphasise how his position distinguishes between the free-market neoliberal view of individualisation and what he calls institutional individualisation (Beck and Beck-Gernsheim 2001: xxi). Our argument, however, has been that neoliberal individualisation should be defined precisely in these institutional terms and that Beck's distinction is therefore no longer valid if we consider neoliberalism as an institutional form of governmentality. Thus Beck's account of individualisation fits squarely within the discourse described as neoliberal governmentality in previous chapters. These accounts work by proclaiming the end of the postwar institutional order, critiquing the role of the state, welfare systems and collective forms of social and political representation: 'We live in an age in which the social order of the national state, class, ethnicity and the traditional family is in decline. The ethic of individual self-fulfillment and achievement is the most powerful current in modern society' (Beck and Beck-Gernsheim 2001: 22). At the same time, 'People struggle to live their lives in a world that increasingly and more evidently escapes their grasp, one that is irrevocably and globally networked' (2001: 25). The world is a runaway world where we must nevertheless try to live a life our own: 'The life of one's own is a reflexive life. Social reflexion – the processing of contradictory information, dialogue, negotiation, compromise – is almost synonymous with living one's own life' (2001: 26).

Giddens is more blatantly neoliberal in his advice: 'In a world where one can no longer simply rely on tradition to establish what to do in a given range of contexts, people have to take a more active and risk-infused orientation to their relationships and involvements' (Giddens 1998: 28). This new, more active and risk-taking orientation is typical of the entrepreneurial spirit we suggested informs the neo-liberal mode of governmentality. Individuals must actively take responsibility for their own futures – no rights without responsibilities – while being encouraged to adopt an entrepreneurial attitude to their life patterns. This is the basis on which a new politics of the self emerges. Beck, by contrast, is less forthright in making these arguments, but they are clearly implicit in his general reasoning. This is underpinned by his deterministic view that 'any attempt to create a new sense of social cohesion has to start from the recognition that individualization, diversity and scepticism are written into our culture' (Beck 1999: 9). This, we should note for now, is quite different from a governmentality-focussed approach that would see such a process in strategic terms. Indeed, by claiming that individualisation, diversity and scepticism are built into our culture, or are conditions of late modernity, Beck's view strengthens such strategies by making them appear to be unavoidable and irreversible.

Individualisation, it is argued, is a structural concept, or at least an institutionalised individualism that replaces previous institutional forms based on community, group and class (Beck and Beck-Gernsheim 2001: 10). Beck talks of a new uncertainty between territorially fixed actors like parties, government, unions, and non-territorial trade, finance and so forth (2001: 11). This opens up the second part of his argument, in that individualism undermines collective forms, but so also does globalisation, which he argues 'implies the weakening of state structures, of the autonomy and power of the state' (Beck 1999: 13). This is reflected in Beck's later work, which realises that risk society should actually be described as a world risk society which 'circumvents and annuls the principles of the first modernity' – not just class antagonism but also national statehood and control over technical and economic affairs (1999: 19).

Just as it is claimed that the social institutions of the first modernity are now thoroughly out of date, so their corresponding forms of understanding are dismissed, with Beck commenting that he 'cannot understand how anyone can make use of the frames of reference developed in the eighteenth and nineteenth centuries in order to understand the transformation into the post-traditional cosmopolitan world we live in today' (1999: 133). The irony here is that Beck's view of individualisation bears comparison with the nineteenth-century theory of Durkheim. When Beck and Beck-Gernsheim say that individualisation is a structural characteristic of highly differentiated societies that rather than endangering integration actually makes it possible (2001: xxi), we wonder what is new here that has not already been covered in Durkheim's (1964) theory of organic solidarity. Unfortunately what is new is that Beck has also taken on board the neoliberal attack on the postwar consensus, turning changes in institutional form into some sort of underlying structural process derived from the nature of modernity itself. However, this sort of understanding of structural process is different from something like Marxism, which focuses on relations of production. Beck ignores this social level and instead has a more general notion of modernity combined with a more surface level of culture. Take the following statement:

> In risk society we must conceive of *relations of definition* analogous to Karl Marx's *relations of production*. Risk society's relations of definition include the specific rules, institutions and capacities that structure the identification and assessment of risk in a specific cultural context. They are the legal, epistemological and cultural power matrix in which risk politics is conducted. (Beck 1999: 149)

The second part of this statement makes it clear that Beck's approach is not at all similar to Marx's relations of production, but works at the cultural level of rules, institutions and capacities rather than the deeper structural level that might help explain the conditions of possibility for these institutional-cultural features. It is precisely because Beck does not want to allow for a concept like relations of production that he is obliged to turn to the concept of modernity for some sort of structural explanation, or is obliged to adopt technological determinism, give globalisation a life of its own and focus on changes in time and space as if they can be 'disembedded' from social relations. Of course Beck's work is not alone in reproducing these ideas. These traits should be familiar to anyone who has read Giddens, Lash, Urry, Castells, Scholte, Bauman and many others.

The argument of this book, however, is not just that these ideas are wrong, or one-sided or overly influenced by neoliberalism's attack on the postwar institutional settlement. It also aims to show how these ideas are useful to actual forms of governance. They are useful in their practical implications for contemporary policy shifts. They reflect what Foucauldians would call a discursive framework or what Marxists would call a particular ideological framework that helps shape contemporary political interventions. We have suggested that this practical effect is best summed up by the notion of governmentality.

Reflexive modernity and the knowledge society in Europe

This section looks at what Beck and Giddens have to say about the EU as well as what the EU has to say about reflexivity and knowledge. Europe is described by Beck and Grande as a new type of empire 'of the second modernity' where sovereignty and the nation state have been transformed (Beck and Grande 2007: 62). Reflexive modernisation for Beck is made up of (1) risk society; (2) forced individualisation; and (3) multidimensional globalisation. This, he believes, is the best way to understand 'Europeanisation' (2007: 3). The development of the EU, it is argued, represents an 'epochal break' in the development of modern societies, among other things, breaking down the distinction between 'we' and 'others', creating a transnationally interconnected society that breaks out of the container of the nation state (2007: 29–31). However, the process also brings with it escalating civilisational risks and new challenges raised by the individualisation of lifestyles, the need for new forms of political participation, the globalisation of markets, security risks and environmental problems, as well as the development of new cultural issues all of which undermine the foundations of the modern nation state (2007: 32). Therefore, globalisation produces a situation where only transnational forms of governance can solve collective problems; Europe in particular is the product of this new situation. It also creates a number of contradictions between different levels of power and sovereignty. Europe, after all, 'was created by the power of side effects, as the unintended product of the reflexive modernization of European national societies' (2007: 136). More specifically, globalisation is said to bring the dissolution of the national basis for the calculation and prevention of uncertainty and risk. According to the theories, this happens in the context of an open, variable spatial structure, a multinational societal structure, horizontal and vertical integration, network power, non-hierarchical decision-making and participation of societal actors in political decision-making, all wrapped up in a cosmopolitan form of sovereignty (2007: 62–72).

So much for the wider context, but what should be done about it? Among other things, Beck affirms the need for a European constitution as a normative foundation for constituting a European civil society and a cosmopolitan regime (Beck and Grande 2007: 228). We have noted before how ideas like cosmopolitanism and civil society have been used to provide ideological legitimacy for much more straightforward political interventions, although even the most ardent pro-European would surely find it hard to take seriously the idea that a constitution – particularly after recent debacles – would provide the basis for a new cosmopolitanism. Giddens, however, is more straightforward in his recommendations for reorganising Europe – and in particular, the health, wealth and well-being of its population. His starting point is the EU's own Lisbon Strategy, noting how the EU has fallen behind the USA according to economic success, GDP per head and unemployment levels. The Lisbon goals were aimed at making Europe become the most dynamic and competitive knowledge-based economy capable of sustaining growth and creating jobs (Giddens 2007: 15).[1] The process encouraged individual Member States to develop certain policy priority areas supported by a Europe-wide framework. The debate over growth and productivity is strongly linked to social cohesion and the sustainability of the European social model. This is picked up on by Giddens, who argues that a new social model requires greater flexibility of labour markets and changes in welfare. Lisbon, he believes, was right to highlight the new economy, but it failed to adequately account for the social transformation needed to go along with it, and in particular the issues of labour flexibility, social justice, welfare and cultural diversity (2007: 27).

On welfare, Giddens writes that the 'post-industrial society is characterized by higher levels of individualism, and by much greater lifestyle diversity than was true before' (2007: 96). He argues that the traditional welfare state transferred risk from the individual to the state, but the state is primarily a social investment and regulatory agency (2007: 97). While the old welfare approach defined benefits in terms of rights, these rights should involve obligations that need to be spelled out in law. This argument should be familiar to followers of the New Labour government in Britain. Dressed in the language of reflexive modernity that argument reads: 'welfare should be redefined in terms of personal *autonomy* and *self-esteem*' (2007: 99).

[1] Lisbon European Council, 23 and 24 March 2000, Presidency Conclusions, www.europarl.europa.eu/summits/lis1_en.htm#b, accessed 20 August 2009.

This means 'empowering' welfare clients by giving them information, choice and personalisation of services (2007: 103). This approach is summarised:

> Policies are based on proactive welfare and investment in human capital ... policies are oriented towards positive life values ... lifestyle change becomes a core concern of the welfare system. Incentives and sanctions are deployed to help secure positive outcomes. These have to be shaped through orthodox democratic mechanisms and should be geared to substantive freedoms. (2007: 103)

In addition, Giddens argues for the Lisbon Agenda to be integrated with schemes to promote social justice and environmental citizenship. Above all, though, focus is on things like scientific and technological innovation, market innovation and collective action in handling new threats (2007: 197). When looking at how innovation, risk and reflexivity come together in the EU, we find a great emphasis on the idea of building a knowledge society. There is no fixed meaning for this term; it can be seen as combining the related notions of information society – that is to say, new developments in information, communications and technology – and the idea of the new economy relating to their application to work, the financial sector and economic growth. Debates within the EU have been concerned with how to harness innovation and knowledge in order to make Europe more dynamic and competitive, while also maintaining the social cohesion of European societies and allowing for differences between various European countries and regions. This was the motivation behind the Lisbon Strategy, which, according to EU policy-maker Maria João Rodrigues, 'can be understood as a strategy for economic and social modernisation in the light of European values' (Rodrigues 2003: 128).

Discussions of the knowledge society often make reference to the need for more reflexive government capable of responding to the challenges and opportunities provided by new uses of information and communication technology, increasingly complex forms of knowledge and more complicated networks across societies, social groups, civil society actors, private companies and governments. These points are made in a recent report to the European Commission which argues that 'Europe's future stability and welfare depend on the development of a collective capacity for open reflection, and perhaps revision, of European policy narratives: in the present case, about the huge, sprawling terrain relating to science, innovation and governance' (European Commission 2007: 73). The document goes on to argue the compelling need for change:

> [A]n important recent policy document 'Creating an Innovative Europe' stated that Europe needs to break out from an unsustainable path. Europe is characterised as a society endemically averse to risk, science and innovation, reluctant to change, and fast becoming unable to sustain its comfortable position in a competitive global knowledge environment. Europe will fall behind with regard to productivity, in capitalizing on new technological knowledge-developments like ICT, biosciences and nanosciences, because commercial knowledge-investors see more rewarding social environments in which commercial technoscience can thrive through consumer enthusiasm for whatever is forthcoming fastest from the global knowledge-factory. (European Commission 2007: 73)

A major factor behind the Lisbon Strategy was the belief that an active effort is needed to shape the transition to a knowledge-based economy and society. This would involve promoting policies to encourage better R&D, structural reform to promote competitiveness and innovation and policies to build an information society aimed at improving standards of living through such things as education, public services, electronic commerce, health and urban management, spreading information technologies in companies, e-commerce, new management tools and democratisation of internet access. Rodrigues sets out how this can be achieved through encouraging the convergence of national R&D policies, building a European area of research through networking programmes and enterprise policies, encouraging innovation, improving financial markets and supporting new investments. The European social model can be renewed, it is suggested, through investment in people, developing new education priorities, open learning centres, active employment policies, expanding skills, making lifelong learning available and modernising social protection (Rodrigues 2003: 17).

All this is justified on the basis of economic and technological determinism, otherwise described as the imperatives of globalisation and technological innovation. The EU's own justification for Lisbon argues:

(1) The European Union is confronted with a quantum shift resulting from globalisation and the challenges of a new knowledge-driven economy. These changes are affecting every aspect of people's lives and require a radical transformation of the European economy.
(2) The rapid and accelerating pace of change means it is urgent for the Union to act now to harness the full benefits of the opportunities presented. Hence the need for the Union to set a clear strategic goal and agree a challenging programme for building knowledge infrastructures, enhancing innovation and economic reform, and modernising social welfare and education systems. (European Council 2000: 1)

Globalisation and new economic challenges are often shorthand for keeping up with the USA, or for competing with China and emerging economies, if not through low wages, then through new knowledge and technological innovation. Being competitive in this new economic environment means Europe developing a common approach to the modernisation process. Hence we return once more to the management of this process through strategies that encourage best practice, sharing of information and benchmarking. The European Commission, we have noted, has a distinctive character as an institution that manages flows of knowledge and expertise and which attempts to shape policies through proposals, recommendations and the preparing of specialist reports. It also promotes best practice, monitoring and evaluation through OMC. For writers like Giddens, this is a positive process that uses peer pressure as a stimulus to change and which rightly emphasises the importance of economic growth and employment policies (Giddens 2007: 165). Indeed, this process should be extended in that it only operates at the intersection between the Commission and Member States. Giddens argues for more horizontal forms of dialogue and policy-making involving a wider variety of groups, organisations and issues networks (2007: 218). As to the role this plays in governing the conduct of states, Telò gives a good summary of how

> [b]y agreeing to take part in the new process, states are also submitted to deep transformations in their preferences, perceptions and respective interests, in the framework of a reciprocal learning process, leading to greater convergence. Moreover, they take risks by agreeing to be judged in this process. (Telò 2002: 261)

Without meaning to, this sounds very much like a governmentality of states since it concerns not only their regulation, but a shaping of their perceptions in line with an underlying rationality which we have suggested is guided by a neoliberal game of competitiveness. We can argue as to whether this represents a governmentality of populations or a governmentality of states, but it seems most likely to be a combination of the two – a governmentality of European populations by means of encouraging states to adapt to a particular agenda and set of targets that reinforce a particular economic programme. This is more a case of institutional reflexivity and risk assessment, although as we shall see in the next section, there is room for both strategies aimed at encouraging the reflexivity of institutions and strategies aimed at individual conduct.

The governmentality of risk

Are there really more risks 'out there', or is it more that we have a greater awareness of risk? Simplifying somewhat, the idea that modern society produces more risks is described as a realist view; the idea that it is our consciousness of risk that has changed is a constructivist position. It is often noted how Beck, in particular, wavers between the two positions although he considers himself both a realist and a constructivist (Beck 1999: 134). To sidestep this kind of discussion we might move from the general issues that Beck raises concerning the way risk is bound to socio-cultural context and conditions of knowledge production to a more Foucauldian focus on systems of representation. This section will push the discussion of risk away from a debate about the conditions of modernity towards the view that risk relates to contemporary forms of governmentality. This type of approach is developed in the work of Michael Power, who opens his recent book on uncertainty by stating that 'managing risk depends critically on management of *systems of representation*, and on instruments for framing objects for the purpose of action and intervention' (Power 2007: 4). Before one can act, one must frame those objects of intervention, and risk is a way of ordering reality and rendering it in a calculable form in order to govern it. In this way we have shifted focus from the general issue of the social construction of risk to the social construction of different practices that contribute to the management of populations.

Power goes on to question Beck's focus on the reflexivity of individuals by suggesting it is better to focus on the risk reflexivity of organisations based on their strategies of risk management. This links risk to managerial and regulatory forms of governing (2007: 4). It is also a way of bringing in normativity to responsibilise decision-making and to deal with social expectations about managing dangers. Often, as we have already noted, this is done through an appeal to the values of science and rationality – risk is interesting in this case because it would seem to be applying these precisely at a time (certainly if we believe Giddens and Beck) when trust in applying these is being questioned. But this would only be a contradiction if we believed that a rationality of risk aims to uncover the truth of something. Instead, risk management is about creating a space of responsibility and 'actionability'. As Power says, we can leave aside the question of who is in charge of Beck's 'runaway world' in favour of a focus on the 'institutionalized frames which underwrite social accounts of the control and manageability of risks' (2007: 6). These frames are different from the 'positivism of numbers and calculations' described by Foucault's work on the origins of statistics; they are represented today, says Power, by the 'administrative positivism of the accountant and auditor' (2007: 179). This section will look at two ways in which risk is managed, starting first with Power's account of auditing, then looking at some Foucauldian work on insurance.

As we have emphasised, a governmentality approach is useful in that it avoids both the idea that things like risk are somehow inherent in the conditions of late modernity but also the instrumentalist approach that claims these things are just tools of particular groups. Instead we must look at the way the already existing (or emerging) procedures 'are displaced, extended, and modified and, above all, how they are invested or annexed by global phenomena' (Foucault 2004: 30–1). For example, Power looks at how many new ideas emerge in the UK in the 1980s, but he is keen to emphasise that this is not simply about the results of Thatcherism, but something deeper, related to the organisation of trust and the establishment of checking mechanisms (Power 1997: xvi). These are things that can then be taken up and organised as part of a government strategy. It is only through such strategy, techniques and discourse that we come to know risk. Indeed, such strategies and techniques produce the 'truth' of risk as a calculative rationality. We have emphasised that the dominant rationality that produces the truth of risk is the neoliberal one. In particular, the neoliberal discourse is concerned with the entrepreneurial subject, although Power notes that there is a constant tension within neoliberal governance between this logic of enterprise and a logic of accountability (2007: 197). The latter is more of a managerial logic with values of auditability that are appealed to in a range of different policy contexts and which provide the basis for establishing cultural and economic authority. The desire for auditability is particularly important in providing authority and reassurance in areas where uncertainty is rife. As Power says: 'The essence of the new risk management is to produce the governance and regulation of unknowable uncertainties via a distinctive kind of organizational proceduralization which prioritizes the audibility of process' (2007: 180).

If audit is going to work it has to present itself in two ways – simultaneously fuzzy and precise. This is because audit works both as an idea and as a technical practice that establishes visible standards of performance. This is a slightly complex process if we follow Power's argument that auditing opens up organisations to external scrutiny and control (1997: 124). It is complicated because it needs to balance the legitimacy derived from the independent external scrutiny of the process, with the control by those with a legitimate right to exercise authority. Hence the legitimising of the practice cannot be such that it is easily replicable by others, otherwise the authority of the auditor will be undermined. In other words, auditing must retain an element of obscurity, something that helps to sustain the 'expectations gap' (1997: 30). More generally we should note how the applicability of auditing works, since 'it is precisely this fuzziness in the idea of auditing that enables its migration and importation into a wide variety of organizational contexts' (1997: 6).

Risk is an important part of the audit process because it provides a way of developing a framework of classification and allows for expectations of decision and action based on management of risk (Power 2007: 180). It develops this classification despite the fact that it deals with things that cannot be easily categorised or classified, hence the prioritisation of correct procedures in order to create the impression that the right thing is being done even if there is no 'truth' to this claim: 'The essence of the new risk management is to produce the governance and regulation of unknowable uncertainties via a distinctive kind of organizational proceduralization which prioritizes the auditability of process' (Power 1997: 180). Auditing and accounting take place in the face of uncertainty in that 'beneath the surface of rational risk management designs, and claims for value-enhancing practice, lurks a pervasive fear of the possible negative consequences of being responsible and answerable, of being required to produce decidability in the face of the undecidable' (Power 2007: 203).

This argument can also be related to processes of insurance. Here, too, it is argued that risk has no precise meaning except as a category or technology of insurance (Ewald 1991: 198). In turn, insurance works to construct a certain social field, what O'Malley calls an 'insurational imaginary' that links abstract techniques of insurance to practicable objects of government (O'Malley 2002: 97). Or in the words of another Foucauldian: 'In its form as a *generalizable technology* for rationalizing societies, insurance is like a diagram, a figure of social organization' (Defort 1991: 215). Risk, then, is essential to the calculations and the juridical definition of insurance and in turn:

> It is characteristic of insurance that it constitutes a certain type of objectivity, giving familiar events a kind of reality which alters their nature. By objectivizing certain events as risks, insurance can invert their meanings: it can make what was previously an obstacle into a possibility. Insurance assigns a new mode of existence to previously dreaded events; it creates value. (Ewald 1991: 200)

Risk and insurance can be seen through the concept of governmentality if we see their calculations as relating to populations, indeed if we see them as ways of helping to constitute populations. Ewald, for example, argues that risk works as a calculation of probability spread over a population and which works to transform the lives of those it covers (Ewald 1991: 200–3). Ewald and Defort provide accounts of the emergence of insurance and the role it plays in offering a guarantee against certain risks and in sharing or distributing the collective burden. At the same time it works in a disciplinary way to open up populations to constant scrutiny; finely classifying and sub-dividing groups on the basis of different categories of risk. This allows people's behaviour and preferences to be monitored and assessed, as well as providing the possibility for introducing a moral aspect to insurance. In light of specific neoliberal forms of governmentality we can see how insurance might work to encourage people to take responsibility for their own affairs, make their own risk calculations and conduct their life in an enterprising way.

We can see how something like insurance has both individualising and societal effects – indeed we could say it is through this individualising effect that the social effect is achieved. As Ewald suggests: 'Insurance provides a form of association which combines a maximum of socialization with a maximum of individualization. It allows people to enjoy the advantages of association while still leaving them free to exist as individuals' (1991: 204). The individualistic rationality of insurance gets people to assume risk, something that is given even greater significance with the shift away from social democratic welfare systems. Now insurance encourages a move away from the state to the private sphere. The state, instead of being directly involved, develops a system of support and advice that encourages us to develop our own self-management strategies. It can do this by presenting such responsibility as a practice of freedom, that is, as freeing ourselves from state intervention, from what Beck and Giddens call traditional social structures, by encouraging our entrepreneurial spirit, giving us autonomy and allowing us to make our own life choices. If we see this in terms of governmentality, then we should pay attention to the ways in which risk creates new subjectivities, redefines relationships, invents new techniques for self-government and assigns responsibilities accordingly (O'Malley 2004: 9). It is true, as O'Malley argues, that the politics of risk and uncertainty have a long history of showing how individuals should conduct themselves in a free-market society, but such a process has been given new impetus by the dismantling of social security systems by contemporary neoliberal governance (2004: 27). Rather than talking of risk as inherent in reflexive modernity, we should take a more Foucauldian approach in seeing risk as a technology with a societal effect:

> The technology of risk, in its different epistemological, economic, moral, juridical and political dimensions becomes the principle of a new political and social economy. Insurance becomes *social*, not just in the sense that new kinds of risk become insurable, but because European societies come to analyse themselves and their problems in terms of the generalized technologies of risk. (Ewald 1991: 210)

It is this, rather than the vague idea of a reflexive stage of modernity, which is key to understanding the role that risk plays in contemporary societies. However, having seen the two explanations of risk through insurance and auditing we find two slightly different although not incompatible accounts, one that emphasises individualisation, the other institutional and managerial practices. Power argues that audit focuses on the organisation rather than the individual and in this sense is different from surveillance – and perhaps insurance (1997: 67). As with other neoliberal trends, we can see auditing as a way of shifting legitimacy away from the direct control of the state. Blurred boundaries between the public and private can be found in things like New Public Management and other shifts in regulatory style. Recent developments like the use of league tables and other metrics represent, as we have seen, attempts to bring in external means of legitimating practices that might also be said to encourage an artificial game of competition. It also works in extending responsibilisation to organisations as well as individuals by focusing on outcomes and performance. The state is then allowed a more detached supervisory role.

However, while this is the case at the national level, things are somewhat different in international politics. Here, if we want to make the concept of governmentality work, we need to move away from the idea that things like risk can be put to work on local populations as we might find in the examples drawn from the EU. Instead we should look at how risk acts as a category to assess the performance of institutions, most notably states. Instead of finding risk assessments at work in the regulation of the daily lives of local people, we find international organisations seeking to compile data on the performance of states in meeting certain targets. A good example is a UNDP report on disaster risk. The report notes how different international organisations, UN agencies, international financial institutions including the World Bank and regional development banks, as well as members of international civil society, have all started to engage in issues of disaster risk and economic development. It makes a number of specific recommendations, including:

(a) Enhance global indexing of risk and vulnerability, enabling more and better intercountry and interregional comparisons.
(b) Support national and subregional risk indexing to enable the production of information for national decision makers.
(c) Develop a multi-tiered system of disaster reporting.
(d) Support context driven risk assessment. (UNDP 2004: 8)

It later outlines three steps to bring disaster risk reduction and development concerns closer together:

- The collection of basic data on disaster risk and the development of planning tools to track the changing relationship between development policy and disaster risk levels.
- The collation and dissemination of best practice in development planning and policy that reduce disaster risk.
- The galvanising of political will to reorient both the development and disaster management sectors. (UNDP 2004: 27)

The report then goes on to throw together all imaginable concepts: 'good governance is a commitment to sharing decision-making power between the stakeholders in a process'. It talks of the state as a 'facilitator in development' rather than having the government as the dominant actor (UNDP 2004: 75). This is supported through civil society and the development of social capital which are no longer exclusively local but are supported by the networks developed by international NGOs and others with similar concerns about risk (UNDP 2004: 80). This matches similar arguments that we have seen in relation to development and aid. When compared to discussions within the EU we can also see comparisons with processes of benchmarking and indexing such as OMC. But the Lisbon Agenda does have real effects on populations across Europe. In this case, the process is actually more of an indexing or auditing exercise. Whether there are any beneficial effects for real people is quite a secondary issue compared to the auditing effect. In relation to the main argument of this book, we can suggest that while processes like the Lisbon Agenda can be found to have affected policy towards populations in the advanced liberal heartlands, such strategies are less likely to be found at work in poorer parts of the world. Instead we find governmentality operating through the interventions of Western-dominated international organisations whose main aim is the evaluation and surveillance of states, governments and local institutions, while using a distant concern with the health, wealth and well-being of populations as a legitimating factor for these interventions rather than as a main priority.

Conclusion

The conclusion to this chapter might be considered a conclusion to the first part of the book in so far as many of the things it summarises are characteristic not only of theories of risk and reflexivity, but also of globalisation theory, networks and flows, social capital, theories of governance, knowledge society and others. We find that instead of providing a clear analysis of risk, approaches such as those of Giddens and Beck effectively contribute to the discourse of the very thing they are meant to analyse and in doing so reproduce a governmentality of risk. A governmentality approach to risk should therefore not only try to account for the role of risk in contemporary society, but also account for the way that different theories contribute to the discourse of risk. This conclusion will do so through various themes that can be found in this literature and which ultimately contribute to the prevailing forms of governmentality – namely, their rejection of class and other social categories; their downgrading of the role of the state and other political institutions; their assumptions about the unstoppable nature of globalisation and the view that we have lost control of macro forces; the accompanying belief that individualisation is taking place to influence the micro level; and a belief that our behaviour at this level should be reflexive not in the sense of being critical of society or the macro changes that are taking place, but in the instrumental sense of working out our life choices and taking responsible decisions.

On the issue of class we can find countless statements from Giddens and Beck that claim that it is no longer relevant, or that it is a product of industrial society, but is being replaced by new sorts of identity. The issue of identity is particularly important since it can be argued that after several years of neoliberal attacks on labour, class consciousness, if not class itself, has been seriously undermined in the advanced liberal societies. Beck and Beck-Gernsheim, however, say that these changes, rather than being the product of a specific neoliberal attack on the organised working class, is somehow inherent in modernity itself. Even the milder Weberian claim that class is related to market position is rejected; ties to a social class 'have typically been pushed into the background. A tendency to individualized lifestyles and life situations forces people – for the sake of material survival – to make themselves the centre of their own life plans and conduct' (Beck and Beck-Gernsheim 2001: 31). Risk itself is lifted from any specific social context and given a universal and unspecific form. Linked to the idea of the knowledge society, Beck argues that the old Marxist adage is reversed; whereas 'in class positions being determines consciousness ... in risk positions, conversely, *consciousness (knowledge) determines being*' (Beck 1992: 53). Individualisation replaces class as the main process of socialisation (1992: 31). Why such an argument might be considered to reinforce rather than question governmentality is because it takes this process of individualisation for granted and sees it as a natural tendency of late modernity rather than as a specific strategy either of government or of business, or more generally of neoliberalism. While it is one thing to analyse contemporary neoliberal strategies of individualisation – for example in the work of Foucauldians on insurance, or Boltanski and Chiapello's work on new management strategies – it is something else to claim that this is a deep-rooted, irreversible and even positive feature of a second modernity. It is easy to attack traditional class roles, of course, but the implications of such arguments are more serious in that they move us towards the assumption that any form of collective politics – especially oppositional politics – is outdated and that we have no choice but to turn to a politics of individual self-interest. It should be obvious why such an argument is fully consistent with neoliberal rationality.

Exactly the same problem can be found if we move on to these authors' discussion of things like globalisation and the role of the state. Giddens and Beck talk of the globalisation of risk as unstoppable and overwhelming: 'In sweeping terms, one can formulate the theory of reflexive modernization: at the turn of the twenty-first century the unleashed process of modernization is overrunning and overcoming its own coordinate system' (Beck 1992: 87). In reality, it is truer to say that it is writers like Giddens and Beck who have been overwhelmed to the point where they are unable to differentiate between the effects of neoliberalism and postwar institutional changes, and the deeper structures of capitalism and the world system. This is what is so dangerous about the idea of reflexive modernity, that it is founded on the belief that it is 'the dynamics of individualization, globalisation and risk [that] undermine the first phase of industrial nation-state modernity and its foundations' (Beck 1999: 152), a claim that fails to look at how any of these three things are themselves socially constituted by economic structure and changes in its mode of regulation as a result of the things that these theories are so keen to deny – things like deep-rooted internal contradictions and the effects of struggles between social groups that both manifest themselves in changing institutional settlements.

While bracketing out the macro level, at the micro level we find these arguments supportive of a neoliberal view of the world and the regulative techniques that support it. Risk society requires us to take a calculating approach to various situations and options we are confronted with. We cannot change our social conditions, but we must adapt our behaviour in a reflexive (read calculative or instrumental) manner. It is also accepted that this places new rights and obligations upon us. In particular, we must take responsibility for our own welfare and security. This is justified on the basis that 'the hazards which are now decided and consequently produced by society *undermine and/or cancel the established safety systems of the welfare state's existing risk calculations*' (Beck 1999: 76). Instead of questioning neoliberal attacks on the welfare state, Beck believes that the encouragement of 'new forms of living reveal dynamic possibilities for the reorganization of social relations' (Beck and Beck-Gernsheim 1991: 98) and opens up an indefinite range of possibilities to the individual (Beck and Beck-Gernsheim 1991: 189). His thesis clearly supports the individualisation of risk and the government strategy of shifting responsibility through such things as private insurance and pension reform, while encouraging the view that this is not so much a new form of governance as a deeper historical process.

At the root of the problem is an imbalance between structural and agential accounts of contemporary social change. At times Giddens, Beck and other writers like Lash and Urry and Castells deny the existence of structure, claiming that it has been replaced by networks and flows. Lash, whom we discussed in the previous chapter, introduces Beck's work in such a way, writing that the first modernity consists of a logic of structures and the second of a logic of flows. The first modernity is one of social systems, the second modernity is one of non-linear systems and chaos (Lash, introduction to Beck and Beck-Gernsheim 2001: vii, xii). Beck himself writes: 'With the emergence of a self-culture, it is rather a *lack* of social structures which establishes itself as the basic feature of the social structure' (Beck and Beck-Gernsheim 2001: 51). Beck's idea of individualisation and Giddens's view of detraditionalisation can be read in such a way. We have seen how they often turn this into a positive argument by focusing on the great potentials offered to an agency freed from the constraint of social structure, or at least, traditional forms of structure.

Giddens is keen to critique poststructuralism for its denigration of the subject, arguing, for example, that the things Foucault describes as disciplinary should be seen as attempts to develop reflexive self-control (Giddens 1991: 160). Beck likewise insists that risk society is not the bureaucratic or technocratic prison depicted by Foucault and the Frankfurt school: 'Unlike most theories of modern societies, the theory of risk society develops an image that makes the circumstances of modernity contingent, ambivalent and involuntarily susceptible to political rearrangement' (Beck 1999: 147). Giddens's answer is his structuration approach, whereby structures and agents are mutually constitutive. A clear example of this can be found in his claim that 'life politics concerns political issues which flow from processes of self-actualisation in post-traditional contexts, where globalising influences intrude deeply into the reflexive project of the self, and conversely where processes of self-realisation influence global strategies' (Giddens 1991: 214). But in fact we find little evidence of the latter process, only an account of life politics that is much closer to Foucault's account of self-regulation under neoliberal forms of governmentality. Hay *et al.* make the more compelling argument that Giddens might be read as overly influenced by the rampant individualism of neoliberalism, and that it is the contemporary social and political climate that is intruding on his sociological analysis (Hay *et al.* 1997: 93).

This means supporting a neoliberal account of the politics of the self as a responsibilised, rational and disciplined actor. But it also means a completely separate structural account of social change. So while structures disappear from an account of social action (now declared a dead traditional form) they reappear in the background as the unstoppable forces of modernity, immune from agents' attempts to influence global strategies. Evidence that these arguments are a reflection of a particular discourse that accepts neoliberalism as an unchallengeable background condition can be found not just in Giddens and Beck, but across the work of all those we have studied – Castells, Lash, Urry, Scholte. Or take this remarkable comment from Bauman in his introduction to Beck's work on individualisation: 'Let there be no mistake: now, as before, individualization is a fate, not a choice; in the land of individual freedom of choice, the option to escape individualization and to refuse participation in the individualizing game is emphatically *not* on the agenda' (Bauman in Beck and Beck-Gernsheim 2001: xvi). This is the great irony for postmodernists and theorists of reflexive modernity alike in that they claim to give an account of complexity, chaos, individualisation and reflexivity, yet premise this on a deterministic account of societal change and a linear view of historical development. We have no control over this process, yet we are told it is liberating us. Moreover, it is a Eurocentric view that prioritises the changes taking place in Western societies while dismissing the rest of world as modern, pre-modern or traditional. These theorists all condemn Marxism for its structural account of social change, while they themselves embrace a far more deterministic, but ultimately empty alternative. The contrast between the two approaches is summarised in Benton's argument that at least Marxism tries to give an account of global changes through ideas like imperialism or the requirements of capital accumulation, whereas such causes are replaced in alternative accounts by an anodyne appeal to the peculiar dynamics of modernity (Benton 1999: 53).

We can argue about whether the ideas of leading intellectuals play any significant role in influencing policy documents. Certainly people like Giddens and Castells have put themselves forward as theorists to different governments and to the EU. We might, however, make the more damaging suggestion that their ideas simply reflect the intrusion of contemporary policy shifts. In that sense, the claims of contemporary social theory and the documentary output of different forms of governance reflect the same dispositif or discursive formation. Within this we find remarkably similar ontological assumptions across a range of different theories, matching the macro-level belief in the unstoppable nature of global trends with the micro-level emphasis on self-reflection and responsibilised individual conduct. We will now go on to shift focus from how these ideas are reflected in international organisations to how international organisations develop these ideas. That is, we will compare some of the documents produced by two such bodies, the EU and the World Bank, and look at how their arguments are part of the same general discourse. However, because of our concern with the wider social context, we will also show how these discourses find themselves having to deal with different contexts and therefore how the ideas discussed in Part I of this book find themselves being deployed in slightly different ways.

PART II

Governmentality and international organisations

6 *Governmentality in the European Union*

In Part I we examined the concept of governmentality and used it to explain the emergence of a series of influential ideas and concepts. We judged these, ultimately, on their practical function. That is to say, rather than simply dismiss them for their conceptual incoherence, we should see how these concepts play an important role in constructing a social imaginary that justifies a series of practical interventions that are in keeping with the neoliberal restructuring of capitalism and its new forms of regulation.

In this second part we look at these ideas in practice by drawing on a selection of documents from two international bodies – the EU and the World Bank. We do not have the space to provide a full range of documents to examine. Instead we will look at a selection of documents, not to claim scientific representativeness, but to try and establish the basis of a common discursive formation. It allows us to make some claims about how governmentality might work in practice and it is useful to compare two very different bodies, the EU and the World Bank, in order to see how similar ideas work in quite different contexts and whether there are modifications to the way that these ideas are used. We should stress that our concern here is with transnational and global governance, not with domestic government, although the nature of domestic social conditions have an important bearing on how governmentality can operate.

For scholars looking to apply the concept of governmentality to an international environment, the EU is an obvious place to start. Here we find a project that goes beyond the confines of particular nation states, which seeks to use new forms of governance, which is multilayered with multiple agents, is a reflexive process and is concerned, above all else, with the management of populations. This last point is ultimately a crucial one. For what we find in the EU is a plausible example of governmentality working with population as its concern and with states called upon to help manage EU policies that target populations, their actions and their well-being. The Lisbon Process, for example, is a prime example of how EU institutions set aims and targets for states, the achievement of which is considered in the interests of the citizens of EU Member States. When we move to the next chapter on global governmentality we will see the same thing going on. But we will find that governance does not always work itself all the way down. In common with the EU we find global institutions working to set targets for states and their governments – now readily identified by these organisations as the central institutions for implementing their policies – but where the effectiveness of this does not always make itself felt at the local or grassroots level. In this chapter, however, we will look at how governmentality fits more easily with local populations because of the particular nature of social conditions across the EU countries. This chapter does not attempt to look at different exercises in governmentality within the Member States, only at the effects of governmentality formulated at the EU level. Moreover, we will mainly look at the European Commission, since this fits most closely with governmentality in practice. However, given more space, there are plenty of other processes going on which could be examined – not least the monitoring and auditing of the EU itself by bodies like the European Court of Auditors.[1] By examining a range of EU documents and statements this chapter suggests that EU bodies are clearly exercising liberal governmentality in a number of ways: through a suggestive form of governance, operating from a distance, responsibilising actors, forming networks, processing information, establishing procedures, setting targets and benchmarking performance.

White Paper on governance

There are countless areas where a governmentality approach to the EU might focus. For reasons of space, we will have to concentrate on a few key areas and provide a general overview rather than an in depth account. There is, however, an obvious place to start. The Prodi

[1] Whereas this chapter is concerned with how the Commission audits the performance of Member States, the European Court of Auditors functions as an external auditing body of the EU, producing, among other things, an Annual Report and various other Special Reports and having a dedicated website at www.eca.europa.eu. The Court of Auditors looks at such things as internal organisation, operating procedures and financial management.

Presidency of the European Commission from 1999 to 2004 really pushed the idea of governance. The most significant document of this period is the White Paper on European Governance, so we will devote this opening section to a study of this document and draw out a number of key themes, before exploring such themes in a range of other documents and practices.

Justifying the need for better European governance, the paper's Executive Summary might be seen as a clear indication of governmentality's concern with the tension between governing too much and governing too little. Noting how the public sees the EU as both too remote and also too intrusive, the paper reflects on how people regard the EU as too complex and difficult to understand. At the same time the document believes that these same people are asking for the EU to show leadership in areas of economic and human development, environmental challenges, unemployment, food safety, crime and a range of issues brought together by the notion of globalisation. The aim therefore is to provide a range of democratic institutions (the issue of what actually constitutes a democratic institution is never explored) in order to better connect Europe with its citizens (European Commission 2001: 3). What follows thereafter is a range of issues raised through an appeal to the well-being of the European population, their connectedness to governance through the idea of citizenship and the continued agonising over the appropriate methods and limits of governance.

The White Paper sets out what it considers to be the most important objectives and principles. The main objectives, it argues, need to be more clearly understood. These include the need for sustainable development, the promotion of human capital, cultivating new knowledge and skills, being able to combine social cohesion with greater competitiveness (in particular, the issue here is the so-called European model), responding to environmental challenges and ensuring peace and stability (European Commission 2001: 28). While some of these are clearly internal to Europe, others relate to concerns about Europe's place in the wider world. We will see that arguments about the latter match the perspectives of various international organisations and emphasise Europe's facilitative role rather than its hard power. The five political principles that are emphasised are openness, participation, accountability, effectiveness and coherence. By now these should be familiar issues and are defined by the paper in the following ways. Openness talks of how the institutions should better communicate about actions and decisions, using language that is understandable in order to improve public confidence in complex processes. This partly helps with the principle of participation, which aims to encourage greater involvement in the policy process, developing an inclusive approach that will create more confidence in the end product. Another theme, that of accountability, tries to clarify legislative and executive roles and urges greater clarity and responsibility in the implementation of EU policy. Effective policies must have clear objectives and be implemented in a proportionate manner. Above all, policies and action must be coherent, especially given the great diversity of challenges and tasks within a complex system of institutions (European Commission 2001: 10).

These self-reflections on the problematic nature of governance are typical of liberal governmentality. The White Paper notes the complex level of detail in much EU legislation which makes adapting it a difficult and time-consuming process. EU documents are continually reflecting on a perceived legitimacy gap, and the document notes that the legitimacy of the legislative process can be damaged by a lack of flexibility and slow implementation by Member States (European Commission 2001: 18). Hence the stress on the importance of more effective decision-making, the need to keep simplifying the regulative process and the call for a more effective understanding of when to intervene and what the appropriate levels of consultation are. The nature of the European decision-making process is such that the Commission works from a distance in pushing national authorities to implement certain measures and improve their performance, complying with EU rules and enforcing them through national institutions. We have already noted in Chapter 4 how the Commission plays a reflexive role in encouraging states to consider their performance and practices and encouraging them to behave in line with certain guidelines and agreements. The Commission functions as the centre of a set of policy networks, influencing the decision-making process through recommendations rather than direct enforcement. This networked form of governance was recognised in a speech made by Prodi to the European Parliament in 2000 where he told MEPs that we must 'stop thinking in terms of hierarchical layers of competence' and instead think of a 'networking arrangement, with all levels of governance shaping, proposing, implementing and monitoring policy together' (Prodi 2000). We can see this networking approach at work in relation to Member

States, but also in relation to other 'levels' of governance, most notably in the EU's considerations on civil society.

Civil society is seen as playing an important role in giving voice to citizens and delivering services that meet their needs. Civil society organisations can mobilise people and encourage social inclusion. Looking at ways to better structure the EU's relationship with civil society, the White Paper suggests a code of conduct to identify responsibilities and improve accountability of all partners. This recognises that minimum standards need to be maintained but that formal rules may slow down procedures. These standards should improve the representation of civil society organisations and engage them in consultative practices and partnership arrangements while also holding them to account. While encouraging greater participation and more open consultation and dialogue, the paper also notes that 'with better involvement comes greater responsibility' (European Commission 2001: 15). Thus civil society must also follow the principles of good governance – including accountability and guarantees of representativeness and openness. To this end the Commission proposes to establish a comprehensive online database to give details of civil society organisations and encourage them to improve their internal organisation. This typifies processes of devolving responsibility while maintaining a watchful gaze through the compilation of data and the requirement to follow certain internal procedures.

There is also the important issue of encouraging the development of civil society in those countries that were then in the process of applying for EU membership. This is seen as part of the process whereby citizens of these countries are informed and prepared and as a way of encouraging greater mutual awareness.[2] We noted above that the White Paper considers the EU's relations with the wider world. Here civil society organisations are seen as playing a useful role as 'early warning systems' for the direction of political debate and allowing for the implementation of things like development policies. The EU's own role in relation to these organisations is seen as one of entering into partnerships with governmental and non-governmental stakeholders while insisting on the principles of responsibility, good governance,

[2] We can see this in ongoing enlargement discussions with Croatia and Turkey. http://europa.eu/legislation_summaries/enlargement/ongoing_enlargement/e50022_en.htm.

accessibility and openness. The EU has developed a vision of itself as a global facilitator, entering partnerships, improving cooperation and openness and promoting new methods of doing things as a complement to 'hard' international law (European Commission 2001: 27). This supports the idea of the EU as a normative power, prompting others to comply with the correct way of doing things, rather than taking a more coercive or disciplinary role in global affairs.

The White Paper is also concerned with how to develop the appropriate networks that can contribute to EU policies. It is argued that networks can play a vital role in achieving greater European integration as well as building bridges to applicant countries and the rest of the world. They reflect cultural changes and global interdependence as well as new technological developments. A tremendous variety of these new networks across Europe link businesses, communities, research centres and regional and local authorities. They have deep roots that reach down into European society. Yet the document notes that many of these may be disconnected from the EU policy process. They require more open and better-structured relations with EU institutions (European Commission 2001: 18).

We will later look in more detail at the EU's understanding of how networks relate to skills, expertise and the knowledge society. The White Paper itself notes the importance of making greater use of skills and practical experience at different levels of governance. For one thing, this is important for the flexible application of EU policies in different local contexts. It also links to the need to build public confidence in the use of expert advice. The EU has set itself the task of putting itself at the heart of a network of experts that can be subject, it is claimed, to public scrutiny and debate as Europe tries to manage a new set of challenges. In particular, this relates to things like food standards, bio-technologies and other risks and ethical questions thrown up by science and technology. Here the EU sees itself playing a crucial role in risk assessment and risk management. It claims to have been developing this role over a number of years by building up its scientific committees, making information and advice publicly available and enhancing its scientific capability, transparency and networking in areas such as food safety (European Commission 2001: 19).

Two years after the White Paper, the European Commission published a report on the progress made. This included the results of a public consultation (only 260 responses received (European Commission 2003: 5)) and further reflections on the theme of good governance, once more defined as openness, participation, accountability, effectiveness and coherence (European Commission 2003: 5). Discourse analysts would note that these are justified through an appeal to 'what the public expects at the beginning of the 21st century' (European Commission 2003: 5), thus reinforcing the common-sense nature of these proposals and attempting to persuade the reader that this is part of bringing politics closer to the people and responding to pressure 'from below'. The report reinforces this point through presenting the importance of 'better involvement' and consultations with civil society, claiming that the issue of low citizen participation and involvement was seen as the most important issue by most respondents (again, let us note that there were just 260 responses!). The idea of bringing governance closer to the people is a constant theme in EU documents and calls for greater public involvement increase even while actual public involvement remains minimal. The report makes a point of calling for greater involvement of non-institutional players as a way of 'bringing the European Union closer to its citizens' and enriching policy deliberations through 'bottom-up involvement' (European Commission 2003: 511). The other major theme of the report is to make the institutions and policies more efficient and effective through this kind of self-monitoring. Hence an impact assessment would be carried out from 2003 onwards to assess all major legislation and policy initiatives.

Finally, the report on the White Paper makes an important point about the way the EU has recognised the social and political importance of networks, defined here as non-hierarchical interaction between individuals and / or organisations, 'where every participant is responsible for a part of the resources needed to achieve the common objective' (European Commission 2003: 17). It notes how the Commission has taken a proactive approach towards networks, working with them to shape decision-making and policy application. It has also started to develop a range of tools to better encourage interactive communication. Noting how economic actors are increasingly organised in networks, it looks at how this can be applied to the process of European governance by developing a framework of transnational cooperation that involves actors at EU, regional and local levels.

Concepts and context

It should be clear how EU discussions about governance relate to some of the conceptual issues introduced in the first part of this book. These concepts work as agenda setters by framing our understanding of governance in a particular manner. For example, the regulative role of the EU is established through an argument about global interdependence and significant cultural changes which justify the kind of networked, facilitative role outlined in the White Paper. The global context acts to frame a set of social, political and economic problems and set limits to the kind of actions possible within this framework. In particular, it supports neoliberal assumptions about how to act in a competitive global environment, taking for granted the idea that agency responds through networked forms of organisation and new types of governance. Assumptions about the inevitability of technological change and the impact of new forms of information also work to depoliticise our understanding of governance, so what we see are technical responses that reflect the technologies of neoliberal governmentality.

This book has tried to show the similarities between the language of governance and the discussions of contemporary social theorists. Naturally this is even more evident when these theorists decide to offer advice to policy-makers. While Anthony Giddens will be best remembered for his closeness to New Labour and his advocacy of the short-lived Third Way, he has also written extensively on the EU and offered advice on how Europe should develop in what he considers to be a more global environment. He talks of how the old Europe has become unsustainable in the face of increased life expectancy, the failure of universalist systems, the massive rise in competition faced by Western societies and other challenges of globalisation (Giddens *et al.* 2006: 1–2). These views, which are commonplace among the documents of bodies like the EU, are rendered more sociological by their assumptions about the deep-rooted societal conditions to which we have no choice but to respond with new, more innovative forms of governance. In this way, Giddens and others legitimise current governance strategies as the only option available, given our changing world. Moreover, they legitimise changes in contemporary forms of governance as not only necessary, but also as positive developments: 'It is too often perceived as being about forcing people to accommodate to a harsher, more competitive world, rather than equipping each and everyone ... with the up-to-date tools to cope with it' (2006: 2–3).

Giddens's argument sometimes comes across as a fairly crude attack on the European social model in line with the Anglo-Saxon neoliberal viewpoint. Europe, it is argued, has a clear choice: either to modernise, or be left behind. Europeans are said to have made a lifestyle choice whereby they traded in a certain level of possible growth for more leisure and stronger welfare. But this is no longer sustainable given a relative decline in average growth, higher unemployment, problems integrating immigrants and a GDP per head no more than 70 per cent of the US level (Giddens 2006: 17). In keeping with the neoliberal reforms of the New Labour government in Britain, Giddens's advice to the EU is to move to a more positive welfare model by promoting education and learning, prosperity, life choice, active social and economic participation and healthy lifestyles. He criticises traditional welfare systems that transfer risk from the individual to the state and community. Taking risks should be seen as a positive thing if it helps people to transform and improve their lives. A more active approach can be found in those labour-market policies which make it clear that the unemployed have an obligation to look for work if they receive state support (2006: 29).

Other contributors to the Giddens *et al.* volume make similar points. The purpose of welfare reform and education reform is to make Europe more competitive in a global marketplace. The importance of childhood development and lifelong learning lies in the creation of human capital capable of making Europe competitive in the new knowledge-based society (Hemerijk 2006: 116). Hence the importance of the Lisbon Agenda and OMC in setting certain goals on competition, growth, labour market and welfare-state modernisation. The objectives and guidelines for intervention should be extended from labour policy to social inclusion, pensions and health care and translated into national action plans, monitoring and evaluation of such plans through peer review and benchmarking and competitive assessment (Ferrera 2006: 267). These can act as instruments for the expansion of what such theorists call the 'lifechances' of Europe's citizens. The focus on lifechances brings in an individualised and rationalised notion of well-being and decision-making which makes citizenship more responsible and active and which, when applied to the European social model, makes it more market compatible and competition friendly. Proposing the need to link competitiveness and growth to expansion of life chances, it is argued that these are not just defined in market terms but also as normative and social bonds (Ferrera 2006: 271). Of course this is a circular point, because we know that such theorists use the idea of social capital to talk of such normative and social bonds and that social capital is a contemporary way by which political economy attempts to measure social relations.

The dual strategy of extending competition into all aspects of social life and shifting responsibility to the individual to take care of their own lifechances is quite clearly a neoliberal project that combines strategies of capital accumulation with the political project to dismantle the institutions of the postwar welfare system. Yet this is presented by theorists like Giddens as some sort of inevitable tendency of late modern society. Rather than being seen as major initiators of these strategies, governments are presented as having no choice but to respond to them. All this is framed under the rubric of modernisation. The need for modernisation brings with it the idea of urgency. With little choice but to follow a necessary path, the question now is how to organise society around the management of these inevitable developments: 'The consequences of the necessary opening to world competition will depend to a large extent on Europe's capacity to organise an adequate common political management of the modernisation process' (Telò 2002: 248). Such a discourse brings with it a strong emotive appeal. Those who do not go along with the modernisation discourse are considered in denial and dismissed as 'traditionalists'. We have seen also how the modernisation project can be presented in a positive way as a new means of empowering individuals to make their own choices and free themselves from overbearing social structures. A modernised European social model would, for example, encourage investment in people and promote those social policies that allow them to exercise their own free choice. Social institutions, meanwhile, will become more reflexive and accountable. Their role in enabling the exercise of human freedom or life choices will be enhanced through a new institutional reflexivity that subjects their performance to constant evaluation by means of best practice, peer review and other social indicators.

Turning now to how these arguments are reflected in EU discourse, we see exactly the same strategies of citing global context, new social problems, the strengths of Europe measured against an urgent need for modernisation and change and a very positive spin on what might otherwise be considered a difficult set of choices. We will look first at a Commission document, *Renewed Social Agenda: Opportunities, Access and Solidarity in 21st Century Europe*. Here we find the context set by a repeat of the argument that globalisation is the 'principal shaping force of our times', and that technological advances and an ageing population are dramatically changing European societies (European Commission 2008a: 4). This pace of change has accelerated, with people developing new values, relationships and working patterns. Today people are confronted with a far greater range of choices and opportunities. The Lisbon Strategy and its focus on growth and jobs, greater market integration and macroeconomic stability, is credited with helping develop these new opportunities, by stimulating employment and mobility (European Commission 2008a: 3). But change is rapid and policies must respond innovatively and flexibly to the new challenges of globalisation, technological advances and demographic developments (European Commission 2008a: 19). Such developments require an urgent review of means, if not ends. The EU is in a unique position to respond to this challenge given its shared values, common rules and solidarity mechanisms. The Commission will 'work in partnership with the Member States and stakeholders and foster cooperation to manage socio-economic change, particularly the change driven by globalisation and technology' (European Commission 2008a: 3). The terms 'stakeholding', 'partnership', 'fostering cooperation' and 'managing change' remind us that the EU's style of governance works to encourage, persuade and enable those with whom it engages. However, this governance through persuasion is based on an adherence to a particular view of the world which is non-negotiable.

This particular view of the world, like that of Giddens and other contemporary social theorists, allows us no say in deciding the nature of the wider social or global context. Instead it takes this for granted while emphasising the new opportunities it offers. As the Commission's statement argues: 'Today a much wider social agenda is needed that allows Europe to take full advantage of the opportunities brought about by globalisation, to help citizens adapt to changing realities and to show solidarity with those who are affected negatively' (European Commission 2008a: 5). Education, health care and other social services need to be reorganised to allow individuals to exploit these opportunities. This depends on a conception of individuals as active participants in the new economy. These reflexive actors are constituted along neoliberal lines as rational decision-makers and risk-takers. As the document says: 'The overriding social issue for the longer term is how best to equip individuals with the right skills to give them a better chance in the modern economy as workers, entrepreneurs and consumers' (European Commission 2008a: 5). Part of the neoliberal rationality is to blur the line between consumers and citizens as well as artificially constructing an entrepreneurial conception of the self. This is fostered through a particular set of educational and labour market policies. Set in the context of a 'rapidly changing world', this approach links people's access to opportunities to a commitment to lifelong learning and ongoing renewal of the skills needed by the labour market (European Commission 2008a: 9). In this way the social agenda is reworked through linking the notions of individual lifechances and opportunities for active participation to social inclusion and enhancing the competitiveness of the EU. Individualism at the micro level produces neoliberal capitalism at the macroeconomic level.

Alongside globalisation, the EU document cites rapid technological change as having a wide-ranging impact on society and requiring a rethinking of social policies (European Commission 2008a: 5). It is claimed that globalisation, technological change and the needs of the new knowledge economy and information society require the EU to act to help Member States modernise and restructure their labour markets. These will be transformed through the promotion of lifelong learning, active labour-market policies and modern social security systems. The Commission calls these policies flexicurity and asks Member States to implement these reforms in line with the Lisbon guidelines (European Commission 2008a: 8). In particular, OMC works as a reflexive tool in measuring performance and achievement of these ambitions. It is seen as key to the EU Social Agenda having encouraged Member States to 'develop a shared vision of social challenges, fostered a willingness to cooperate and learn from each other's practices, created a new dynamism in furthering and implementing reforms, and promoted more knowledge-based policy making, geared towards openness, transparency and participation' (European Commission 2008a: 16).

Looking at another document on the EU's growth and jobs strategy, it is all too clear how the discourse of global change works to justify the neoliberal agenda of competitiveness and free-market policies. In the EU's discourse there is simply no alternative but to implement policies designed to improve Europe's competitiveness in the global economy. Trade barriers should be removed and new rules and approaches to trade policy should be developed as part of the Lisbon Strategy of encouraging cooperation between the Commission and among Member States. The development of the single market is vital in making European companies more competitive. It works to impose discipline, predictability and transparency, encouraging innovation and the efficient allocation of resources and has, according to the relevant Commission document, 'fostered the development of high-quality rules and standards which help shape global norms' (European Commission 2006: 3–4). European economic openness to global trade and investment is seen as the best way of exploiting the benefits of the single market by maintaining competitiveness and encouraging jobs and growth. It is seen as the best way of exposing domestic economies 'to creative competitive pressures', encouraging innovation and increasing incentives for investment (European Commission 2006: 4). These themes of competitiveness, performance and individual responsibility are seen most clearly in the Lisbon Process, which is the focus of the next section.

From Lisbon to 2020

The Lisbon Agenda set out to establish a collectively agreed framework and set of policy instruments that could be applied to the economy, the use of information and technology, employment policies and the social model. Wim Kok's mid-term report, *Facing the Challenge: The Lisbon Strategy for Growth and Employment*, notes the difficulties in achieving many of the goals and stresses the urgency of applying the strategy along the lines discussed above. It bases this urgency on the perceived need to compete more effectively with North America and Asia, citing a widening gap in growth rates along with the now familiar specificities of Europe's ageing population and low population growth. 'Time is running out', it urges, 'there can be no room for complacency'. Better implementation of policies is required in order to make up for lost time (European Commission 2004a: 6). The document pays particular attention to the knowledge economy – something we will focus on in the following section. It argues that in order to compete with Asia, it is necessary for European countries to commit to developing the knowledge economy as a way of gaining specialism, excellence and comparative advantage, but in doing so Europe will also find itself confronted with the dominance of the United States (European Commission 2004a: 12).

By now it should be obvious that these sorts of arguments – with their urgent promptings that something must be done to respond to inevitable and unstoppable global changes – work to justify a set of strategies and programmes designed to bring about social restructuring. In the case of Europe this always concerns the economic market, labour relations and the social-welfare programmes covered by the European social model. Setting the social and global context in a problem-solving way, the report asks whether the ambition of the Lisbon Strategy is wrong. It answers its own question:

> The ambition is needed more than ever, whether to meet the challenges of enlargement, an ageing population or the intensified global competition – let alone the need to lower current levels of unemployment. Is Lisbon over-ambitious? Again no. Even if every target were to be hit on schedule, Europe would not be on safe ground. Competitor countries and regions are moving on as well, threatening Europe's position in the global economic league table. Europe must find its place in a global economy, which will nonetheless enable it to uphold its own distinctive choices about the social model that it rightly wants to retain. Whether it is life expectancy, infant mortality rates, income inequality or poverty, Europe has a much better record than the US. The objective of Lisbon is to uphold this record in an environment where the challenges are multiple and growing. (European Commission 2004a: 11)

The backdrop of the competitive demands of the global economy provides the basis for pushing through a social agenda that emphasises the importance of competition, performance targets and changes to the European social model, while presenting these changes in a depoliticised form. While change must come from within, the demand for change comes from without. The imperative to adapt to external changes works to legitimise a modernisation agenda that can be presented simultaneously as technical in nature and also in an emotive way. The Lisbon Strategy is presented as 'Europe's best response to these multiple challenges', representing a framework that sets out what targets and changes are needed to sustain the European economy and create new jobs and trade. This can be achieved only through innovation and operating 'at the frontiers of technology'. The report calls on us to show more awareness of the high cost of not following this path (European Commission 2004a: 16). At risk, it argues, is the sustainability of European society itself, by which is meant the European social model. Here we clearly find the powerful combination of technical demands to modernise and emotive language about social and political choices:

> Europeans have made choices about how to express the values they hold in common: a commitment to the social contract that underwrites the risk of unemployment, ill-health and old age, and provides opportunity for all through high-quality education, a commitment to public institutions, the public realm and the public interest, and that a market economy should be run fairly and with respect for the environment. These values are expressed in systems of welfare, public institutions and regulation that are expensive in a world where low cost and highly efficient producers are challenging the old order. If Europe cannot adapt, cannot modernise its systems and cannot increase its growth and employment fast enough then it will be impossible to sustain these choices. (European Commission 2004a: 16)

These sorts of appeals present the Lisbon Agenda as an inclusive project that brings all Europe together. 'We must *all* take action' to deliver the Lisbon goals, this 'require[s] everyone to engage'. The European institutions and Member States must show greater political commitment and do more to deliver. There must be a 'broader and deeper engagement of Europe's citizens' (European Commission 2004a: 6). To ensure that this happens, the Commission takes it upon itself to coordinate the process by pressurising Member States to exert peer pressure on one another, keeping information on each state's progress and publishing these results. Given that different Member States start from different positions, the Lisbon goals require interpretation according to the particular national context.

The Lisbon Strategy was conceived as a way of mobilising stakeholders within the EU to respond to the challenges of the knowledge economy by combining economic competitiveness, employment and social cohesion. Responding to the challenges of globalisation and interdependence should be in line with the EU's values and experiences, something claimed by the 'Declaration on Globalisation', adopted by the December 2007 European Council. The Commission's 'Strategic Report on the Lisbon Strategy' of December 2007 emphasises how globalisation must be built more effectively into the delivery of the Lisbon Strategy (European Commission 2008b: 15). However, the final assessment of the Lisbon Strategy is not particularly positive. It failed to achieve its main targets, such as the 70 per cent employment rate, and 3 per cent of GDP spent on research and development and failed to close the productivity growth gap with other industrialised countries (European Commission 2010a: 3). While there were some 'tangible benefits', and some consensus around the EU's reform agenda, the Commission's final evaluation document notes a serious 'delivery gap between commitments and actions' where some Member States pressed ahead with ambitious reforms and others fell behind (European Commission 2010a: 4). It notes that the role of the European Council was not clearly defined, and that while guidelines for National Reform Programmes (NRPs) were useful tools, the approach to NRPs was significantly different across the Member States. Nor was the starting position of different countries taken into account. The combination of too many targets and too many vague commitments led to serious problems with ownership (European Commission 2010a: 5).

The Lisbon Strategy is summarised as a response to the challenges of globalisation and ageing (European Commission 2010a: 2). However, it was not until the world was shaken by profound economic crisis that the Commission had to admit that its strategy was too inward-looking and too focused on preparing the EU for globalisation rather than trying to shape it (European Commission 2010b: 7). The EU's next project – Europe 2020 – claims to address these issues more effectively and learn from the lessons of Lisbon. However, an examination of the latest arguments does not reveal too much new thinking. The Europe 2020 agenda mentions the very same issues of globalisation, lack of productivity and an ageing population, and outlines three priorities – a 'smart growth' economy based on knowledge and innovation, a competitive economy that is greener and more resource efficient, and a high-employment economy with social and territorial cohesion (European Commission 2010b: 3). Among seven flagship initiatives is one of 'Innovation Union' that aims to improve finance research and innovation that can create growth and jobs. Another is 'an agenda for new skills and jobs' that involves modernising labour markets and talks of 'empowering people' by developing their skills and the mobility of labour (European Commission 2010b: 4).

Similarly, we find a dominant focus on the instruments of governance and a reflection on standards of performance. Dealing with bottlenecks in the single market, for example, leads to a discussion of how to ensure single-market measures are enforced properly through reinforcing structures, better network regulation and legislative and supervision packages. The Smart Regulation agenda will be promoted by better use of regulations rather than directives, as well as evaluating existing legislation, updating rules, monitoring markets, reducing administration and improving the business environment. There is also a call for the development of new financing instruments, raising additional funding for innovative and growing businesses and developing a European venture capital market. Exactly the same language is used to justify the 2020 strategy. There is a call on 'all parties and stakeholders (e.g. national / regional parliaments, regional and / or local authorities, social partners and civil society, and last but not least the citizens of Europe) to help implement the strategy, working in partnership, by taking action in areas within their responsibility' (European Commission 2010b: 28). There is the same monitoring process by which the Commission will report annually to the European Council on the progress towards the targets using 'international benchmarking'. Then there are five headline targets on R&D investments, education, energy and climate change, the employment rate and reducing poverty. These set out to define where Europe should be by 2020. Whether or not the EU countries meet these targets, the important thing is the method of governance that is being consolidated. We move now to look in more detail at some aspects of this.

Information society and networks

Discussion of these issues is helped by examining the SOWING project and its final report *Information Society, Work and the Generation of New Forms of Social Exclusion*, which was a Europe-wide collaborative research project within the EU's Fourth Framework Programme of Research and Technological Development. This is interesting in so far as it connects the EU's policy approach to some underlying theoretical discussions. Not surprisingly it starts with the familiar claim that we are living through a period of profound social and economic change, and adds that there is uncertainty as to the type of new economy and society that is emerging. However, it settles on the idea of information society as the one that in recent years has most clearly 'set the tone' in scientific and public debates about the socio-economic direction of Europe (European Commission 2004b: 5). This concept, it is noted, became an increasingly political term in the 1990s, especially within EU policy-framework discussions. It was presented as a strategy for overcoming social and economic stagnation and lack of competitiveness in relation to the United States and Japan. EU discussions looked at how the idea of the information society could be used to press for greater development of information and communications technology, especially in relation to the organisation of the European labour market (European Commission 2004b: 13; and see Bangemann 1994). The 1994 Bangemann report notes the need to 'master the risks and maximise the benefits' of the profound changes in societal organisation and structure. The 'revolutionary tide, sweeping through economic and social life' leaves Europe with no time to lose (Bangemann 1994: 8). Information technology revolutions were called for in areas like telecommunications, but above all, the EU started to note how these changes could be related to European labour markets and the wider economy. The debate over the information society went hand in hand with the project of deregulating the European economy and flexibilising its workforce. The combination of neoliberal economic and labour-market policies and developing the information society is seen as the best way to promote economic growth and employment (European Commission 2004b: 13). The SOWING document argues that in fact it is information rather than communication technology that is the main source of change. The process of 'informatisation' is highlighted as explaining the way these changes are more than purely technological ones. What we are now witnessing is the reorganisation of all economic sectors and industries through the effects of collecting, processing, interpreting and disseminating information (European Commission 2004b: 5).

There are countless EU documents we could draw on to show the significance of the information society concept in EU policy discussions. If we continue with the Kok report we can see how it stresses the importance of developing the information society through new regulatory frameworks, research, education and human capital investment. These provide links to policy areas like research and development, e-commerce, mobile communications technology and education and training systems – in particular, the promotion of lifelong learning (European Commission 2004a: 19). At the same time, the report stresses that the concept of the knowledge society is much more than any one of these areas and 'covers every aspect of the contemporary economy where knowledge is at the heart of value added' (European Commission 2004a: 19). Because of this, technological innovation demands large-scale organisational and institutional restructuring. The crucial point, therefore, is the way that the issue of the information society is used as a means of intervention into workforce relations. Thanks to the unstoppable forces of information, the workforce must become more agile if it is to 'exploit the new trends'. The strategy must therefore be to 'secure more flexibility and adaptability in the labour market' while bringing in the type of active welfare policies previously mentioned, which 'help the growth of employment and productivity rather than hinder it' (European Commission 2004a: 8). This is partly done through a new approach to education and skills as ways of creating an active and mobile labour force. The spread of information is also connected to new, networked forms of organisation and more flexible organisational structures that are better able to respond to the fast pace of innovation. The Kok report argues that 'possibilities for wider economic structures to create the network economy and society and a fundamental re-engineering of business processes are being opened up by ICTs' (European Commission 2004a: 8). This connection between information and organisation leads us to the related concept of networks.

The SOWING authors note the significance of the work of Castells and Lash on new organisational logics, the network approach and reflexive production. Rather than seeing the network concept as fully explaining the features of the new economy, they prefer to see it as an explanatory framework that informs the way that people interpret the new pressures of objective economic developments (European Commission 2004b: 7). This is what shapes the process of organisational restructuring. In a similar vein, the authors claim that they do not see information technology as the main cause of change, but look instead at the role it plays in facilitating change. They go on to say that their 'hypothesis is that the new emerging technological practices can be characterised by the application of network technology, decentralised and integrated organization forms, innovation as the key company aim, trust-based organisation culture and increasing demand for communication skills' (European Commission 2004b: 109). However, like Castells, the authors end up promoting the idea of an 'organisational logic', which, while not dependent on technological change, can play just as strong a role in determining the 'historical foundation of the information economy' (Castells 2009: 164). The conceptual aspect of this logic is something that the SOWING report develops when looking at new ways of coordinating and controlling work processes. It talks of a change from the traditional bureaucratic logic of coordination to something termed 'discursive coordination'. Rather than being centrally controlled, this new logic coordinates through a collective learning process based on 'mutual adjustment' and 'continuous discourse on a decentralised basis'. Using familiar terms of EU coordination and control, we find the report talking of the importance of 'systemic discourse, performance agreements and benchmarking via automatically generated performance standards ... [in order] to reach an agreement on general strategic orientations concerning markets, output, human resources, and planned budgets (European Commission 2004b: 6). The report shows some caution about changes in work practices, noting that there are limits to the extent to which labour has been casualised or contract flexibility has been brought in. Nor can we really talk of evolution towards the 'flexible firm model' (European Commission 2004b: 10). The real issue, however, is the way that arguments about the emerging information economy are used to justify strategic interventions by government in order to attack things like full-time employment, standardised working hours, collective wage agreements, job security and other gains made by working people.

The EU seized on these ideas back in the 1990s to push through their interventions into the way the workforce is organised. The White Paper *Growth, Competitiveness, Employment* suggests that changes in information technology will have far-reaching effects on the organisation of production (European Commission 1993) – a discursive strategy that works to depoliticise what is a conscious project to reorganise the workforce. Restructuring implies a continuous process of organisational renewal and learning in which all members of the workforce have to be involved. As the Green Paper *Partnership for a New Organisation of Work* states, we can identify a shift from fixed systems of production to a flexible, open-ended process of organisational development (European Commission 1997). To pick out one document from this period, *Living and Working in the Information Society: People First*, the EU starts to push the idea that we are living through a historic period of technological change in order to reorganise work along flexibilised and deregulated lines. By presenting technological change as inevitable, it creates the impression that it is work relations that must therefore be adapted, thus using technological change to justify neoliberal restructuring as the only reasonable option. In terms of management techniques, traditional approaches must be replaced by 'a new industrial and enterprise culture characterised by flexibility, trust, commitment and ability to anticipate and harness change' (European Commission 1996: 8). In practice, this means putting more pressure on the trade unions and workers' organisations to accept more flexible conditions. In a thinly veiled attack on workers' rights, it argues the need for

> the right legal and contractual framework (labour law, collective agreements, industrial relations etc.) to allow firms and individuals more flexibility, while providing adequate security to workers. Member States' labour laws based upon the standard model of full time, workplace-based employment of indefinite duration, can no longer respond entirely to the needs of a more knowledge-based production of goods and services. (European Commission 1996: 10)

Yet the document disguises the fact that it is really about the restructuring of the relationship between capital and labour by using the language of freedom and equality. The top-down attacks on workers' rights are presented through the prism of network theory as if '[e]nterprises are being transformed from hierarchical and complex organisations with simple jobs, to less hierarchical, more decentralised and network-oriented organisations' (European Commission 1996: 9). The ideological effect of this is enhanced if we consider that hiding the real effects of restructuring behind the compulsion to meet the needs of the information age is combined with neoliberal governmentality's appeal to the individual to make the most of their new opportunities through responsible decision-making and the right lifestyle choices.

Moving to a more recent document, *Taking European Knowledge Society Seriously*, we can see the development of another theme, the intersection of informational society with theories of risk. This document notes the emergence of a new and distinctively European approach to risk governance, centred on policy debates on the 'precautionary principle', 'public and stakeholder-engagement' and 'participatory deliberation'. It notes how the EU is playing a leading role in various areas of risk and uncertainty, the limits of scientific knowledge and the need to raise awareness and public engagement (European

Commission 2007: 36). Interestingly, the document follows the constructivist approach on the relationship between science and governance, claiming that issues of social and policy concern – and here it lists such things as sustainable development, precaution, and biodiversity – 'are conventionally assumed to focus on independent objects which exist "out there" in nature and are knowable through science' (European Commission 2007: 81). By contrast, the authors of the document believe that these issues, rather than being 'out there' awaiting scientific discovery, are 'essentially humanly constructed' in the way that 'their boundaries are framed, their dimensions selected and their meanings defined' (European Commission 2007: 82). This constructivist notion of risk is important because it allows this approach to be related to the idea of reflexivity:

> This means, we suggest, that new ways should be found to promote 'reflexive' thinking about the multiple meanings and normatively salient dimensions of these objects of attention. In other words, there needs to be explicit acknowledgement and deliberate public exploration of the socially and normatively constructed dimensions and characteristics of issues and their objects that lie at the intersection of science and governance. The way to achieve this is the adoption, both in the governance of science and the use of science for governance, of new institutions and procedures for more inclusive and pluralistic discussion, learning, and challenge. (European Commission 2007: 82)

This sociological understanding of risk and reflexivity we know, following Giddens and Beck, is institutionally grounded, and thus fits perfectly with the projects of institutions like the European Commission. Indeed, according to this particular document, the very future and welfare of Europe depend upon a reflexive policy narrative in relation to a vast new terrain of science, innovation and governance (European Commission 2007: 73). The ultimate aim of these theories of risk and reflexivity is to justify a neoliberal economic agenda. The context is provided by the claim that Europe is 'characterised as a society endemically averse to risk, science and innovation, reluctant to change, and fast becoming unable to sustain its comfortable position in a competitive global knowledge environment' (European Commission 2007: 73). Thus Europe is considered to be falling behind with regard to such areas as productivity and developing new technology, losing out to other parts of the world that give greater rewards to enterprise. This is intended to filter right down to the micro level. In short, governmentality works here to responsibilise both governments and individuals. As an early document says:

> Nothing would be more dangerous than for Europe to maintain structures and customs which foster resignation, refusal of commitment and passivity. Revival requires a society driven by citizens who are aware of their own responsibilities and imbued with a spirit of solidarity towards those with whom they form local and national communities. (European Commission 1993: 6)

Putting this in terms of governmentality inside the EU, we can see familiar processes operating at different levels. We clearly see an attempt at governance among states (such things as responsibility to implement legislation), which in turn is encouraging internal dynamics of transformation within Member States. Also, at the micro level, we find strategies to responsibilise the activities of citizens and encourage particular types of behaviour. This is important in relation to our next chapter on the World Bank, where we shall see that the same discourse works at the macro level in attempting to govern the activities of governments and states, but does not necessarily find resonance at the micro level of individual citizens, civil society and grassroots activities. In Europe we find social relations much more responsive to these techniques and strategies, although we find this type of governmentality constantly aware of its own limits and failings.

Reflections on governance

The previous sections have shown how certain ideas reproduce governmentality by virtue of the picture of the world they help to create. Particularly important is their taking for granted what are considered to be underlying social conditions and the accompanying claim that government practices must be adapted to these conditions. This hides the way that these conditions are in fact contestable strategies of governance. Most of the prominent discourse on themes like networks, information society and global competitiveness works precisely by denying their strategic nature and the fact that instead of being an underlying condition, as the theory might suggest, they are really a part of the neoliberal restructuring of the European institutional framework. As we have said, this restructuring is something that reaches right down from the governance of the EU to national governmental strategies, especially in Northern Europe, to company management, workplace organisation and individual self-reflection. However, while this works to further strategies that reproduce governmentality, it is necessary to say something about more conscious, self-reflexive exercises in governance. In particular, this section is concerned with the way that governance reflects on its role and limiting its own role – the idea that one always governs too much. This also links with the idea of governing from a distance through the encouragement of others to govern themselves. We have already looked at OMC and we will not repeat this in detail, but concentrate on how it is part of reflexive government's consciousness of its own role and limits.

The European Commission's White Paper on Governance talks of OMC as an important part of the process of achieving objectives, establishing reporting mechanisms, disseminating information and deciding if legislative action is needed. It helps clarify EU policy objectives and improves the effectiveness of EU policies, sets out the conditions for EU regulation and refocuses the roles and responsibilities of Europe's institutions. Reflecting the nature of the EU, it combines formal legislation with non-legislative and self-regulatory solutions to better achieve those objectives (European Commission 2001: 22, 33). The approach is intergovernmental rather than supranational in so far as it works through consensus-building and peer pressure. It is promoted in positive terms as making policy-making more inclusive and accountable, connecting the EU more closely with its citizens and civil society, promoting a stronger interaction with local and regional government and, in general, employing persuasion rather than coercion to pursue common policy discourse. This is also in keeping with the principle of subsidiarity (European Commission 2001: 4–8). OMC fixes various EU targets and goals with appropriate quantitative and qualitative indicators and benchmarks, but it has to take into account national and regional variations. The idea is that states take responsibility for these goals and try to learn from one another through monitoring, evaluation and peer review. Rather than imposing collective discipline, these procedures can be promoted as a means to disseminate good practice, although the SOWING report warns that simply copying good practices can have undesired effects and that the method of benchmarking must be applied carefully to take account of the different organisations and institutions within which the practices are embedded (European Commission 2004b: 130).

The Commission, however, credits OMC for fostering willingness to cooperate and learn. Its report, *A Renewed Commitment to Social Europe*, which looks at the social impact of OMC, claims that the overall assessment among Member States and stakeholders is largely positive. It talks up OMC as an innovative tool of European governance whose policy impact and effectiveness is assessed through the Social Protection Committee, through dialogue with civil society stakeholders and through the reports of independent experts (European Commission 2008c: 3). Thus, seeing OMC as a robust analytical tool, it is regarded as the best way of making progress towards commonly agreed goals, while also taking account of diversity and different national context. For this reason, Member States are themselves able to define national targets and to identify which other counties share similar situations or problems. The stated objectives of OMC for social protection and social inclusion fit squarely with our conceptions of governmentality as concern for populations through the ideas of social cohesion, social equality, social inclusion and adequate social protection and economic growth, but these will be achieved by promoting such things as good governance, transparency and involving stakeholders in the design, implementation and monitoring of policy (European Commission 2008c: 9).

Another paper on growth and employment also focuses on good governance and transparency as the best way to involve stakeholders, which in turn is seen as the best way of achieving key objectives. We know by now that this is part of a key aim of responsibilising actors, and the paper calls for an overview of the intended measures each government will take to achieve transparency. Each Member State is called upon to develop a national action programme setting out how it will achieve the Lisbon targets, how it will ensure coherence and consistency in measures taken and how it will involve all stakeholders in the process. Heads of state must signal their commitment and national parliaments must take ownership of the Lisbon Agenda and interpret it for their publics (European Commission 2004a: 40). There follows the familiar message that the need for reform 'has to be explained especially to citizens who are not always aware of the urgency and scale of the situation'. OMC provides benchmarking and peer pressure to improve performance and deliver competitiveness – the only way, we are told, that the social model can be preserved and improved (European Commission 2004a: 42).

Another report on the promotion of decent work in the world also stresses the importance of strengthening policy coherence from the national and regional levels through to multilateral and global relations. It claims to be following the recommendations of the World Commission on the Social Dimension of Globalisation and cites a number of initiatives for policy coherence and better global governance including organisations like the ILO, IMF, World Bank, regional development banks, WTO and UN (European Commission 2008b: 10). The document uses the term 'flexicurity' to describe an integrated strategy that can promote both flexibility and security in the labour market, helping employers and employees 'to seize the opportunities globalisation offers'. It notes the 'different pathways' for implementing the flexibility approach and adapting it to different political, economic and institutional frameworks in 'partner countries'. OMC here works as part of the social protection and social inclusion strategy to combat poverty and create jobs across Europe. But reflecting on its achievements, the report notes how more must be done to improve social cohesion and reach those on the margins of society, urging what it calls an 'active inclusion approach' to give the excluded better access to labour markets (European Commission 2008b: 13–14).

A brief look at these documents shows how the EU's method of governance is constantly aware of its own limitations and urges continual review of policy achievements both by the Commission and by the Member States and other institutions and organisations it is working with. This continual review of policy achievement, part of a reflexive approach to governance, is reinforced by a stream of review documents where the EU reflects on its role as a regulator. To pick out one such document, the *Third Strategic Review of Better Regulation in the European Union* sets the scene by noting the significance of better regulation across the EU in order to achieve a wide range of benefits such as proper functioning of markets, ensuring a level playing-field for companies and financial institutions and protecting workers and consumers, health and the environment. But the costs of this have to be minimised. The Commission notes that it must ensure that regulation works properly to stimulate entrepreneurship and innovation and allow companies to compete more effectively. To do this it sets out a Better Regulation agenda (European Commission 2009: 2). Among the practical conclusions the review suggests are thirty-three new simplification initiatives in 2009 aimed at dealing with things like late payment of commercial transactions and enforcing civil and commercial judgments (European Commission 2009: 6). Similar documents show how the Commission is continually concerned with the effectiveness of its regulative measures and procedures and engages in a continual process of re-examination and reconsideration.

To summarise, we can see key features of governmentality at work in these governmental practices and self-understandings. This governance tries to operate from a distance by encouraging Member States and others to meet certain targets and exercise responsibility in directing their own actions. It maintains control over the process by playing the role of network manager. The Commission works by coordinating the exchange of information (using tools like OMC), which is a means of steering and coordinating a range of actors and policies. It makes proposals which are then implemented by national governments with the Commission scrutinising from a distance. Indeed, we could follow Haahr in seeing the Lisbon Strategy as a sort of contract which formulates various objectives and specifies certain obligations which must be met. It states certain mutual commitments, but leaves it to Member States to try to meet these (Haahr 2004: 217). These methods are operating upon states and their governments rather than upon individuals or populations, but they work on governments by invoking the governance of populations as their target in so far as they invoke the whole population in the production of wealth through employing more competitive and innovative means. In Europe, therefore, this relationship between transnational governance, national and regional government and local population and workforce is a fairly meaningful one that reaches right down to everyday activity. In the next chapter we will suggest that the World Bank's global governance is slightly different in so far as the governmentality of local populations is more of a means (of governing the behaviour of states) rather than an end in itself.

Risk and security

This brings us to the final topic of this chapter where we can perhaps begin with an apology for not covering the crucial issue of security in more detail. We know that Foucault claims apparatuses of security to be the essential technical means by which governmentality works as a complex form of power (Foucault 2007: 108). We know that in a Foucauldian social ontology, security is seen as straddling matters of law, economy, police and social order (Neocleous 2008: 13). But to do justice to the specific issue of security would require a whole volume in its own right. Likewise in the next chapter it will be impossible to cover all aspects of governmentality in different parts of the world. Thus we have limited these two chapters to a study of aspects of transnational governmentality in order to compare methods of governing through such things as benchmarking, constructing artificially competitive environments, the development of networks and the use of ideologies of global change. Therefore, in this final section on the EU we will limit our study to considering a few security measures in order to show how these fit with the argument that governmentality connects questions of security to the exercise of freedom and then look at an expression of the security agenda from a trans-European perspective through the Hague and Stockholm programmes.

The 1997 Amsterdam Treaty is an important stage in the development of a European security policy. Controls on borders, asylum, immigration and judicial cooperation were moved to the first pillar and the treaty sets out to establish an area of 'freedom, security and justice'. While setting out the conditions for the free movement of peoples, the Treaty also addresses the need to develop common measures to tackle racism and xenophobia, terrorism, trafficking in people, drugs and arms and combating corruption and fraud. It notes how these objectives will be achieved through cooperation of police forces, customs authorities and other border agencies. It also calls for closer judicial cooperation, coordination of investigative mechanisms and approximation of rules on criminal matters. One specific area worth considering is that of asylum, where the Treaty raises the need to determine which Member State is responsible for asylum applications, the minimum standards for receiving asylum seekers, the minumum basis for refugee status and agreed standards for granting or withdrawing this status.[3]

The development of an Area of Freedom, Security and Justice (AFSJ) is clearly something that could provide numerous issues for

[3] For a summary of the Amsterdam treaty see http://europa.eu/legislation_summaries/institutional_affairs/treaties/amsterdam_treaty/a11000_en.htm.

governmentality scholars to analyse, especially in terms of how the concept of freedom works within the social imaginary. The basic claim of the AFSJ is to establish the basis for the free movement of peoples within the EU. In order to protect this, the process requires harmonisation and minimum standards across the different Member States. It is on this basis that a strong connection exists between security, freedom and methods of governance. Putting this in positive terms, the EU asserts its commitment to freedom based on human rights, democratic institutions and the rule of law and notes that integration is rooted in common values. As well as protecting EU citizens against crime, it talks of involving civil society through the principles of transparency and democratic control.[4] The EU has deepened this process with the subsequent Hague (2004) and Stockholm (2009) programmes.

The Hague Programme sets out a huge list of aims including guaranteeing fundamental rights, developing minimum procedural safeguards and access to justice, providing protection to persons in need, regulating migration flows and controlling the external borders of the Union, fighting organised cross-border crime, countering the threat of terrorism, developing Europol and Eurojust, carrying further the mutual recognition of judicial decisions in civil and in criminal matters and improving police and judicial cooperation in order to implement a Common Asylum System (European Council 2004: 3). It goes on to say:

> The European Council considers that the common project of strengthening the area of freedom, security and justice is vital to securing safe communities, mutual trust and the rule of law throughout the Union. Freedom, justice, control at the external borders, internal security and the prevention of terrorism should henceforth be considered indivisible within the Union as a whole. An optimal level of protection of the area of freedom, security and justice requires multi-disciplinary and concerted action both at EU level and at national level between the competent law enforcement authorities, especially police, customs and border guards. (European Council 2004: 4)

We can see how this fits with the idea of governmentality as setting out positive tasks of government to encourage the exercise of freedom by its citizens – that is to say, the right of all EU citizens to move and

[4] See a summary on the Freedom, Security and Justice website at http://ec.europa.eu/justice_home/fsj/intro/fsj_intro_en.htm.

reside freely in the territory of the Member States – but at the same time strengthening security controls. The European Council encourages an open, transparent and regular dialogue with Europe's citizens, in particular through their representative associations and civil society in order to promote and facilitate citizens' participation in public life (European Council 2004: 7). These sorts of arguments are familiar from other areas of EU policy. However, in the realm of security, the EU can exercise more coercive power against those who do not exercise their freedom in what is considered a responsible way, who are not active participants in civil society and, especially, those who fall outside the boundaries of the EU. Hence the Council emphasises the need for intensified cooperation and capacity-building both within the EU and especially on its southern and eastern borders. It euphemistically claims that it wants 'to enable these countries better to manage migration and to provide adequate protection for refugees' (European Council 2004a: 13), which really means improving surveillance techniques and data recording to make sure that people cannot get in unnoticed.

The Stockholm Programme, like its predecessors, also promotes itself positively as creating European citizenship rights based on freedom, security and justice. If we follow up on the question of migration policy, this document raises the matter in terms of the responsibility to protect citizens. It calls for the development of a migration policy based on responsibility, solidarity and partnership. In reality, its main concern is how to combat illegal migration from the southern border, but this is packaged as a technical matter of how best to maintain credible and sustainable immigration and asylum systems (European Council 2009: 4). There are also familiar expositions of how to govern more effectively through evaluation of the legal instruments adopted, and it proposes an Action Plan for substantially raising the level of European training for police, judges, prosecutors, border guards and others responsible for implementing the procedures. The Programme presents a reinforced and proactive external policy dimension based on forming partnerships with third countries, cooperating closely with neighbours, actively developing and promoting European and international standards, developing the exchange of information, making more effective use of resources, using a full range of instruments, stepping up monitoring and evaluation and promoting policies described as encouraging solidarity, coherence and complementarity (European Council 2009: 74). The overall package can be summarised as giving

Europe's citizens the freedom to live in a law-abiding society, with the authorities prepared to act against those who threaten it.

It is possible to interpret these developments in different ways depending on the literature one is following. For some this represents an intergovernmental framework for cooperation. But we can also develop this through the networks metaphor, looking at the intersection of numerous bodies concerned with policing, border control, justice and law – most notably Frontex, Eurodac, Eurojust and Europol. These different bodies can only really work as part of a network and through combined means of intervention. Between them they develop and deploy new forms of surveillance and monitoring techniques like profiling, intelligence-led policing and the carrying out of risk analyses. In particular, we see the development of intelligence-led surveillance or 'dataveillance', new surveillance assemblages combining public authorities and private companies, the computerisation of personal data, biometrics and new procedures for visas, passports, identity cards and the monitoring of air passengers. There is a strengthening of the ways that individuals can be traced and of course, post 9/11, new laws on counter-terrorism. The Schengen area works through the networking of different agencies, something Walters and Haahr describe as a liberal form of policing because it connects existing agencies as part of a lighter and more economical way of governing rather than developing extensive new bureaucratic agencies (Walters and Haahr 2005: 105). Security is maintained, despite the abolition of border controls, by developing common checks, harmonising entry conditions, developing common rules to examine entry applications and harmonising surveillance measures. The development of databases like the Schengen Information System and Eurodac allows for the better exchange of information and the promotion of common practices and harmonisation of standards and procedures. Walters and Haahr point out that alongside the development of networked governance is a constant fear of flows which might take advantage of the gaps in the network:

> It is not the fear of drugs, illegal immigrants or terrorists per se. More specifically, it is the concern that these threats – understood as 'flows' or as 'transnational networks' which operate across the smooth, borderless spaces of the new Europe – will take advantage of, and prosper from the gaps, discontinuities, incompatibilities and miscommunications between its various police and security agencies ... The governmental task is not to replace the national

agencies but to provide a framework which minimizes the risk of incoherence, miscommunication or disjuncture. (Walters and Haahr 2005: 106)

This constant fear of 'incoherence, miscommunication and disjuncture', of 'discontinuities and incompatibilities' is a driving feature of EU governance in all areas of policy. It is easy, therefore, to see how this might be considered through the governmentality lens as consistent with a constant awareness of the limits of the methods used, the techniques deployed or the need for continuous appraisal of how governance occurs.

We have avoided the question of fighting terrorism and concentrated instead on the issue of how migration is constructed as a security issue, threatening the freedoms offered by the EU. This works through the various issues discussed throughout this chapter, such as the way networks are coordinated, the way technology allows for new practices of profiling, screening, electronic surveillance and the development of databases. Risk works through what Bigo calls the 'management of unease'. For him, it transforms misgiving into a form of rule where technologies of surveillance employ profiling to decide who is watched (Bigo 2002: 82). This is consistent with governmentality's emphasis on being proactive, anticipative and using moralising techniques. But we also clearly see that governmentality does more than set out the positive tasks of government. It also works negatively through the idea of misgivings. There is of course the positive presentation of freedom and the idea of citizenship. But the neoliberal construction of active citizenship works to give it various duties and responsibilities and in so doing forces immigrants to integrate or risk exclusion. This 'governmentality through misgivings' with its shift away from the more protective and enabling discourse (Bigo 2002: 85) to a discourse of unease does of course have much in common with those discourses associated with the threat from terrorism, and it is here that we find the real meaning of governmentality with its excluded other and its less than liberal tactics of discipline and surveillance, which are at the same time necessary for the discourses of freedom and security to function.

Conclusion

We should conclude by re-emphasising how European governance fits with the concept of governmentality, but also note the significance of the wider context. There are clearly many more things that could have been covered in this chapter. Rather than try to cover as much detail as possible, we focused on aspects of the dominant EU discourse on governance and examined projects centred on the Lisbon Strategy in order to tease out the kind of ideas promoted by the EU and their relation to a set of strategies and techniques designed to influence policy-making in a number of areas. It should be clear how the discourse of the EU fits with a range of ideas covered in the first part of this book. The basis for justifying a certain set of methods or tools of governance is constructed out of ideas like globalisation, international competitiveness, technological change, information society and risk management. These are presented as inevitable developments over which we have no control. The actual strategies that are then employed are legitimised as reflexive responses that enhance people's choices, free them from the constraints of past social structures, encourage creativity, initiative and innovation, bring governance closer to the people, involve civil society and a wide range of actors and work through networks and partnerships in a mutual and pluralistic way. The reality is a managerial response that presents itself in technical terms and which works to depoliticise the process so that actually people's active involvement is extremely limited.

We can also see how this works as *liberal* governmentality. In particular, the European Commission operates from a distance, making suggestions, recommendations and promptings, but also operating through establishing the correct procedures, methods, aims and objectives with progress and performance measured through a set of targets, or through peer review and benchmarking. Having effectively defined what the agenda should be, the Commission steps back from this as if its role is that of a neutral observer that encourages Member States to act correctly and helps them to do this by offering technical support, information and a network of knowledge-sharing practices. Benchmarking is done through processes like OMC, which encourages peer review and the sharing of good practice. While results show that actually the targets are often not met, it is perhaps more important that states are locked into a network of governance that shapes their behaviour and conditions their way of thinking. This process works to responsibilise actors, and works through the familiar ideas of responsibility, reflection, ownership and partnership – issues, as we will see, that extend into the arena of global governance.

It might be suggested that the fact that many Member States failed to meet their Lisbon targets does not undermine the idea of governmentality, but highlights the fact that this is governance from a distance that tries to work through persuasion and encourages actors to do the right thing without having the power of compulsion. This meets with the idea that governmentality works to construct 'free subjects' who are encouraged, from a distance, to reflect upon their conduct and exercise their freedom in the right way. In any case, with OMC we are dealing with the governance, not of individual citizens, but Member States. It may be that OMC targets individuals in the form of state personnel, or it might even work by creating a new set of individuals within the state bureaucracy who differ from the traditional professionals of the welfare-state era. However, it comes up against the fact that states are not unified entities, but complex institutional ensembles containing within them a variety of different apparatuses and agents who may often have conflicting interests. The Gramscian literature best gets at this idea through its notion of the state as a strategic terrain upon which are acted out hegemonic projects that are made up of a diverse range of social agents.

Being more historically specific, we need to consider a wider set of changes, not fully explained by the governmentality literature, relating to the failure of the institutional settlement of the postwar era to offset the crisis tendencies in the capitalist economy through particular forms of regulation and a set of social compromises embodied in a complex historical bloc. How this process unfolds is a result of different social and historical conditions. Consequently, the impact of particular forms of governmentality will be different in different places according to their own socio-economic conditions and history and balance of social forces. It is inevitable, therefore, that if we are looking at governmentality across different countries, as we are with the EU, we will find it more entrenched in some places rather than others. We also find that governmentality operates at different levels. In the UK, where forms of governmentality are now almost a way of life, we find deep-rooted monitoring, safety and resilience assessments, government targets and benchmarking. Particular sectors like education are now governmentalised to such an extent that teachers and lecturers are required to continually assess their performance, monitor the delivery of their classes, measure the satisfaction of students and, in the case of higher education, measure their research in terms of outputs, outlets, audience, impact and financial reward. The governmentalisation of different sectors has reached different levels of development depending on the country. While the process has been going on throughout Europe, it is undoubtedly stronger in the Anglo-Saxon countries and those more influenced by the neoliberal model. Across Europe the acceptance of the neoliberal model as the only option has been pushed by the EU, but meets with some inertia and resistance. The fact that some countries are more protective of their economies, or that their state bureaucracy functions differently, or that they have different systems of welfare and, especially, where the labour movement and political opposition is organised and strong, inevitably reflects itself at the EU level and explains the unevenness of developments, as reflected in an assessment of the Lisbon Strategy. We have also recently seen the limits of governmentality in relation to deeper socio-economic processes that are not those constructed by the governmentality discourse itself, but separate developments like the economic crisis. The reaction to this, too, is different depending on different expressions of class consciousness, as reflected in mass protests in Greece and a quite different reaction in Germany and elsewhere.

That the functioning of governmentality is patchy and uneven points to the need to study the wider social context within which governmentality operates. Governmentality is not monolithic. It is one among a number of features of our complex social environment. This chapter has tried to suggest ways in which governmentality works inside the EU. More precisely, we should say that it is about how the EU would like governmentality to work. But the EU's own conclusions on Lisbon point to the fact that governmentality does not always work as well as the EU would like. The EU's ideology tries to hide this by simplifying the wider context and claiming a common purpose. But the underlying issue of different social contexts and different economic, political and cultural actors and environments really cannot be ignored as it affects the ability or even willingness of the governments of the EU Member States to implement strategies and achieve targets and benchmarks.

Ultimately the willingness of Member States to implement these measures is an internal matter. Rather than seeing the relationship between the EU and Member States as one of outside-in, it should be seen as inside-out. That is to say, the Commission is in effect encouraging what are ultimately strategies of state transformation (or governmentalisation of the state). The dynamics for change come from within these Member States rather than from outside (as the literature confusingly suggests). The failings of the Lisbon Strategy reflect differences across the different members of the EU relating to the degree to which this process of state transformation is taking place.

Whether the Lisbon Strategy should actually be considered a failure is a matter for discussion. The failure to achieve uniform results across the whole of the EU could actually work to strengthen the case for governmentality. The EU's response to its practical failings is to call for even more reflection, fine-tuning and consideration of appropriate measures. Qualitatively, however, the response to Lisbon has been an uninspiring offer of more of the same. This suggests that for governmentality, process is perhaps more important than the outcome. At least, however, we can see the significance of the relationship between domestic forms of governmentality within the Member States and the efforts to coordinate these changes at a transnational level. As we shall go on to see, with the World Bank and other attempts at global governance, not only is process more important than outcome, but the areas in which this actually works is more severely limited by actual social relations.

7 *Global governmentality and the World Bank*

This and the previous chapter try to illustrate how the ideas discussed in Part I play a role in the documents of international organisations. By choosing the examples of the transnational governmentality of the EU and the global governmentality of institutions like the World Bank we can also compare governmentality in different contexts. The previous chapter, in looking at the EU, suggested that the results of attempts to implement governmentality are uneven and that this is a consequence of governmentality existing across different societies with their different political, economic and cultural environments. However, it is certainly true to say that the governmentality approach of the EU finds some resonance in the societies of Member States and that this sort of governmentality can clearly be seen to have evolved as a form of rule within the 'advanced liberal societies'. The transnational governmentality of the EU is part of a 'multi-layered' governance that includes the EU institutions, civil society and the private sphere and which embraces the micro level of individual conduct. But perhaps most crucial of all – and something that the idea of multi-level governance does not really capture – is the degree to which the governmentalisation of the state is occurring within each of the Member States.

This chapter, like the last, focuses on governmentality across a number of different states rather than at a more grassroots domestic level. The actual approach to things like partnerships, benchmarking and peer review is quite similar. The difference lies in the way that international organisations like the IMF and World Bank impose techniques of governmentality on various countries from the outside without there being the same inside-out dynamic within the states themselves. This is an imposition, because this governmentality lacks an organic relationship to the particular social conditions within these countries. By highlighting the importance of social context, the argument of this chapter is also directed at the global governmentality literature by insisting that such an idea needs to pay attention to the disparity between the governmentalising impulse of international institutions, which inevitably reflects the rationality of the countries where they are based, and the actual social conditions where deployment takes place. This disparity draws attention to the uneven nature of international relations and the exercise of power by dominant countries over weaker ones through an outside-in dynamic. This latter idea means that there is a shift in focus of governmentality from the techniques that concern themselves with populations, to the regulation and disciplining of state behaviour in the interests of a neoliberal international agenda. To illustrate this, the chapter draws on the documentary output of various international organisations. Obviously there is too much to cover in one short chapter, so there will be more of a focus on the arguments of the World Bank, while introducing other international organisations in less detail to highlight similarities. The aim is to show how the arguments of these organisations reflect the ideas discussed in Part I, how such ideas cannot always hope to be fully implemented in relation to populations but also how they can be used to regulate the behaviour of states. This section will rely heavily on quotations from official reports and policy papers in order to show how the thinking of these organisations is set within a general discourse that reflects issues highlighted by theories of governmentality.

Building institutions for markets

To understand the current thinking of the World Bank, the best place to start is with its annual World Development Reports. These have been produced since 1978 and reflect the organisation's thinking on a range of different development topics. These reports are the Bank's main analytical statements and thus reflect particular changes in thinking. In 1997 the World Bank chose to address the role of the state in its World Development Report, *The State in a Changing World*. This came out following a number of World Bank documents in the 1990s on the concept of good governance. It was followed in 2002 by the World Development Report entitled *Building Institutions for Markets*. These two reports reflect, perhaps more than any other document, a new way of thinking inside the World Bank, something that has come to be known as the post-Washington consensus. This change in approach is reflected on some years later in another World Development Report:

Although the resulting 'Washington Consensus' is sometimes interpreted as anti-state, this is not the main message that survives after more measured consideration. Instead, just as events in the 1990s confirmed that markets were essential for development, they also showed that good governments are essential for well-functioning markets. Markets operate within a framework determined by institutions, and they work only as well as those institutions do. They work best, therefore, when a capable state maintains order within the rule of law, provides effective regulation, macroeconomic stability and other public goods, and corrects other market failures. (World Bank 2005a: 226)

This new approach is often simplistically attributed to a change in leadership inside the World Bank and the new line that was pushed by the then president, James D. Wolfensohn, and chief economist, Joseph Stiglitz. The latter talks of a new agenda of seeing markets and governments working together, of taking a 'special responsibility for government to create the institutional infrastructure that markets require in order to work effectively' (Stiglitz 2001: 346) – such things as laws, legal institutions, property rights, competition and antitrust enforcement. He discusses the need for financial regulation to guarantee the safety of banking (an ironic comment in light of subsequent events), and the need for government to mobilise capital, allocate investment, support education and training, develop technology and promote equality (2001: 347). In turn, governments become more effective if they make proper use of market mechanisms. Since these reflections are in a volume edited by Giddens, he emphasises the importance of reflexive government, especially in relation to the use of regulations (2001: 348). While this might be more likely in developed economies, he considers the World Bank to have a vital role in helping poorer countries develop the necessary institutional infrastructure required to attract capital, especially through advising on the best practices for successful development (2001: 352).

Noting, therefore, how countries in sub-Saharan Africa are suffering from a crisis of state capabilities, the World Bank now places priority on rebuilding state capacities by overhauling public institutions, reasserting the rule of law and checking the abuse of state power (World Bank 1997: 14). This emphasis on state capacity-building is clearly a big change from the structural adjustment programmes of the 1980s, whose pro-free market emphasis might be said to be against the role of the state. The change in emphasis in the 1990s now sees the state playing a crucial role in providing a macroeconomic and a microeconomic environment, developing an institutional infrastructure and ensuring basic education, health care and the physical infrastructure required for economic activity (1997: 31). This approach can be summarised as one of 'rais[ing] state capability by reinvigorating public institutions' (1997: 3). In the opening of *The State in a Changing World* this is explained in terms of

> designing effective rules and restraints, to check arbitrary state actions and combat entrenched corruption. It means subjecting state institutions to greater competition, to increase their efficiency. It means increasing the performance of state institutions, improving pay and incentives. And it means making the state more responsive to people's needs, bringing government closer to the people through broader participation and decentralization. (World Bank 1997: 3)

These themes should be familiar to us as key features of governmentality – limits on state behaviour, reflection on the exercise of state power, judging institutions by their performance, introducing economic measures to judge effectiveness, decentralising power and appealing to the idea of civil society and public participation to understand government effectiveness. We will start with the most important feature of contemporary governmentality, the idea of the limitations of state activity. The first and most significant of these limits is one of the imagination, for one could be forgiven for thinking that the world of the World Bank is one where everything must be judged against the market. While the state may exist in a 'changing world', there can be no other basis for assessing the credibility of government than through how it relates to markets:

> [M]arkets and governments are complementary: the state is essential for putting in place the appropriate institutional foundations for markets. And government's credibility – the predictability of its rules and policies and the consistency with which they are applied – can be as important for attracting private investment as the content of those rules and policies. (World Bank 1997: 4)

The framework imposed by thinking of things in terms of the rationality of the discourse of political economy means that the state is always regarded as a potential threat to the proper functioning of markets.

Ironically, the first stage of limiting the exercise of government is through the reflexivity of government itself; that is to say: 'Institutions that limit the state's capacity for arbitrary action will improve its ability to provide institutions that support broad-based markets' (World Bank 2002: 100). The second way that government is seen as limited is through the role of competition. As the World Bank says: 'Competition is an important force in promoting institutional change as well as economic development and growth. Competition can create demand for more effective institutions, and it can sometimes also substitute for complicated regulation' (2002: 149). We know that while the World Bank might want to present competition as a normal, healthy state of affairs, there is nothing natural about it – indeed seeing it through the governmentality lens means recognising its artificial nature as something imposed on different social spheres. Likewise, the third way the World Bank suggests limiting government is to forcibly impose decentralisation of powers while simultaneously invoking the empowerment of civil society and local partners:

> Decentralizing state power and resources seems a logical continuation of the many recent efforts to bring government closer to the people. Like the broad range of participatory mechanisms described earlier, decentralization offers the chance to match public services more closely with local demands and preferences and to build more responsive and accountable government from below. (World Bank 1997: 120)

As well as these three ways of limiting the state's power – reflexive government, competition and civil society – this issue of limits of the state's power is conceived through an inside–outside dichotomy. From the outside the state is influenced by the 'global events and international agreements [that] are increasingly affecting its choices' (World Bank 1997: 12). Sometimes this takes the form of 'partnerships' with external stakeholders, at other times it is the competitive pressure of markets that makes itself felt in state institutions. Things like flows of capital expose developing countries to danger, making it essential for states to develop sound macroeconomic policies, a strong legal system and a transparent regime of investors' rights and regulations (World Bank 1999: 6–7). The context for this discussion is the assumption that globalisation is an external pressure that states have no choice but to adjust to. They must make themselves 'good homes for long-term foreign investment' by developing the sort of institutional structure best able to work with global economic and financial markets (1999: 7). The inside–outside dichotomy is expressed through the familiar idea of the global and the local:

> Responding to these new forces of globalization and localization requires robust mediating institutions, especially when countries commit to take actions in a crisis, separately or collectively. Institutions serve to balance the diverse interests of society and to determine how the forces of development distribute their benefits and advantages, their costs and risks. (1999: 174)

These same dynamics are therefore also said to be present inside the country. As might be expected from a governmentality perspective, this is conceived of in terms of measuring state capability and meeting performance criteria. The advice of the World Bank is that:

> State capability will also be improved by institutional arrangements that foster partnerships with, and provide competitive pressures from, actors both outside and within the state. Partnerships with and participation in state activities by external stakeholders – businesses and civil society – can build credibility and consensus and supplement low state capability. Partnerships within the state can build commitment and loyalty on the part of government workers and reduce the costs of achieving shared goals.
>
> The flip side of partnership is competitive pressure – from markets and civil society and within the state itself. Such pressure can improve incentives for performance and check the abuse of the state's monopoly in policymaking and service delivery. Similarly, competitive or merit-based recruitment and promotion are crucial for building a capable bureaucracy. (World Bank 1997: 78)

We know by now that inside countries the idea of civil society is something to be appealed to by the 'good governance' discourse in order to provide a link, as Abrahamsen says, between the idea of democratisation and the drive to economic liberalisation, to provide a counterbalance to the state sphere and to safeguard against corruption and bad practice (Abrahamsen 2000: 52). This discourse weaves together the ideas of competition and accountability, somehow presenting the situation as one where states most show their accountability – principally in the interests of fostering market competition – while the accountability of markets is of course never raised. As the World Bank puts it:

> At the local level, states should focus on the processes and incentives for building accountability and competition. Where local governments are weakly accountable and unresponsive, improving both horizontal accountability (to the public) and vertical accountability (to the center) will be a vital first step toward greater state capability. (World Bank 1997: 130)

Hence all talk of encouraging civil society must be seen not as an end in itself, but as a way of supporting markets. Given the weakness of many states, especially in Africa, a new orthodoxy emerged within these international organisations that claimed to be building governance from the bottom up, using civil society as a way of pressurising states to reform and open up their mechanisms of governance. We will examine this focus on civil society in a later section. But while this emphasis was new, the reasons for it were the same – faith in the free market as the best way to encourage development. So a 'strong and capable state is necessary to support markets, and an arbitrary and corrupt state can impede their development' (World Bank 2002: 26). Therefore, 'good political institutions limit the arbitrary use of power by individuals, encourage competition in the political process, delegate responsibility and promote accountability' (2002: 100). If all this works, then such institutions would better be able to channel information about market conditions, define and enforce property rights and increase competition (2002: 8). Summarising all this:

> Good governance includes the creation, protection, and enforcement of property rights, without which the scope for market transactions is limited. It includes the provision of a regulatory regime that works with the market to promote competition. And it includes the provision of sound macroeconomic policies that create a stable environment for market activity. Good governance also means the absence of corruption, which can subvert the goals of policy and undermine the legitimacy of the public institutions that support markets. (2002: 99)

There is a partial recognition that this is more likely in rich countries, in that higher per capita incomes, stronger property rights and an absence of corruption to some extent reflect a 'greater capacity of rich countries to provide good institutions' (2002: 99). But still the free-market ideology suggests that if states can somehow support the process of economic liberalisation, then this will provide the best basis for improving living standards in poorer countries, 'providing opportunities to engage in productive activities, and by empowering citizens ... [in order to] promote growth and reduce poverty' (2002: 26). This: 'Competition improves efficiency, increases incentives for innovation, and promotes wider access' (2002: 76). Unfortunately, the World Bank's own examples of countries who have been able to do this always name the same select few like Botswana, Chile and Mauritius (World Bank 1997: 41).

Yet whether or not such strategies are successful on the ground, we can certainly see that the World Bank has a particular discourse that fits well with our study of governmentality. The mix of government, civil society and the market is prominent in the new discourse of empowerment and social capital. Take this statement from the *Attacking Poverty* World Development Report:

> Opportunity, empowerment, and security have intrinsic value for poor people. And given the important complementarities among them, an effective poverty reduction strategy will require action on all three fronts, by the full range of agents in society – government, civil society, the private sector, and poor people themselves. (World Bank 2001: 33)

We will see in a later section how this concern with poverty reduction strategies is expressed through auditing and benchmarking processes. Here we will concentrate on the conceptual framework used by the World Bank. We find, as mentioned, numerous references to civil society:

> The benefits of greater consultation and partnership with civil society show up in improvements in the process of public policymaking, in the quality of service delivery, and, in some instances, in improved rates of return. They also manifest themselves in the greater flexibility afforded to public agencies and officials in the way they intervene. (World Bank 1997: 120)

This in turn is founded on the kinds of technological and infrastructural developments discussed in earlier chapters. Advances in technology are said to provide greater flexibility, transparency and protection against monopoly abuse. Open information flows allow for the sharing of ideas and information and so further encourage institutional reform (World Bank 2002: 182). The World Bank sees its role as a knowledge bank, helping countries to develop their policies through linking local knowledge with international experience. In particular, it is keen to link open information flows and technological development to concepts like human and social capital (2002: 27).

All this is brought together by the key idea of empowerment. According to the World Bank definition: 'Empowerment means enhancing the capacity of poor people to influence the state institutions that affect their lives, by strengthening their participation in political processes and local decision-making' (World Bank 2001: 39). Responsive states and social institutions are required to facilitate access to market opportunities and public services. The empowerment of poor people 'is part of the broader agenda of sound governance and accountability of state institutions to their citizens' (2001: 39). This is said to allow better access to jobs, credit, roads and health (2001: 6), while enhancing security and reducing vulnerability to economic shocks, natural disasters (2001: 7) (we will cover these issues later). The state is responsible for encouraging private investment through creating a transparent business environment, developing stable fiscal and monetary policy and investment regimes (2001: 8). Thus the best way of promoting opportunity is to make institutions more accountable and responsive, reduce both physical and economic vulnerability and stimulate growth through building people's assets.

This latter idea brings us back to the terrain of social capital, a key concept that was taken up inside the World Bank and which is prominent in many World Development Reports. We will also see the role social capital plays in the discourse of other international organisations like the UN. For the World Bank, a simple definition of social capital 'refers to the networks and relationships that both encourage trust and reciprocity and shape the equality and quantity of a society's social interactions' (World Bank 1999: 18). The World Bank's emphasis on things like civil society, local networks and voluntary associations suggests both ways to protect against the worst effects of exposure to the global economy and how to move forward with a development agenda that links markets to public institutions as poor people draw on social capital, social norms and networks to move out of poverty (World Bank 2001: 10). As we have seen, the concept of social capital manages to simultaneously emphasise the social while promoting individual self-maximising behaviour; it claims to be based on social norms, while reducing these norms to economic conditions. As a statement by the World Bank puts it:

Social capital refers to the internal social and cultural coherence of society, the norms and values that govern interactions among people and the institutions in which they are embedded. Social capital is the glue that holds societies together and without which there can be no economic growth or human well-being. (Grootaert 1998: iii)

The problem, however, is that if it is true that social capital is something that is formed over time and deeply embedded in common understandings, then even if we were to accept the World Bank's arguments, this concept is radically at odds with the way that intervention by international organisations takes place. This is hinted at in Ostrom's contribution to a World Bank discussion of social capital and economic development, where she writes:

> It is these mutually reinforcing sets of relationships between private and public sector investments and activities that one can call economic development. Social capital plays as essential a role in achieving that development as physical or human capital. It does not represent, however, a quick fix that can be created by external or top-down processes. (Ostrom 2000: 202)

This is a very serious point given our argument that global governmentality is largely an imposition on poorer societies rather than something that organically develops within them. While much work has been done on how social capital works in Western societies, one really has to wonder whether such models can have explanatory power in places where civil society does not conform to the Western model and where local networks are often bypassed or ignored if they do not immediately fit with the free-market agenda of Western development partners. While the World Bank claims to be adopting a bottom-up approach, we will go on to look at how the differences in the nature of civil society mean that the World Bank has to construct or fabricate something more suitable to its policies.

Here, then, lies an important issue in the deployment of concepts. For the idea of social capital played a key role in the World Bank's literature, but then suddenly lost its influence because of some of the problems mentioned above. Ultimately the concept got caught between the Bank's hard-core economists and those seeking to use the concept to promote a more social agenda. Hence the explanation for the use of the concept of social capital has more to do with discussions inside the institution rather than whether it can really succeed in practice (especially outside of the Western liberal context where the idea developed). This point needs some qualification in so far as the advocates of a social-capital approach inside the World Bank were indeed concerned with how the social-capital discussion could influence operational strategy. They believed that these discussions could allow people to talk more openly about the role of local organisations and social networks in helping development and poverty reduction. But whether the concept is really that important in and of itself, or whether its deployment was more of a strategic move by a group of researchers inside the Bank is an issue now raised by the reflections of a number of these insiders who say that the influence of the concept 'is the outcome of more than a decade of network and alliance building – initially around concepts such as participation, environment, and sustainability, and more recently around terms such as empowerment and social capital' (Bebbington *et al.* 2004: 57). While these comments reveal the strategic nature of the social-capital debate, their reference to other ideas like participation and empowerment points to wider institutional matters. For critics like Ben Fine, the use of the concept of social capital should ultimately be understood as little more than a rhetorical device for smoothing the transition from the Washington to post-Washington consensus (Fine 2010: 126). The fact that the concept could mean almost all things to all people helps explain its rapid rise. But it also explains why it is that once a wider literature on development had emerged, the concept started to lose its significance.

The Comprehensive Development Framework and Poverty Reduction Strategies

Recognising failing growth rates, the World Bank launched its Comprehensive Development Framework (CDF) in 1999, shifting the focus from conditionality to ownership and donor coordination. It now cast the role of international organisations as one of providing technical assistance to promote capacity-building and encourage greater participation in the poverty-reduction process. It has four principles which by now should be very familiar – each country should have ownership of the policy agenda; this should be in partnership with stakeholders; attention should be paid to social and structural concerns; and a long-term holistic approach should be taken (World Bank 2001: 195). The idea of country ownership requires that each country should be able to direct its own development agenda and should encourage the participation of its citizens and local groups. Partnership with stakeholders means coordination between governments, donors, civil society and other groups. This focus on civil society, social capital and local empowerment is seen as the most effective way of bringing people together and building social cohesion. The argument for long-term infrastructural goals rather than just short-term macroeconomic stabilisation and balance of payments comes across most strongly in the national poverty-reduction strategies. The World Bank and IMF together launched the Poverty Reduction Strategy (PRS) in 1999 with the aim of helping what are called the Heavily Indebted Poor Countries to improve their national development strategies. As a follow-up, the 2005 Paris Declaration on Aid Effectiveness gives twelve indicators for managing mutual accountability. The Declaration argues that aid partnerships must be based on mutual accountability, with aid recipients expected to improve their policy-making (World Bank 2007: xi). This section will largely focus on the way such organisations emphasise indicators and targets without necessarily doing anything to improve the lives of real people. This is in keeping with our idea that the actual health, wealth and well-being of populations is less the target than the means by which governmentality can be imposed on states by getting them to agree to a monitoring process that subjects them to governance through the exercise of their agreement to abide by certain norms of behaviour and responsibilised self-conduct.

The new approach to aid emphasises the idea of partnership. Thus an aid relationship is seen as a reciprocal one, implying mutual accountability:

> [A]id recipient countries are expected to make efforts to improve their policies and policymaking while their development partners are expected to provide more and better aid, aligning their support with country-owned policies and relying to the extent possible on countries' own systems and national institutions to deliver the aid. (World Bank 2007: 1)

Establishing a framework for mutual accountability means, for the World Bank, putting in place mechanisms for monitoring performance and measuring progress (2007: 2). Hence, the Paris Declaration brings in country-wide monitoring of data on development outcomes, measures performance and emphasises domestic accountability and government credibility. This is packaged in terms of a development 'partnership' that helps improve country ownership of development strategies (2007: xii). As with other forms of governmentality, this relationship is seen in calculable and instrumental terms: 'Governments and external partners will need to shift their overall balance of attention towards developing results-oriented frameworks during the coming years' (2007: xvi). While this results-orientated framework sounds like it is concerned with improving the well-being of populations, it is really all about monitoring states' behaviour. Results are judged by level of compliance rather than any sort of success on the ground. In talking of major objectives, the World Bank lists the collecting of statistics, its support for the implementation of country statistical strategies and the need to develop communication strategies and improve dissemination efforts (2007: xvii). In terms of measuring success, the World Bank makes claims such as how in 2007, 13 per cent of 62 countries covered by the review had a largely developed operational development strategy (2007: 6). When the framework talks of the need to develop a unified strategic framework with a coherent long-term vision, it means that countries must set themselves long-term development targets based on national ownership of development strategy. Again, success in this field is measured in terms of the degree to which such measures are implemented – for example, that by 2003, almost 60 per cent of countries had taken some action towards reaching agreement among government and stakeholders on a national development strategy (World Bank 2005b: 4).

What we see with these strategies is typical of exercises in governmentality that focus on monitoring, auditing and benchmarking as ends in themselves or as processes that govern their own standards of legitimacy. The aim is less that of actual poverty reduction, than setting up reporting processes and sectoral monitoring. Governments following Poverty Reduction Strategies are required to produce an annual progress report for every year of PRS implementation and to meet various objectives relating to government performance in poverty reduction and government accountability to citizens. Various government institutions are required to give regular administrative reports, with more developed sectoral monitoring and reporting required in areas like health and education. Additionally, governments are charged with the responsibility of improving their use of surveys and statistics on poverty outcomes (see Wilhelm and Krause 2008: 43, 46).

Combined with this focus on 'government leadership and coordination across the executive and local governments', the PRS 'has encouraged many countries to reach out to stakeholders in an unprecedented way, sometimes building on other movements that have resulted in permanent mechanisms for stakeholder participation' (World Bank 2005b: 17). A World Bank report by Wilhelm and Krause brings together a number of themes such as government accountability, stakeholder partnerships, monitoring, evaluation and reflexivity:

> The Poverty Reduction Strategy (PRS) approach aims to enhance accountability by promoting the participation of domestic stakeholders in the formulation of clear and realistic development goals. Institutions for monitoring and evaluation, including annual progress reports, are designed to trigger learning and improved performance. (Wilhelm and Krause 2008: 1)

This idea of domestic stakeholders brings us back to the promotion of civil society participation, which for the World Bank 'brings elements of legitimacy, accountability, and continuity to national development strategies'. This brings legitimacy to the strategy in so far as 'stakeholders' inputs and assessments are accounted for, signalling that the government and key national stakeholders are broadening their areas of agreement' (World Bank 2005b: 19). Even this aspect is monitored, although the actual outcomes are predictably weak – according to the World Bank, civil society participation in shaping PRS is largely developed in just one tenth of the countries (notably Tanzania and Uganda), although it is claimed that 'two-thirds of the countries have taken action to systematically involve civil society organizations in dialogue with the government' (2005b: 19).

We will summarise these arguments later. But what the CDF and PRS initiatives tell us is that international organisations have moved to force countries to regulate themselves through a combination of responsibilised ownership and partnership, both of which rely on the idea that the recipient of assistance will 'do the right thing'. Recipient countries are required to develop realistic plans to tackle poverty. They may draft their own PRS but, as Lyakurwa says, stakeholders' perceptions are important in determining how these plans are implemented, while the role of institutions like the IMF and World Bank is clouded by their claim that their new role is to advise and support programmes, while letting countries find their own way to implement policies (Lyakurwa 2005: 169, 174). In fact it is quite clear that the World Bank and IMF have the power to veto a country's PRS, resulting in countries losing their aid and trade credits. Governments have to submit their Poverty Reduction Strategy Papers (PRSP) to the executive boards of the World Bank and IMF, and an assessment is made on whether the strategy qualifies for concessional assistance (Klugman 2002: 4). Thus, countries are free to find their own policies only in so far as they find the right ones, while support for institutions must always be with the aim of encouraging markets to develop.

The construction of civil society

The promotion of civil society has to be understood in the context of strategies to regulate state actions and decentralise service provision. The World Bank's understanding of civil society involvement is premised on the belief that Civil Society Organisations (CSO) can deliver services more efficiently than centralised governments (World Bank 2006: 1). The Bank's review of its engagement with civil society notes the growing importance of its relationship to civil society in shaping policy dialogue and country-level operational cooperation. It suggests that this dialogue is an open and horizontal form of collaboration that has opened up new and profitable ways of designing, implementing and reviewing things like PRS and other areas of Bank–government–civil society engagement (2006: 67). Civil society is seen as a way of getting local involvement in development policy loans, improving governance and setting up accountability mechanisms. CSO involvement, therefore, is seen in explicit terms as a way of introducing 'social accountability mechanisms' and monitoring performance (2006: 49).

Two of the World Bank's most prominent examples of civil society involvement are Ghana and Tanzania. The Bank talks of the participatory nature of Ghana's PRSP revision process, noting the involvement of NGOs, trade unions, the government and private sector in extensive consultations at national and local levels. It also notes the extensive use of public forums, for example focus groups, workshops and broad use of the media (2006: 93). In Tanzania the first PRSP was followed by a one-year consultation process which likewise involved local and national groups in workshops and training sessions. It is noted how stakeholder workshops included 'representatives from district council secretariats, faith-based organizations, persons with disabilities, NGOs, community organizations, persons living with HIV/AIDS, trade unions, and businesses' (2006: 99). Village-level consultations also took place alongside a large-scale opinion survey and radio and television communication. Extensive use of the Internet was also evident.

This brings us to the more general issue of involving civil society groups through workshops, training, the media and new information technology. The World Bank makes this a prominent feature of its reports. It also fits with the idea that the World Bank provides support for 'capacity-building', both through training and workshops for government officials and civil society groups, and through information sharing and use of knowledge and information flows. However, it should be recognised that this gives international organisations and donors a new form of authority. Returning to the two examples of Tanzania and Ghana, we see this relationship in operation.[1] For example, Claire Mercer suggests that the prohibitive costs of online connections in Tanzania means that local networking is very difficult and that international NGOs based in Western countries can effectively act as information gatekeepers, and that information, once 'corporatised', is filtered down to local NGOs (Mercer 2004: 54). A fetish for IT means that local NGOs are cherry-picked, often on the basis of 'trendy' development issues rather than providing more mundane administrative support. The consequence is that NGO involvement reflects the interests of donors and international organisations rather than local people, while emphasis on things like information technology appeals to a small urban NGO elite rather than a broader grassroots constituency (2004: 56, 58).

This kind of dependency relationship means that CSOs are either a product of the development process, or else they soon lose their autonomy as they enter into partnership with governments and aid donors. In looking at the situation in Ghana, Julie Hearn suggests that the result is that such groups end up building consensus and adjusting to poverty rather than challenging it (Hearn 2001: 45). If this is really the case, then what role do such organisations actually play? Hearn's

[1] The World Bank's *Civil Society Engagement Review* of 2006 contains the following summary of its involvement in Ghana:

> The revision of the first PRSP was based on a one-year consultation process led by the government and involving the general public. The Association of Local Authorities of Tanzania played a lead role in the first round of nationwide consultations held in December 2003. This was followed by a series of training-the-trainers workshops for the facilitators who were then deployed in the country. District-level consultations were conducted through multi-stakeholder workshops, which included representatives from district council secretariats, faith-based organizations, persons with disabilities,

suggestion is that they play the role of implementers and monitors. This means that rather than challenging the government, such groups play a role in ensuring that services are delivered efficiently and accountably. In partnership with donors and governments, CSOs act as external monitors who lend credibility to the implementation of poverty reduction policies (2001: 50–1). Operating in this manner, members of local NGOs attach themselves to the aid process, not so much to raise grassroots demands as to access funding opportunities presented by outside interventions. The consequence, as Lazarus notes, is to direct resources to the better-off, better-organised and most articulate actors, normally a professional urban elite (Lazarus 2008: 1210).

All this points to how little involvement local people really have in a process designed and enforced by outside organisations that gather a local elite around them simply as a means of regulating state actions, decentralising service provision and monitoring performance. While the World Bank talks of the need to encourage wider participation, in reality, the agenda is nearly always set in advance, with little scope for genuine discussion, and no real possibility of criticism. International organisations use a highly technical and depoliticised language, with the main proposals established in advance and little opportunity for any significant period of consultation (Fraser 2005: 326). For all the talk of engaging civil society, studies have shown that processes like the PRSP involve very few local groups, indeed that very few such groups can be expected to emerge from domestic social processes. The nature of international intervention maintains such a situation rather than enhancing local involvement. As Fraser neatly summarises:

> The problem of a lack of 'capacity' in civil society can, therefore, be understood as a lack of capacity to rehearse political arguments in the form of 'planning knowledge'. And 'capacity building' can be understood as a

NGOs, community organizations, persons living with HIV/AIDS, trade unions, and businesses. Village-level consultations were also undertaken through village assemblies. The inputs received at the village and district levels were then consolidated to form a region-wide feedback report. Broader communication was also carried out via radio, television, and the Internet, as well as through an opinion survey that was distributed to about 500,000 throughout the country. Reports of the first-round consultations were consolidated into the first PRSP draft, which was then posted on the Internet for additional feedback from stakeholders. Further deliberations on the second draft were made during a national workshop held in September 2004, which brought together representatives from government, civil society, and the business community. (World Bank 2006: 99) process of teaching elite cadres within civil society to express themselves in an appropriate and professional manner – to perform as a version of Western 'good citizens'. (2005: 330–1)

Lazarus is equally scathing, claiming that local participation amounts to no more than limited consultation, often staged simply to satisfy donor demands. The politics of donorship require the rhetoric of local involvement accompanied by strategies designed to keep this process limited to a few privileged participants (Lazarus 2008: 1207).

All this suggests that the sort of civil society international organisations wish to engage with is at best a selected one, at worst a fabrication based on the imposition of a private-sector development model. The capacity-building process creates a professional elite that is entirely tied to the aims of international organisations rather than grassroots people. International intervention might involve partnerships with urban elites who engage with the state and are involved in issues like human rights and democracy promotion, but usually ignores more traditional associations based on family, clan, tribe and religion (Howell and Pearce 2001: 188). As Howell and Pearce note of civil society programmes in Ghana, South Africa and Uganda, the power of the urban elites is strengthened because they share with donors an interest in economic liberalisation and procedural democracy, but the interests of local peasants and farmers will in all likelihood be ignored (2001: 189). This also reflects liberalism's conventional attachment to a 'modern middle class' as the basis for a stable liberal-democratic system, regardless of whether this really exists (Ayers 2008: 15). The civil society approach therefore functions in order to support certain strategies and techniques used by international organisations to impose a sort of discipline on these societies. The grassroots effects may be marginal, but these interventions can work at the national level to discipline governments and emphasise the need for social consensus, particularly in relation to economic strategies. Indeed, it might be suggested that the main aim of these strategies is not to give local ownership but to force local groups to give their support to these programmes (Ruckert 2009: 65).[2] The technical approach of international organisations allows for

[2] Ruckert (2009: 65) gives as an example the IMF's claim that this process 'will make it easier to generate domestic political support for the program, since it is likely to be seen, at least in part, as an indigenous product, rather than a foreign imposition' (IMF 2001: 14).

the exclusion of potentially hostile groups who have political agendas outside the strategic remit, and also enhances the power of organisations like the World Bank, which exerts leverage through its role as a knowledge provider with privileged access to information flows and technical expertise. The local consequences of these civil society projects, as many commentators have noted, are the production of lopsided local dynamics of very little use to local populations. Craig and Porter, for example, look at the case of Uganda, a country that has made considerable efforts to meet PRSP requirements, and note how the focus on technical requirements like best practice rules and accountable delivery of resources has had a detrimental effect on the functioning of local political authorities (Craig and Porter 2003: 66). Even the more supportive literature on this topic – an assessment by Cheru, for example, which is positive in regarding the PRSP approach as a unique opportunity for African governments – nevertheless concludes that there are serious problems with implementation, participation and achievement of goals (Cheru 2006).

This returns us to the argument that global governmentality involves the targeting of local states, but that the techniques used are entirely inappropriate for the governance of local populations. The follies of the argument for devolving state power to an artificially constructed civil society are noted by Marcussen's comment in relation to sub-Saharan Africa:

> If development strategies in Africa are built on a minimalist state in combination with a strengthened civil society in many respects replacing the state – an effort which to a great extent is funded externally and implemented through northern and southern NGOs – the result may well be an anomaly, artificially constructed and externally driven. The resulting asymmetry might easily risk being not only unsustainable, but even unstable and perhaps violent. (Marcussen 1996: 421)

But while Marcussen goes on to suggest that more support should be given to those local NGOs that have the appropriate knowledge of local conditions, we are suggesting that such a solution cannot work, as helping local groups assist local populations is not the main intention of international intervention. Since the main aim of intervention is not to improve local conditions, but to impose a form of global governmentality that regulates the behaviour of states and their governments in the interests of global capital, what goes on in civil society is entirely dependent on the mechanisms used to govern states. Rather than starting with local populations and looking at how they can be helped, we should look at how global governmentality is directed at states, seeking to regulate them through appearing to be concerned with the health and welfare of their populations. Leaving aside questions of whether the concern of international organisations is genuine, albeit misguided, our analysis sees the construction of civil society as a means of raising the issues of self-limitation of government, devolution of state power and, most importantly, promotion of free and open markets.

Dealing with risk

As well as making states responsible for their poverty-reduction strategies, international organisations intervene in a governmentalising manner by trying to make states responsible for developing their own national programmes capable of responding to what are described as financial and natural macro shocks. This process, which combines deliberations on how to best protect the poor with the promotion of free-market risk-taking, is described by the World Bank as one of designing pro-growth systems of social-risk management (World Bank 2001: 11). Indeed, the discourse of risk-taking has a runaway character, moving swiftly from protection to free-market opportunism: 'Providing protection for poor people (reducing vulnerability in dealing with risk) not only makes them feel less vulnerable – it also allows them to take advantage of higher-risk, higher-return opportunities' (2001: 15). At least it is recognised that some places have greater vulnerabilities. Focusing on poorer countries, we see how World Bank and IMF papers develop the notion of shock; that is, an event with an unexpected impact on their economies that is beyond the control of the government. These shocks may range from market volatility, fluctuations in interest and exchange rates and shocks to commodity prices, to natural disasters, diseases and conflict-related events (Martin and Bargawi 2005: 44). The consequence of these events can be to make debt unsustainable, cause uncertainty in public and private sectors and reduce the scope for poverty reduction strategies (2005: 53). In these cases the IMF uses Poverty Reduction and Growth Facility (PRGF) loans and Exogenous Shocks Facility arrangements and suggests the adjustment of macroeconomic policy. The World Bank intervenes through donor support via its Poverty Reduction Support Credit (PRSC). Both link to the PRSP discussed earlier and stress the involvement of civil society and other development partners, as well as making the inevitable references to a good-governance approach that encourages the private sector.[3] To summarise the new World Bank and IMF approach we can quote a World Development Report, *Attacking Poverty*, which states: 'In addressing risk and vulnerability, the issue once again is whether public interventions and institutions work well – and in the interests of poor people' (World Bank 2001: 40). The post-Washington consensus approach of these institutions is to assess these interventions and institutions through the good-governance agenda that in turn is based on an assessment of how well these institutions can work with the free market.

The World Bank also does work on individual and household risk using a Social Risk Management framework to link risks to welfare levels. It covers specific regions through Poverty Assessments and various development reports. Strategy Papers make risk and vulnerability assessments and attempt to identify formal and informal coping mechanisms. The risk and vulnerability assessments identify gaps in various public risk management programmes and not surprisingly find solutions to these problems in the development of a new set of vulnerability indicators and a more rigorous form of data collection (Kozal *et al.* 2008: 32). We could go into a lot more detail on this area of World Bank activity, but to give an indication of the scope of the governmentality discourse within international organisations, we will switch from looking at the World Bank to looking at similar arguments presented by the UNDP in *Reducing Disaster Risk: A Challenge for Development*. Although this is a document specifically about risk – itself a significant means of exercising governmentality – we see that it also divides neatly into other key themes already discussed, such things as capacity-building, good governance, stakeholder partnerships, social capital, networks and civil society and, above all, the use

[3] See the World Bank and IMF websites for more details on these. For example, the IMF page www.imf.org/external/np/exr/facts/prgf.htm, accessed 19 December 2009, and the more detailed account of the IMF's role in the PRF at www.imf.org/external/np/pdr/prsp/poverty2.htm, accessed 19 December 2009. For the World Bank's webpages on Poverty Reduction Support Credits see www1.worldbank.org/publicsector/civilservice/acrext/vol1page3.htm, accessed 19 December 2009.

of data for benchmarking and monitoring performance. On the capacity-building front, the UNDP claims that it has made considerable progress in building programmes in disaster reduction and recovery. The UNDP supports the implementation of the International Strategy for Disaster Reduction agenda at a national and regional level,[4] reinforced by partnerships with various international organisations and UN agencies like the Office for Coordination of Humanitarian Affairs. The UNDP goes on to talk of the importance of international financial institutions like the World Bank and the regional development banks that link the question of disaster risk with economic development. The document also stresses the linkage with international civil society and organisations which, it is claimed, have moved the disaster management agenda from mitigation and preparedness, towards deeper integration with development processes (UNDP 2004: 18). All this, then, fits with the good-governance agenda and a belief in stakeholder partnerships:

> At the heart of good governance is a commitment to sharing decision-making power between the stakeholders in a process. This must be built on the political will to accept power-sharing and see the state as a facilitator in development. This contrasts with the conception of the government as the dominant actor shaping development and disaster risk management. (UNDP 2004: 75)

The idea of the state as a facilitator fits with the capacity-building role and with the idea of a networked state based on partnerships with stakeholders. The UNDP document emphasises the role of social capital and civil society, both domestically and internationally, claiming that civil society and social capital are not only local institutions, but have support within networks throughout the world (2004: 80). The UNDP definition of social capital tallies with the previously mentioned World Bank conception:

> Social capital refers to those stocks of social trust, norms and networks that people derive from membership in different types of social collectives. Social capital, measured by levels of trust, cooperation and reciprocity in a social group, plays the most important role in shaping actual resilience to disaster

[4] See the website www.unisdr.org.

shocks and stress. Local level community response remains the most important factor enabling people to reduce and cope with the risks associated with disaster. But community ties can be eroded by long-term or extreme social stress. (2004: 7)

In the context of risk, the concept of social capital is used to emphasise the importance of building social or community bonds in order to reduce vulnerability. Such things as social cohesion, inclusiveness and open participation in decision-making are all mentioned as means of achieving development in communities at risk from disaster (2004: 24).

These community issues are also developed through the deployment of a relatively new term – resilience. Social capital is mentioned in the document as the best way to build resilience within those communities threatened by shocks and disasters (2004: 80). Resilience is a concept that might be understood alongside capacity-building as the means and abilities a community or individuals within it might have to withstand shocks and indeed to bounce back and flourish. Seen through the governmentality lens we might say that the concept is best understood less through the focus on external shocks and more through the idea of encouraging particular forms of self-organisation, responsibility, adaptability, learning and governance.[5]

The building of a disaster-risk index allows for calculation of risks relating to populations, for example the average risk of death per country from disasters such as earthquakes, tropical cyclones and floods and the identification of different socio-economic and environmental variables that correlate with risk to death (2004: 30). This aims to enhance global indexing of risk and vulnerability, encourage national risk-indexing for the benefit of national decision-makers and to develop a multi-tiered system of disaster reporting (2004: 93). This makes certain issues 'thinkable' in particular ways, while encouraging 'responsible' management of the problems.

All of this provides plenty of evidence to those who would use a Foucauldian framework to look at how the UN and other organisations govern through risk and uncertainty, compiling cross-country

[5] For a more lengthy account of the UNDP's idea of resilience see *World Resources 2008: Roots of Resilience* (UNDP 2008). For a governmentality account of the concept see Lentzos and Rose (2009).

and regional data while using a biopolitics of populations to encourage local participation. For example, Phillips and Ilcan have argued that the management of risks – particularly in the area of biotechnology[6] – can work to mobilise the agency of local people around the world and to frame interventions to encourage local participation (Phillips and Ilcan 2007: 104). Looking at the UN, they suggest that it governs through risk and uncertainty, using its expertise about biotechnology to identify and manage those at risk and to encourage appropriate decision-making and responsible conduct (Phillips and Ilcan 2007: 109). The governmentality approach can therefore be seen to explain the actions of a number of international organisations, working through ideas like risk, vulnerability, resilience, preparedness and overall good governance.

In Larger Freedom

Continuing the focus on the UN, this section looks at the document *In Larger Freedom: Towards Development, Security and Human Rights for All*, a well-known statement, actually billed as the Report of the Secretary-General, Kofi Annan. This document is important because it reflects on progress in meeting the Millennium Development Goals (MDGs) – the eight international development goals promoted by the UN and supported by international institutions like the G8, World Bank and IMF. However, it also raises important issues concerning security and human rights and indeed reflects on the role of the UN itself, presenting the need for some fairly substantial reforms. Again, our strategy is to quote from this at length in order to show how, despite its reflexive nature and its concern with human rights and security, its discourse reflects such familiar themes as accountability, responsibility and partnership. The essence of the document, and why it should be considered a clear reflection of the governmentality discourse, can be found in the following quotation, which explains that freedom is actually a form of responsibility and accountability and that states,

[6] Phillips and Ilcan look at the way international organisations like the Food and Agriculture Organization (FAO) and the United Nations Educational, Scientific and Cultural Organization (UNESCO) use risk and uncertainty as a way to engage populations in debates about biotechnology and even manage populations considered at risk (Phillips and Ilcan 2007).

civil society, markets and international partners can be assessed in terms of performance:

> In our efforts to strengthen the contributions of States, civil society, the private sector and international institutions to advancing a vision of larger freedom, we must ensure that all involved assume their responsibilities to turn good words into good deeds. We therefore need new mechanisms to ensure accountability – the accountability of States to their citizens, of States to each other, of international institutions to their members and of the present generation to future generations. Where there is accountability we will progress; where there is none we will under-perform. (United Nations 2005: 7)

This chapter has rather taken for granted the idea that all these arguments are underpinned by an uncritical acceptance of the ideology of globalisation, so we should perhaps start by noting how the document sets the scene by stressing global interconnections and interdependence.

> In our globalized world, the threats we face are interconnected. The rich are vulnerable to the threats that attack the poor and the strong are vulnerable to the weak, as well as vice versa. A nuclear terrorist attack on the United States or Europe would have devastating effects on the whole world. But so would the appearance of a new virulent pandemic disease in a poor country with no effective health-care system. (2005: 81)

Passages like this are indicative of a familiar strategy that we find in much of the globalisation and global governance discourse and which emphasises our common future even if this is shaped by threats and risks. Behind the commonality, though, lies the fear that we now live in an age where things that happen in poorer countries can spread and pose new threats to richer countries – things like disease, terrorism, immigrants or refugees. But we should not be fearful because the conditions are in place for us to live in harmony, the international is reimagined as an arena where we all share common concerns as well as vulnerabilities. Hence the idea of interdependence is talked up as a positive thing that binds all states together and gives us common cause. Moreover, we can all enjoy a global abundance of resources if only we can find a way of overcoming the divides between rich and poor and ensure that our resources are able to benefit all peoples (2005: 3).

Of course the effect of this is ideological in that it hides the true nature of the capitalist world system and what Cammack (2009), Gruffydd Jones (2006) and others would call the systemic exploitation of the poorer countries by the richer ones, not least under the neoliberal free-market approach that Western-dominated international organisations are encouraging the poorer countries to accept as part of their development strategy. We know by now that the exploitative relations between North and South are hidden by an ideology of partnership that claims that richer countries can offer support to poorer ones – in terms of finance, technical support and expertise – that is non-exploitative and mutually beneficial. This is reflected in the Millennium Development Goals, explained in the UN document in the following terms:

> In the Millennium Declaration, world leaders were confident that humanity could, in the years ahead, make measurable progress towards peace, security, disarmament, human rights, democracy and good governance. They called for a global partnership for development to achieve agreed goals by 2015. They vowed to protect the vulnerable and meet the special needs of Africa. And they agreed that the United Nations needed to become more, not less, actively engaged in shaping our common future. (United Nations 2005: 4)

But there is no peace, freedom or security without responsibility. The idea behind partnership is to ask countries to freely accept responsibility for implementing the recommendations of outside partners. These recommendations take us away from the ideals of peace and human rights and back to the familiar theme of implementing the good governance agenda and market-friendly policies. Although this is a UN statement, it reads just like a World Bank promotion of the idea of building institutions for markets

> Developing countries should recommit themselves to taking primary responsibility for their own development by strengthening governance, combating corruption and putting in place the policies and investments to drive private-sector led growth and maximize domestic resources to fund national development strategies. (2005: 55)

Countries are given clear targets to meet. They are told to put in place bold ten-year goal-orientated policy frameworks in order to meet the MDG targets, described in terms of 'scaling up of public investments, capacity-building, domestic resource mobilization and, where needed, official development assistance' (2005: 12). If developing countries are prepared to implement the recommendations of their international partners, they will receive increased development assistance:

> While there are clearly capacity constraints in many developing countries, we must ensure that those countries that are ready receive an immediate scale up in assistance. Starting in 2005, developing countries that put forward sound, transparent and accountable national strategies and require increased development assistance should receive a sufficient increase in aid, of sufficient quality and arriving with sufficient speed to enable them to achieve the Millennium Development Goals. (2005: 17)

A harsher way of putting this is that those countries that do not do what their international partners tell them to do will be punished by receiving less donor support. Again, this is a matter of responsibilising governments, claiming to offer freedom and partnership, but backed up with the threat of withdrawal of donor support, particularly when it comes to following the correct economic policies:

> Each developing country has primary responsibility for its own development – strengthening governance, combating corruption and putting in place the policies and investments to drive private sector-led growth and maximize domestic resources available to fund national development strategies. Developed countries, on their side, undertake that developing countries which adopt transparent, credible and properly costed development strategies will receive the full support they need, in the form of increased development assistance, a more development-oriented trade system and wider and deeper debt relief. (2005: 12)

There then follows the normal set of benchmarking initiatives designed to make countries meet their MDG commitments, which are presented as unproblematic and universally accepted indicators:

> The Millennium Development Goals have galvanized unprecedented efforts to meet the needs of the world's poorest, becoming globally accepted benchmarks of broader progress embraced by donors, developing countries, civil society and major development institutions alike. As such, they reflect an urgent and globally shared and endorsed set of priorities that we need to address at the September 2005 summit. (2005: 10)

The first thing to note is how passages like this judge progress not in terms of actual poverty reduction, but in terms of the degree of implementation and adherence to various governance indicators. Talk of universal acceptance fits with the idea of governmentality as a drive to standardise measurement while denying of the power relationship behind the compliance of the recipient country by making the relationship look free and fair – in fact a responsible exercise of freedom. Reading between the lines, it is clear that failure to comply with guidelines drawn up by donors and development institutions will lead to a withdrawal of donor support. In a shift from the structural adjustment approach, these new suggestions move, in the words of Paul Cammack, from 'economic shock therapy' to a new form of 'institutional shock therapy' (Cammack 2004: 203). This can more easily be presented as something with broad support – everyone, after all, is in favour of institutional accountability. It can be presented as something carried out by the free will of governments, with support from a broad range of partners. Behind this, however, is not a free exercise of power, but the exercise of coercive pressure by those who enjoy greatest influence in the international system.

African governance and peer review

This section looks at governance and institutional reform in Africa in order to explore the impact of unfavourable local conditions. As noted, the World Bank and IMF turned to a more institutional approach following the failure of structural adjustment programmes. In Africa, figures suggest that the growth rate of 5.5 per cent between 1974 and 1977 had fallen to 0.9 per cent by 1992 (Lyakurwa 2005: 167). This clear failure to achieve results led the World Bank and IMF to develop the new approach described above, based on country-led PRSP. The World Bank continued to argue that if countries can get their macroeconomic policies right – by encouraging competition and sorting out balance of payments, inflation and exchange rates – then higher productivity and efficiency would follow. The neoliberal free-market approach is clearly still dominant in the advice that the solution 'requires unleashing markets so that competition can help improve the allocation of economic resources' (World Bank 1994: 61). African governments should be encouraged to deregulate prices and markets and to make wise use of scarce institutional capacity, giving priority to 'reforms that minimise unnecessary government involvement in markets' (1994: 9). What is new is that alongside these economic recommendations, the World Bank and other international organisations demand things like investment in human capital, infrastructure, institution building and better governance, civil service and public sector management (1994: 2, 120). The World Bank's *Adjustment in Africa* document admits that results show the difficulty in achieving these policy reforms, especially given the weakness of institutional capacity, and the serious limits on technical capacity, accountability and transparency (1994: 183–4). But it is claimed that adjustment works in those African countries that are prepared to undertake major policy reforms (1994: 1).

Although we have stated that international organisations seek to impose governmentality on African states and then package this as a mutual partnership, we should at least examine the idea that initiatives like the New Partnership for Africa's Development (NEPAD) and the African Peer Review Mechanism (APRM) are more regional processes run for Africans by Africans. As with other forms of governmentality already discussed, NEPAD and APRM contain the familiar list of ambitions and targets, focusing on governance, political stability and economic management across the continent. Recognising that there might be specific problems relating to this agenda, the NEPAD core document notes:

> In part, Africa's inability to harness the process of globalisation is a result of structural impediments to growth and development in the form of resource outflows and unfavourable terms of trade. At the same time, we recognise that failures of political and economic leadership in many African countries impede the effective mobilisation and utilisation of scarce resources into productive areas of activity in order to attract and facilitate domestic and foreign investment. (NEPAD 2001: 7)

The NEPAD document goes on to cite all the standard arguments for global governance, tying itself in with the international agenda of the UN and the Millennium Goals. Thus the agenda is already set and the task for Africa is to meet such expectations. It particularly emphasises the importance of stable conditions in order to 'enhance resource flows into Africa', including aid, trade and private capital (2001: 9). For this to occur, African states must take responsibility for developing conflict-prevention mechanisms, promoting democracy and human rights, maintaining macroeconomic stability, enforcing law and order and transparent regulatory frameworks, providing education and training and promoting the role of women (2001: 10–11).

Coming out of the 2001 summit of the Organisation of African Unity, the peer-review process is designed to assess the quality of governance in relation to various standards, conventions and protocols. African countries voluntarily agree to participate in a process of monitoring in order that 'the policies and practices of participating states conform to the agreed political, economic and corporate governance values, codes and standards contained in the Declaration on Democracy, Political, Economic and Corporate Governance' (OAU 2002: 1). The structure of the review process is composed of a Heads of State Forum (of presidents or prime ministers from the twenty-six participating countries) that meets twice yearly and a Panel of Eminent Persons appointed to oversee the review process and make recommendations. The first stage comprises a base review, followed up by periodic reviews every two to four years. Country review teams produce high-profile reports on national situations, looking at system failings, commenting on practices and procedures, considering fair principles and best practices and looking into the best ways to build trust and national consensus. This is recorded in the Country Review Reports, which provide an assessment of best practices and governance. All this is done with the assistance of three Technical Partners who provide support and advice. These are the United Nations Economic Commission for Africa (UNECA), the United Nations Development Programme (UNDP) and the African Development Bank (ADB).

Results thus far have been patchy at best, with only Ghana getting consistent praise for its efforts (Herbert and Gruzd 2008). The same commentators, who write that Africa is starting to recognise the need for improving the quality of its governance and the importance of stability, sustainable development, economic growth and the protection of rights (2008: 101), also note how wary countries are of the process, how inconsistent their reforms, how patchy their responses to recommendations. While Ghana is held up as an example of how the process can be used to legitimate significant government reform, it is noted with concern how half-hearted South Africa's efforts have been (2008: 108). This lack of engagement is in part due to the perception that the APRM's recommendations comprise a series of best practices that reflect the thinking of international organisations and which consequently do not fit with national conditions and, moreover, as Mathoho notes, would require significant resources to properly implement (Mathoho 2003: 6). While Herbert argues that APRM offers 'a valuable opportunity for civil society to get key problems and solutions onto the national agenda' (Herbert 2007: 1) and recommends APRM as a useful 'advocacy tool', others raise the sorts of issues noted by Mathoho that there is uncertainty over how it will operate and concern that it is elitist and exclusionary, often ignoring existing civil society (Mathoho 2003: 6).

This is precisely the problem. Writers like Abrahamsen are absolutely correct to show how the APRM fits with a governmentality approach, but serious questions must be asked about the effectiveness of this. Abrahamsen's argument is part of a more general case that governmentality operates through so-called partnerships. As she says:

> [T]he PRM can be seen as an institutionalised form of self-discipline. African countries are asked to subject themselves to detailed reviews and although entirely voluntary, the result is likely to be used by donors to decide whether or not they qualify for development partnerships. The policies and standards they are asked to live up to are those contained in the NEPAD document, which conform by and large to the liberal development goals of international donors, stressing the need for good governance, economic liberalism, peace and security. (Abrahamsen 2004: 1461)

But whether APRM succeeds even in this respect is open to question. We have suggested that rather than being an effective way to address populations on the ground, such processes can, like other forms of global governmentality, be seen as ways of disciplining states and their governments in the way suggested by the extract from Abrahamsen. That is to say, the process works by suggesting states 'voluntarily' agree to engage in a review process that is 'mutually agreed' and ultimately 'empowering', where empowerment is neoliberal code for making oneself attractive for donor support. In order to play this game, states must link their reforms to goals of market liberalisation, fighting corruption and promoting the private sector – that is to say, states must adjust their practices to meet with the neoliberal agenda of international organisations. But, still, we must ask if this is effective. Almost all country reports suggest that the process is not being taken fully seriously. As Mathoho starts to suggest, this might be something to do with underlying social conditions:

[T]he effectiveness of the APRM will depend on the states under review. It is likely to be ineffective where a state is repressive, has a weak civil society, and an unorganised private sector. This condition is common to many African states. The fact that the findings and recommendations of the APRM will not be binding, and implementation not obligatory, may result in states not taking seriously the recommendation that flow from the process. (Mathoho 2003: 12)

The NEPAD document itself is aware – certainly more so than the World Bank documents – that there are serious problems in the actual implementation of good governance and capacity-building practices. While paying lip-service to the ideas, these problems are clearly recognised:

State capacity-building is a critical aspect of creating conditions for development. The state has a major role to play in promoting economic growth and development, and in implementing poverty reduction programmes. However, the reality is that many governments lack the capacity to fulfill this role. As a consequence, many countries lack the necessary policy and regulatory frameworks for private sector-led growth. They also lack the capacity to implement programmes, even when funding is available. (NEPAD 2001: 19)

It is little wonder, therefore, that the NEPAD and APRM processes are riddled with contradictions and half-hearted commitments. Those writing from an African perspective are certainly more aware of the contradictions that exist between the recommended governance strategies and the actual conditions that might enable this to work. For example, while Western-backed international organisations stress the importance of information flows and technological innovation, the NEPAD document notes how Africa suffers from 'poor ICT infrastructure, combined with weak policy and regulatory frameworks and limited human resources', and that consequently 'Africa has been unable to capitalise on ICT as a tool in enhancing livelihoods and creating new business opportunities, and cross-border linkages within the continent and with global markets have been constrained' (NEPAD 2001: 25). The NEPAD document also questions another cornerstone of the global governmentality argument, that economic risk-taking is key to African development:

The low level of economic activity means that the instruments necessary for the real injection of private funds and risk-taking are not available, and the result is a further decline. In this self-perpetuating cycle, Africa's capacity to participate in the globalisation process is severely weakened, leading to further marginalisation. The increasing polarisation of wealth and poverty is one of a number of processes that have accompanied globalisation, and which threaten its sustainability. (2001: 7)

There is also recognition in the document that Africa faces an uneven playing-field and that what is termed globalisation – in effect, the free-market approach – places African economies at a disadvantage.

On the other hand, greater integration has also led to the further marginalisation of those countries that are unable to compete effectively. In the absence of fair and just global rules, globalisation has increased the ability of the strong to advance their interests to the detriment of the weak, especially in the areas of trade, finance and technology. It has limited the space for developing countries to control their own development, as the system makes no provision for compensating the weak. The conditions of those marginalised in this process have worsened in real terms. A fissure between inclusion and exclusion has emerged within and among nations. (2001: 7)

All this raises very serious questions about the feasibility of these strategies in those parts of the world with difficult socio-economic conditions, especially when advocacy of free-market policies puts African economies at a severe disadvantage.

Conclusion

The underlying theme of this chapter is the way that international organisations have developed a new approach to issues of development, aid, donor support, macroeconomic advice and other matters on which they intervene. In particular, we saw how institutions like the World Bank and IMF moved from the structural adjustment policies of the 1980s and 1990s to an approach that claimed to be more consensual, based on mutual understanding and partnership, where the recipient country would be offered ownership of its development strategy in return for a responsible exercise of its new freedom. It moves to recognise the importance of state institutions, civil society, social capital, networked governance and capacity-building as well as using the latest discourse of New Public Management. Our contention is that this new approach, far from representing a break, is consistent with the structural adjustment era as far as the overall neoliberal goals are concerned. There remains the neoliberal belief in promoting free markets, reining in the state and disciplining labour. But the new approach is much more governmental in its approach, using the kinds of techniques discussed throughout this book in order to discipline state behaviour.

The post-Washington consensus is distinctive in arguing that successful free markets need supportive states, sound institutions and good governance. The new approach of the World Bank, we noted, is summarised by the phrase 'building institutions for markets'. This relationship is presented as mutual: 'What is required is to step beyond the debates over the roles of governments and markets, recognizing that they need to complement each other' (World Bank 1999: 2), but of course the essential idea is that states support markets and remove obstacles to the movement of capital, not the other way around. The reason why the World Bank has rediscovered the state is because it has drawn the conclusion that effective and accountable governance can make markets produce the best results (World Bank 2005a: 227). That does not mean that states have been given a free hand to exercise power. They must be limited by their own mechanisms of governance, as well as their relations with civil society and other partners, and, most crucially, through their relations with markets and their duty to make markets work for their populations. Rather than representing the decline of the state, this suggests that states are recognised as the main source of social and economic regulation and that control of the state (in this case through external monitoring) is as important as ever.

The World Bank notes the new ideas of the 1990s – the ideas we have covered in the first part of this book – that emphasise the role of institutions both for development itself and the empowerment of those people for whom development is taking place (World Bank 2005a 227). This idea of empowerment is crucial if we are to see these issues through a governmentality lens. We know how Foucault suggests that empowerment is a key way of seeing the productive exercise of power. It creates the impression that we are freely exercising our will and improving the quality of our lives. If this concept can be applied to states and governments, then it helps explain how the new discourse of development is underpinned by the belief that states and governments can freely enter into partnerships and set their own development agenda. However, we know that in reality this ownership is extremely limited – it amounts to states following the advice given to them by their partners, while taking responsibility for implementing these ideas and being judged according to a series of agreed targets and benchmarks. This is governmentality of states based on appealing to the exercise of their freedom, but with the effect of regulating and monitoring their behaviour and responsibilising those in government. The World Bank uses the notion of accountability to bring together issues of ownership, willingness to implement recommendations and capacity to deliver. All this is backed up with the coercive threat of withdrawing aid and donor support should things not be done correctly.

The matter of whether these interventions by international organisations really work needs to be posed in a particular way. Instead of focusing on the stated aim of improving the conditions of the local population through poverty reduction or development, we need to see these in relation to the different objective of securing open markets across the globe. The neoliberal view is that liberal markets and poverty reduction go together; as the IMF suggests: 'Countries that align themselves with the forces of globalisation and embrace the reforms needed to do so, liberalizing markets and pursuing disciplined macroeconomic policies, are likely to put themselves on a path of convergence with advanced economies' (IMF 1997: 72). This argument has been questioned by a number of writers. Kiely, for example, notes that a belief in the importance of openness to global markets seriously underestimates the ability of developing countries to break into new export markets, suggesting that in fact these policies increase uneven development by giving competitive advantage to already developed countries (Kiely 2007b: 434). But because the World Bank and IMF are wedded to the view that openness to the global market is the solution to all problems of development, then if, for some reason, such pro-market policies do not result in economic growth and poverty reduction, this must be considered something to do with the country itself, its own internal practices, lack of democracy, lack of empowerment of women and local groups, lack of transparency and overreliance on the wrong type of regulation and state intervention. The market is never to blame.

We are continuing to bring this under the description of governmentality. But this is clearly quite different from the idea of governmentality working on local populations. It is true to say that explaining the failure of governmentality to improve the conditions of local populations is part of the task. This can be done through exposing the dogma and social conditioning of international organisations and their personnel. The bureaucrats, officials and policy-makers who populate these institutions are themselves subjects whose understanding has been constructed within a particular discursive field which makes them see the world in a particular way even if this is wholly inappropriate to problem-solving in less developed countries. If the idea of global governmentality is to have any sort of meaning then it should be considered in relation to the techniques aimed at regulating the behaviour of states and governments. This chapter has shown how this takes different forms – benchmarking and indicators, peer review of practices like good government and transparency and openness to the discipline of global markets. This has been noted, if not consistently so, by some of the governmentality theorists in IR. Fougner is most explicit about this:

> While much governmentality research has focused on how neoliberalism has come to inform multiple practices on the part of state authorities, the argument here is that states are themselves increasingly subjected to a form of neoliberal governance in the contemporary world political economy – in the sense that they are constituted and acted upon as subjects with a rationality derived from arranged forms of entrepreneurial and competitive behaviour. (Fougner 2008a: 308)

For Fougner and others, this would represent some sort of governmentality once-removed in so far as the issue is not really that of the regulation of populations; indeed it may not even matter to the international organisations that liberal techniques of governmentality are not effective in different local contexts so long as a system of global governmentality can be established which is successfully able to regulate the behaviour of states. By arguing that this is governmentality once-removed, we are suggesting that global governmentality is aimed at states rather than populations, but that this way of regulating state behaviour takes place *through* the targeting of populations by means of the stated aims of poverty reduction and development. Concern for populations exists as means rather than ends.

The bigger question is why regulate states? Here the governmentality theorists have less to say, and we are forced to turn to those working with historical materialism to find an answer. For Paul Cammack we should see the broader approach as one of globally embedding the disciplines of capitalist competitiveness, securing the hegemony of capital over labour and pressuring poorer countries to accept a new institutional infrastructure that supports the neoliberal consensus. The employment of new techniques is a recognition that the original macro-economic focus was too narrow and required a greater emphasis on states and other institutions as a means of making markets more competitive (Cammack 2009: 30). Stephen Gill uses the term disciplinary neoliberalism to illustrate the combination of the structural power of capital at the macro level and the micro dimension of power as found in the Foucauldian disciplinary practices that sustain this. It is institutionalised at the macro level of international political institutions (a 'new constitutionalism') and the discourse of global economic governance, and works through intensified surveillance practices, pressuring the state as well as the labour force to conform to market discipline (Gill 2003: 130–1). What is missing from Cammack's account is a recognition of the role a Foucauldian approach can play in explaining the techniques used to achieve the bigger goal of maintaining the conditions for global competitiveness. What is missing in Gill's account is a distinction between disciplinary power and governmentality. We would suggest that disciplinary practices can be applied to both local populations and their governments through what Foucauldians tend to call biopolitics. But the move from Washington to post-Washington reflects the belief that regulating states can be better achieved by more subtle techniques of governmentality.

While the World Bank recognises the weakness of formal institutions in poor countries and notes how many poor people have to rely on informal institutions like community networks and trust-based relationships, even this is turned into an argument for supporting free-market activities: 'Informal institutions develop to spread risk and to raise relative returns from market transactions. They do this by improving information flows, defining property rights and contracts, and managing competition' (World Bank 2002: 172). The new language of networks, flows and risk is imposed on traditional social relationships so that, like the idea of social capital, everything is turned into an economic resource for maximising personal gain. While one might expect to find this sort of approach in the discourse of economic institutions like the World Bank, IMF and OECD, this chapter has tried to show that such a discourse is endemic in all international organisations. To conclude by re-emphasising that these arguments apply as much to other international organisations as they do to the World Bank or IMF we find the UN making identical arguments about how the quality of institutions matters for economic growth and social cohesion. Indeed the argument moves from the idea that institutions make society more fair and stable, securing the adequate provision of public goods, to the idea that they help the functioning of markets and encourage calculated risk-taking (United Nations 2006: 125). Whether there is any truth behind any of these claims is now largely irrelevant. The governmentality effect is achieved, not by results on the ground, but by the establishment of widely agreed standards of compliance.

8 *Conclusion*

There are two main issues that we wish to emphasise in this conclusion. The first relates to the role of social theory and the second to global governance and governmentality. However, because the main focus of this book has been on social theory, we will discuss this issue only briefly in order to spend more time discussing how the argument of this book might contribute to an understanding of global governance and the role of governmentality in the international domain.

Social theory in the global

Rather than taking the conventional route and developing a 'post-positivist' account of IR, we started from a different puzzle – what role does contemporary social theory play in global politics? That is what we mean by the social in the global. We address this question via the concept, or perhaps we should say the practice, of governmentality. We found a number of contemporary social theories extremely influential. Because they have been picked up and used by international organisations, IR scholars should be interested in them even if these are terms that do not always fit with the typical IR vocabulary. For IR scholars should be interested in the idea of a governable space called the global, and therefore in how social theory helps construct this.

Of most significance are the ontological claims that these theories make and the picture of the world that they create. Indeed, it is by painting a certain picture of contemporary social life that these claims do most harm. We have picked a number of approaches that claim to be radical and emancipatory – something that makes them more appealing and also more dangerous. The four most damaging aspects of their common social ontology might be considered to be (1) their ontological shallowness – lacking social depth or an account of social relations and causal mechanisms; (2) a deterministic account of social change – based either on economic and technological determinism, the inevitability of globalisation or some progression through the stages of modernity; (3) embracing TINA – there is no alternative, so we must make the best we can of it; (4) their individualistic focus – we must adapt our behaviour at the micro level to take account of these new social conditions and the absence of effective collective agency. These ideas come together to create a picture where on the one hand we are overwhelmed by social and global change, yet on the other our response to these changes is focused at the micro level of individual responsibility. The processes of change are seen as unstoppable forces over which we have no control. A postmodern emphasis on social fragmentation and a questioning of collective forms of agency reinforce this lack of control. Unlike postmodernism, these theories present our situation as some sort of liberation. We are urged to embrace a micro politics of the self as if this represents a liberating move or even a 'return to politics'.

Against such claims, we have suggested that such an individualisation of political problems fits perfectly with neoliberalism and helps reinforce the status quo by attacking collective politics, the state, political parties, trade unions and other social forces that have traditionally helped bring about social transformation. As well as confusing us at the level of agency, these arguments also present a confusing picture of social structure – sometimes denying it all together, or suggesting it has been replaced by social networks – but also presenting a shallow, surface account of the social world, where processes are seen as things in themselves, separate from underlying causes. Such theories are either unable or unwilling to provide a causal account of the processes they describe and in so doing accept the world as it appears in its surface forms and as it seems to us through our experiences.

It is a peculiarity of these contemporary social theories that they simultaneously manage to do three seemingly contradictory things: (1) give an account of the world that focuses on surface appearances; (2) give an account of the world based on a belief in deep-seated changes; and (3) deny any causal account of these changes. Our explanation for this ontological confusion is that these theories all confuse practice with process. They present what are actually social projects and political strategies as if they were deeper underlying conditions. In doing so, they are unable to provide an account of the conditions of possibility for such projects for they are now taken as the conditions themselves. The result is to naturalise their effects as if they were the result of some deep-seated development in modernity itself, rather than the consequence of a very specific social and historical context. The concepts covered in this book are actually the product of very specific institutional changes in the advanced liberal societies arising out of the unravelling of the postwar settlement. Critical social theorists have tried to give meaning to these changes by focusing on their institutional nature and the relationship between institutional change, political or hegemonic projects and underlying conditions of capitalist production. Bob Jessop, for example, sees such things as competitiveness and innovation not as inevitable features of a second modernity or a risk society, but as a result of institutional change that promotes the Schumpeterian workfare state (2002) as an alternative to universal welfare provision. Other concepts like social capital fit with these processes by which liberal governments push through institutional reform that rolls back the role of the state (see Roberts and Devine 2003). Foucauldian approaches would likewise seek to explain these changes through the movement from centralised government to a form of governance that increasingly devolves power downwards to local bodies and upwards to transnational institutions. They would see this, if not wholly in institutional terms, then as a changing rationality of governance that does not deny the role of the state, but sees how it develops more subtle and sophisticated techniques for the management of populations and territory. What these more critical approaches can offer is an explanation of the importance of things like globalisation, networks, risk and social capital as strategies and techniques of governance rather than as deep-rooted changes in the nature of modernity. These strategies work to 'instrumentalise the real' (Gordon 1980: 251) through exploiting the possibilities that they discern and create themselves. They thus lend theoretical legitimacy and practically rationalise the very social and political changes they are claiming to describe.

When we extend this to international politics we find ourselves confronted with a range of different constructions that are legitimised or actualised in this way, the most significant of which from an IR point of view are globalisation, global civil society and global governance. It is imperative that critical IR scholars engage with these ideas and question the way they have been constructed. The emergence of the concepts we have examined is not accidental. They accompany very specific changes in the advanced liberal societies. They support these changes through their deterministic, near-fatalistic accounts of these changes. They claim that these changes represent some unstoppable process (globalisation) or deep, underlying condition (of modernity), making us think that there is nothing we can do to challenge or reverse them. This denies the strategic nature of these developments and reminds us of Margaret Thatcher's 1980s acronym TINA, which suggested there was no alternative to free-market capitalism. We have offered an alternative account of these changes as social projects in the context of institutional restructuring as a result of deeper capitalist social relations. The theories we discussed take these capitalist relations as given, whereas we have suggested that these relations are reproduced through the complex intersection of different forms of regulation, discourses, strategies, techniques and projects.

Taking this argument in a discursive direction explains something (though not everything) of what is going on. Foucault talks of a 'regime of veridiction'. He says that doctors in the nineteenth century said many stupid things about sex, but that the important question to ask is what it was that allowed them to present these things as truths (Foucault 2008: 36). We will not go so far as to call the things discussed in this book stupid. But if governmentality is seen as a regime of veridiction, then we can see why these ideas nevertheless have an important reality. This book has analysed how a range of contemporary social theories contribute to this regime of veridiction. It is particularly concerned with the fact that these theories often present themselves in radical terms, claiming to offer progressive solutions to the world's problems. In doing so they paint a particular picture of the world as a field for intervention. In practice, it can be shown that the radical claims that these theories make are mistaken and that their view of the world obfuscates where power really lies. Instead – and by virtue of this – they contribute, not to improving the world, but reinforcing a regime of veridiction associated with dominant forms of governmentality.

Global governance as global governmentality

Having gone through various issues and arguments it is perhaps time to try and make some sort of attempt at explaining what global governance means. If we have learned anything it is that global governance is a difficult concept to define and perhaps an even harder idea to implement. Our rather paradoxical suggestion is that ultimately global governance is easier to grasp once we stop trying to define it, or to measure it by its success or failure, strength or weakness.

This book has used the term global governance in the absence of a better way to describe the role of international organisations. Clearly the concept refers to much more than this. In fact, it probably covers too much and consequently finds itself alongside a lot of other general ideas that lack clear and precise meaning. The concept sometimes fills a void left by the absence of world government and often refers to different systems of rule-making, political coordination and global policy-making. This leads theorists of global governance to emphasise such things as its multi-layered and pluralistic nature. At its worst, the idea combines with globalisation theory to suggest that power has shifted away from the nation state to international institutions and regimes. When it does highlight the role of states, this is usually in the form of regime theory, often accompanied by various questionable assumptions about the nature of states and their behaviour. Given the problematic nature of both these positions it is tempting to give up on the notion.

Unlike ideas like globalisation and global civil society, however, it is possible to say that there is global governance going on 'out there'. The various things associated with global governance are clearly in operation – not just international organisations but also NGOs, civil society groups, private actors and, most importantly, states. Certainly the governance part of the concept is taking place, although we have raised issues about the meaning of this term and how it works in practice. The global part is more problematic, and we have striven to raise doubts about the actual global scope of many of the organisations and their practices. There is certainly a tendency in the global governance literature to overstate the extent to which global governance, as this literature understands it, is either taking place or being successful in its activities. But then global governance might be understood differently from how this literature understands it. It might be understood as a rationality or way of thinking about the world. Or, more conventionally, as a set of international regimes composed of self-interested states who find common interest. Or else, as Gramscians might say, a hegemonic order, or, as perhaps regulationists might say, a global mode of regulation.

We wish to hold on to ideas like hegemonic order and mode of regulation and indeed have used these to explain the institutional arrangements that organise and support the capitalist economy both nationally and internationally. But we would distinguish between these and actual governance (as we do in the next section). In our view, therefore, the best way to understand governance is not in these terms, but through the idea of governmentality. By applying the concept of governmentality to global governance we feel that we can give the term meaning while avoiding some of the difficulties concerning what it actually is. Instead, the idea of global governance as an international form of governmentality draws attention to its underlying rationality as well as to the various technologies and techniques that it deploys.

While recognising that Foucault's work contains an understanding of governmentality in general, we argued that it makes sense to look at forms of governmentality in their specificity. In today's world that means governmentality takes a predominantly neoliberal character, particularly in the advanced liberal societies. A major argument of this book has been that this neoliberal character is especially prominent when looking at international organisations. Of course not all international organisations are like this. But the governance commonly referred to as part of the post-Washington consensus does tend to show this character.

We suggest that international organisations do so in two ways. First, they tend to reflect power in world politics. The postwar settlement was dominated by the United States. It continues to play the dominant role in the international domain despite the unravelling of this settlement. It continues to dominate in three major areas – providing the world's key currency, supplying a large open market and enjoying military supremacy. While the crisis of the 1970s revealed a long-term problem of US hegemony, it is actually possible to say that the relative decline of the USA (weakening currency, massive trade deficit and military overstretch) reveals to potential rivals just how much they rely on the US-led system and just how difficult it would be to offer an alternative leadership in any of these areas (see Norrlof 2010). Given that the USA continues to dominate in economic and military areas, it is not surprising to see this reflected in the institutional architecture of the postwar period. This has been analysed first in terms of the influence of 'Americanism' or Fordism and Keynesian state intervention; then, following the crisis of this system of regulation at home and abroad, of the rise of neoliberal ideas and policies.

If the first source of neoliberalism in these institutions is a result of the dominance of the international system by the United States and therefore by the dominant economic model in the USA, the second sense is more reflexive. Neoliberalism has had two major reflexive phases. The first was as an aggressive reaction to the postwar settlement and its economic models. Internationally this was reflected in the Washington consensus with its championing of free markets, privatisations, rolling back the state and structural adjustment programmes. The second was a phase of institutional re-embedding which rediscovered the role of the (enabling) state in providing institutional support for markets and guaranteeing the rule of law, combined with an emphasis on civil society and NGOs.

We looked at how this found expression in global governance by examining some of the work of the World Bank. Our conclusion is that the dominant ideas inside this organisation reflect the dominant ideas inside the United States and other Western countries, where the majority of its staff have been educated and trained and where most of the funding and influence comes from. These ideas are not necessarily best suited to the actual conditions in the places where they are deployed. When seen in terms of global governmentality, we can say that they reflect the dominant rationality of the advanced liberal states but that there might be something of a credibility gap between their arguments and their actual deployment around the world.

This issue was not examined in detail because our concern has been with the global governance aspect of global governmentality. But a case-by-case study would reveal the kind of problems we found in Hearn's (2001) and Mercer's (2004) accounts of civil society issues in Ghana and Tanzania, or the chaotic security provision in Kenya (Abrahamsen and Williams 2006). Here the limits of governmentality are much clearer, because in most cases the techniques that are encouraged or imposed by outside organisations and international donors are not particularly effective at the local level, certainly if judged in terms of the ideas of 'conducting conduct' and managing populations 'from a distance'. What we see in such cases is governmentality lifted out of context, or very artificially trying to construct new actors and agents.

It has been argued that for a variety of reasons, interventions by international organisations have settled down into the management of states and governments. This matches with the new approach of the post-Washington consensus, with international institutions encouraging partnership, local responsibility and ownership through a retargeting of the state as the main vehicle for the governance agenda. We tentatively suggest, therefore, that global governance is most meaningfully understood as the governmentality of states and their governments – through international organisations, donors, development partners and other national governments.

But why should this governmentality of states occur? Quite simply, because rather than being undermined by economic developments as the globalisers claim, the state is essential for neoliberal strategies at both national and global levels. States are the main bodies capable of regulating capitalism, so if the state itself can be regulated, then the reproduction of capitalism can be guaranteed. The state is also the main protector (of capital) against instability and security threats. The state therefore plays a crucial role in ensuring the conditions for the global accumulation of capital, and given the global nature of this process, global standards of regulation have to be achieved. Ultimately it is impossible to understand issues like good governance, accountability, the rule of law, the construction of civil society and democracy promotion without seeing this bigger picture of the need for institutionalising the process of global capital accumulation.

However, this too is limited in its effectiveness. It can clearly be seen, especially across sub-Saharan Africa, how these projects are often met with even greater half-heartedness, as for example in the results of the PRSPs and African Peer Review. It is also important to emphasise that there are alternatives to meeting the requirements of these international organisations, particularly with the emerging 'Beijing consensus'. In contrast to its Washington counterpart, this offers African states a chance to get trade, investment and loans without having to meet a lot of conditions and hence without having to deal with a lot of governmentality requirements. In 2009 Chinese Premier Wen Jiabao promised $10 billion in low-interest loans to Africa. By then trade between China and Africa had risen tenfold to almost $107 billion.[1] But there are still significant limits to the scope and reach of the Beijing consensus. This trade is still far lower than China's trade with regions

[1] 'China Pledges $10bn Concessional Loans to Africa', *Guardian*, Sunday, 8 November 2009, www.guardian.co.uk/world/2009/nov/08/china-pledges-10bn-loan-africa, accessed 18 August 2010.

like the EU and Japan. Africa's trade with China is still heavily concentrated in certain regions. Eighty-five per cent of Africa's exports to China come from five countries – Angola, Equatorial Guinea, Nigeria, Congo and Sudan – and it is still heavily focused on oil, ore, metals and raw agricultural goods (Broadman 2008: 97). Hence, again, we see evidence of global unevenness, with some states better placed to avoid global governmentality than others.

If global governmentality is problematic in such cases, what of governmentality across the advanced liberal societies? We argued that in the EU governmentality exists at all levels from the individual to local, to national to transnational. But even in the EU, those ideas and practices that we have described as governmentality find themselves up against certain limits. The Anglo-Saxon nature of much of the governmentality discourse might be influential inside the EU bodies, particularly the Commission, but that does not mean it will enjoy equal success in all Member States. The European social model maintains a strong hold despite attempts to governmentalise it. Outside the UK and those places at the forefront of the neoliberal changes of the 1980s, we find different political traditions. Some countries still have combative workers' movements or strong corporate state models. Governments may be reluctant to implement changes, whether because of ideological opposition, half-heartedness or even as a result of incompetence. This is evident in the failings of the Lisbon Strategy and its uneven effects across Europe. It is very clear, even in the neoliberal heartlands, that there is more to the management of populations than just governmentality. It intersects with other important socio-economic processes, and the outcome is a complicated matter.

So the lesson to learn is that while governmentality is a powerful presence, we should be careful not to overplay its strength. Its success depends upon the willingness of states to engage with it. While there is certainly an unconscious conditioning element to governmentality in so far as it pre-exists those who act and shapes their interests and outlook (one need only look into the beliefs of World Bank staff to see this), it is not the case that it exists 'above the state' (Neumann and Sending 2010: 1) as some sort of omnipotent entity, or what Hardt and Negri's followers might call empire. Governmentality stands behind the state rather than above it. To see its relative success or failure, we have to look at the other entities through which it must work.

Global governance in social context

The emergence of neoliberal governmentality can only be explained by locating it in social and historical context. There is no doubt that neoliberal governmentality expresses deeper social relations; this much is clear in the way it seeks to govern through imposing the logic and rationality of the market. But it is equally true that it can do this only because of particular historical developments. The rise of governmentality in its present form is a product of the economic crises of the 1970s and the restructuring that resulted from these. The development of new forms of capitalist regulation, new state strategies and new hegemonic projects allowed for neoliberal governmentality to flourish. This governmentality is rooted in and emergent from these deeper social relations, but it cannot be reduced to these conditions. The particular form it takes is dependent on a range of different historical and conjunctural factors.

We have suggested that governmentality is emergent rather than constitutive. That is to say, it is not the underlying rationality that underpins all other aspects of the social. Rather, it exists alongside a range of other social processes and its particular character is emergent out of these relations. This position is suggested by some of Foucault's own comments on the relationship between capitalist development and the emergence of governmentality. We therefore suggest building a bridge between the central importance of capitalist accumulation, the social conditions within which this accumulation takes place, the institutional framework necessary for the organisation and regulation of capitalism and the types of norms and patterns of conduct characteristic of disciplinary power and governmentality. Disciplinary power, for example, can help explain the individualisation and fragmentation of labour power and the distribution of disciplinary space (Foucault 1979: 145). If disciplinary power provides a 'physics' or 'anatomy' of power (1979: 215), then governmentality, as an encouragement of the responsible exercise of free choice, helps explain part of the moralisation of the population which Foucault claims is equally important in the protection of capitalist wealth and maintaining the domination of the bourgeoisie (Foucault 1980: 41, 203). This is particularly appropriate to an understanding of how neoliberalism works on the individual subject. We have criticised theories of risk and reflexivity for fetishising the exercise of this freedom without looking at its relation to underlying capitalist social relations – indeed, they tend to ignore this matter exactly at the time when the logic of capital invades every aspect of our lives. Two parallel processes – in social theory and neoliberal practice – make this turn to a conception of the self which, in the words of Colin Gordon, represents 'the managerializing of personal identity and personal relations which accompanies the capitalization of the meaning of life' (Gordon 1991: 44).

If this is how governmentality works at the individual level, we suggested that it could be seen to be working at the institutional and state levels as well. If we follow Paul Cammack's arguments, then tackling global poverty is not so much the primary goal of organisations like the World Bank as the means by which to 'embed the disciplines of capitalist competitiveness on a global scale' (Cammack 2009: 7), forcing countries to develop their institutional capacities in line with the needs of the global economy and international capital accumulation. Cammack goes on to argue that this means securing the hegemony of capital over labour, and maximising the capacity of healthy and well-educated workers to enhance the competitiveness of their economies (Cammack 2009: 14). We would argue that this is partially true, but it is truer of the Lisbon Strategy of the EU than it is of global governance elsewhere. This is because the uneven nature of global capitalist relations means that projects like the PRSPs that aim to enhance the health and productivity of the workforce often meet with very little success on the ground and that the purported concern for the health and well-being of the population becomes more of a means for influencing the behaviour of states. Indeed, while neoliberalism requires skilled, healthy and productive workers, it also needs a large amount of cheap and expendable labour. Thus the issue, in many parts of the world, is not so much creating a healthy workforce as ensuring market openness and expendable labour. This is achieved by pressuring governments. On a global scale, while governments of poorer counties might be subjected to governmentality from a distance, neoliberal capitalism subjects the multitudinous poor of these countries to something closer to disciplinary power and coercion.

Capitalist development relies as much on cheap, coerced labour as it does on the exercise of free choice and governance from a distance. The control of populations through biopolitical means should not necessarily mean the same thing as governmentality. The two ideas are often conflated. Foucault's lectures claim that he found it impossible to talk of biopolitics – the problems of population – without seeing it through the framework of liberal political rationality (Foucault 2008: 317). There are two sides to liberalism and neoliberalism, and the concern with the limits of government and exercise of free conduct is matched by the security needs of the capitalist system. Mark Neocleous talks of the 'deadly *complicity* between security and capital' (Neocleous 2008: 144), which is nevertheless hidden behind a security fetish that hides the strategy of managing capitalist contradictions and class struggle and the constant policing of civil society (2008: 155).

While we could write extensively on the domestic aspect of this relationship between security, capital and the state, it is perhaps even clearer in international relations thanks to the heavy imbalance of power relations between the North and the South. Clearly the reconstruction of Iraq has relied heavily on disciplinary power and naked coercion and is more meaningfully understood through ideas like disciplining the population, reorganising the workforce and forcibly opening the country up to capitalist markets. This is the flip side of liberalism; a relationship where governmentality and coercive power go hand in hand, as might be seen in the case of Iraq, or neoliberalism's use of state terrorism to gain access to resources and markets (Blakeley 2009) or how biopower and security apparatuses deal with the 1 billion-plus people living in slums, often by a politics of exclusion (Davis 2006). We have not looked at these issues in much detail, because implicit in our argument is the view that the techniques used to exploit, discipline, control and, if necessary, exclude these large populations, while representing biopolitics, are not best described as governmentality. While the language of security provision often reflects the language of governmentality, the actual interventions are usually based on a more coercive approach. This, in our view, is not so much governmentality as the flip side of governmentality, the other face of neoliberal power, the bigger picture of global politics. It is indicative of the way, as Majia Nadesan puts it, totalitarianism haunts liberal governmentalities, of how they claim to reject the exercise of centralised, coercive power, yet rely on this, and exclusionary principles, for securitising everyday life (Nadesan 2008: 210).

A lot of the global governmentality literature leaves the issue of coercive force, disciplinary power and the weakness of governmentality relatively under-theorised. Nadesan is a notable exception. Her work examines the issue through the idea of a neoliberal regime and argues that brute force is needed for those who cannot be incorporated, particularly where economic and political security is at risk. This derives from the contradictory imperatives of neoliberal governmentality, which seeks to work from a distance, but which, through the promotion of free-market expansion, creates new security risks, especially from displaced populations (2008: 91). Despite this concern to govern from a distance, we therefore need to consider this 'martial face' which, according to Nadesan, is relatively under-theorised, but increasingly visible, especially when, as recently, neoliberal logics were combined with US neoconservative ones (2008: 38). In summary, this shows the inescapability of the nexus of government, discipline and sovereignty as different aspects of power, and the need to oppose those accounts, both in sociology and IR, that claim that state power is being weakened, decentralised and dispersed, or that disciplinary power is somehow being replaced with less coercive forms of social regulation.

Who is in charge?

We finish by raising some questions about the status of governmentality and the possibility of challenging it. Unfortunately we have concentrated so much on what governmentality is that we have not said much about resistance to it. This does not mean that we accept the view, common among many poststructuralists, that we should remain neutral on this matter and simply describe how governmentality works without offering an alternative perspective. What we have at least done is challenge the view put forward by many contemporary theories that there is no alternative to the situation they describe, taking for granted our social conditions without considering how we might change them, which reflects the ideology of neoliberalism by asking what individual gains we can make, not how we can change society for the better. We have shown that the conditions these theories take for granted are in fact strategic relationships. These are reversible. As Foucault says, 'between a relationship of power and a strategy of struggle there is a reciprocal appeal, a perpetual linking and a perpetual reversal' (Foucault 2001c: 347).

This does not mean we can get rid of governmentality any more than we can get rid of hegemony, the state or other essential power relations. Foucault shows governmentality to be deeply rooted in the emergence of liberal societies and their structures and apparatuses of power. But it is certainly possible to challenge the dominant neoliberal form of governmentality by exposing its limits and weaknesses. Just as the process of governmentalising more and more social relations continues, so it comes up against more and more obstacles. How we challenge governmentality – indeed whether we can ever really escape it – is a difficult issue, but we have at least shown – particularly by extending the concept to the global plane – that it is not a monolithic, all-conquering logic. Governmentality is full of gaps, weaknesses, crisis points, failings and contradictions. All of these can be challenged given the right sort of project. Points of resistance will continually emerge. For Foucault, 'every intensification or extension of power relations intended to wholly suppress these points of insubordination can only bring the exercise of power up against its outer limits' (2001c: 347). Governmentality is a hugely significant feature of our contemporary world. It is also something that can, and should, be challenged.

Challenging something is not, however, just a matter of exercising the human will. To look for points of resistance, we need to look at the bigger picture that governmentality is just one part of. We see that the techniques of governmentality may struggle or even fail because they do not match with the material conditions in those areas where they are being applied. This may be down to various reasons – most generally, to social conditions, more specifically, because of things like the balance of social forces, the different nature of social groups, organised opposition, vested interests, specific economic conditions, socio-economic inequalities, poor access to resources, certain political practices and customs, cultural conditions and so on. Having emphasised the power of governmentality, it is important to look at its limits and the fact that the world is more than just a product of some sort of dominant rationality, but an intersection of different structures, practices, ideas and material conditions, played out across an uneven geopolitical terrain.

Examining the limits and obstacles to governmentality is as important as examining its influence. To do this we need to look at the relationships between state, markets and civil society to see how governmentality is situated. Globally we find governmentality working at the level of states and their regulation by international bodies, but we also need to examine how the most powerful states and the social forces within these states dominate these institutions. This means that governmentality continues to find itself in a relationship with sovereign power as well as with other disciplinary techniques. The complex and uneven relationship between these elements always leaves gaps and weaknesses, which alternative strategies must try to exploit.

Nor should capitalist social relations be taken for granted. In the postwar period these were institutionally secured through specific historical blocs that reflected the relative strengths and weaknesses of different social groups. These blocs, as Gramsci notes, form a link between deeper structural conditions and particular expressions of human activity (Gramsci 1971: 366). These deeper social relations shape and condition the activities of agents. Under normal conditions, social agents routinely reproduce these relations through their everyday practices. But the fact that social relations are reproduced through human action means they are potentially transformable under conditions of heightened consciousness and political awareness. Of course this works both ways. Under conditions where 'incurable structural contradictions have revealed themselves' we find the dominant politics forces 'struggling to conserve and defend the existing structure … making every effort to cure them, within certain limits, and to overcome them' (1971: 178). This helps explain the situation the dominant groups found themselves in when developing new neoliberal projects in the 1970s and 1980s. Their actions were shaped by deeper social conditions, but also by their own efforts to find solutions.

If we insert neoliberal governmentality into this picture we can see how its rise to prominence is dependent upon these particular conditions. It relationship to human agency is more complex. On the one hand, it is dependent on a set of political actors pursuing a particular hegemonic project that develops neoliberal ideas. On the other hand, governmentality is a rationality that cannot simply be taken up and used in an instrumental way in order to solve certain problems. As a rationality, it pre-exists and shapes the ideas and actions of those who support it. This is why those who study the emergence of neoliberal tactics in the 1980s talk of them as 'contingent lash-ups of thought and action' which gradually took a coherent form as part of a neoliberal rationality (Rose 1999: 27). The rationality that emerges as the dominant one represents a sort of background condition that shapes the particular agents who develop particular policies. It enables political action to take a coherent form, but at the same time it plays a decisive role in conditioning those who act. This makes it difficult to answer the question, who is in charge? Governmentality itself is not an actor. It relies on people to do the acting. But as a condition of possibility for the coherence of their actions, it shapes and conditions people in a decisive way. Like other things that pre-exist individual agency, it is both enabling and constraining, constitutive and conditioning.

Rationalities, however, come and go. While Foucault is right to emphasise the importance of governmentality as a rationality, we have tried to show that this rationality takes a particular form dependent on wider social circumstances. Indeed, there is no one single rationality, but different rationalities connected to different social practices and interventions. But rather than following this route into a relativist philosophical position that claims there is no one way of seeing the world, we should take the realist philosophical route of linking these rationalities to wider social relations and suggesting that some rationalities become dominant because of the nature of these relationships and the fact that power resides in the wider social system, not just as an internal feature of discourse.

It is the tendency to see power as internal to the practices and discourses themselves that leads Foucauldians into a position where resistance seems impossible. By taking the step of linking governmentality to other social practices and projects (like hegemony) and to an ensemble of different social institutions (like the state) and to situate it within a set of deeper social relations (like mode of production), we break out of this internalising logic and thus offer more hope for social transformation.

To take these three connections in order. First, economic conditions have inherent contradictions that create moments of crisis. This necessitates social regulation and institutional intervention, but also provides grounds for institutional crisis and hence challenge. Any rationality that is associated with these deeper economic conditions is likely to be called into question. Second, the state is the key institution for organising intervention. State strategies perform this task and strategically select the right techniques for intervention. However, there is no necessary correspondence between the needs of the system and the actions of the state. This means that governmentality may well be undermined by a disjuncture between economy and state. Further, if we see the state as a strategic terrain for the unfolding of particular struggles and political projects, then there is always a basis to challenge the existing order. Third, hegemony is the best way to conceive of these relations. Ultimately, it is through the success or failure of particular hegemonic projects and, on a longer-term basis, of particular historical blocs that the fate of particular forms of governmentality is decided. That is not to say that governmentality is secondary to hegemony, far from it. Governmentality acts back upon hegemonic projects and shapes the way particular actors behave and hence the projects they develop. Through looking at neoliberalism as a rationality, we have tried to suggest that actors do not create projects afresh, but that their actions are conditioned by rationalities that pre-exist them. So hegemony and governmentality overlap with one another rather than having a mono-linear causal relationship. This is often a tense relationship, as are the relations between state, society and economic conditions. Here lies the basis for optimism. Once we step outside governmentality and look at these wider social relations, we see both its conditions of possibility, and the conditions of possible challenge and change.

Bibliography

Abrahamsen, Rita (2000) *Disciplining Democracy: Development Discourse and Good Governance in Africa*, London: Zed Books

(2004) 'The Power of Partnerships in Global Governance', *Third World Quarterly*, 25, 8: 1453–67

Abrahamsen, Rita and Michael C. Williams (2006) 'Security Sector Reform: Bringing the Private In', *Conflict, Security and Development*, 6, 1: 1–23

(2007) 'Introduction: The Privatisation and Globalisation of Security in Africa', *International Relations*, 21: 131–41

Adler, Emanuel (2010) 'Europe as a Civilizational Community of Practice', in Peter Katzenstein (ed.), *Civilizations in World Politics*, Abingdon: Routledge: 67–90

Adorno, Theodor (1973) *Negative Dialectics*, London: Routledge

Aglietta, Michel (1987) *A Theory of Capitalist Regulation: The US Experience*, London and New York: Verso

Archer, Margaret (1995) *Realist Social Theory: The Morphogenetic Approach*, Cambridge University Press

Axford, Barrie (1995) *The Global System: Economics, Politics and Culture*, Cambridge: Polity

Ayers, Alison (2008) 'Imperial Liberties: Democratisation and Governance in the "New" Imperial Order', *Political Studies*, 57, 1: 1–27

Bangemann, Martin (1994) *Europe and the Global Information Society: Recommendations to the European Council*, Brussels: European Commission

Barnett, Michael and Martha Finnemore (2004) *Rules for the World*, Ithaca, NY, and London: Cornell University Press

Barnett, Michael and Raymond Duvall (2005) 'Power in Global Governance', in Michael Barnett and Raymond Duvall (eds.), *Power in Global Governance*, Cambridge University Press: 1–32

Bartelson, Jens (2000) 'Three Concepts of Globalization', *International Sociology*, 15, 2: 180–96

(2006) 'Making Sense of Global Civil Society', *European Journal of International Relations* 12, 3: 371–95

Bauman, Zygmunt (2000) *Liquid Modernity*, Cambridge: Polity
Bayart, Jean-François (2009) *The State in Africa: The Politics of the Belly*, Cambridge: Polity
Bebbington, Anthony, Scott Guggenheim, Elizabeth Olson and Michael Woolcock (2004) 'Exploring Social Capital Debates at the World Bank', *Journal of Development Studies*, 40, 5: 33–64
Beck, Ulrich (1992) *Risk Society: Towards a New Modernity*, London: Sage
(1998) 'The Politics of Risk Society', in Jane Franklin (ed.), *The Politics of the Risk Society*, Cambridge: Polity: 9–22
(1999) *World Risk Society*, London: Sage
(2000) *What Is Globalization?* Cambridge: Polity
Beck, Ulrich and Elisabeth Beck-Gernsheim (2001) *Individualization: Institutionalized Individualism and Its Social and Political Consequences*, London: Sage
Beck, Ulrich and Edgar Grande (2007) *Cosmopolitan Europe*, Cambridge: Polity
Bell, Daniel (1973) *The Coming of Post-Industrial Society*, New York: Basic Books
Benner, Thorsten, Wolfgang H. Reinicke and Jan Martin Witte (2005) 'Multisectoral Networks in Global Governance: Towards a Pluralistic System of Accountability' in David Held and Mathias Koenig-Archibugi (eds.) *Global Governance and Public Accountability*, Oxford: Blackwell: 67–86
Benton, Ted (1999) 'Radical Politcs – Neither Left nor Right?', in Martin O'Brien, Sue Penna and Colin Hay (eds.), *Theorising Modernity: Reflexivity, Environment and Identity in Giddens' Social Theory*, London and New York: Longman: 39–64
Best, Jacqueline (2007) 'Why the Economy Is Often the Exception to Politics as Usual', *Theory, Culture and Society*, 24, 4: 87–109
Bevir, Mark and Frank Trentmann (eds.) (2007) *Governance, Consumers and Citizens: Agency and Resistance in Contemporary Politics*, Basingstoke: Palgrave Macmillan
Bigo, Didier (2002) 'Security and Immigration: Toward a Critique of the Governmentality of Unease', *Alternatives* 27: 63–92
Blakeley, Ruth (2009) *State Terrorism and Neoliberalism: The North in the South*, Abingdon: Routledge
Bøas, Martin and Jonas Vevatne (2004) 'Sustainable Development and the World Trade Organization', in Martin Bøas and Desmond McNeil (eds.), *Global Institutions and Development: Framing the World*, London and New York: Routledge: 93–107
Boggs, Carl (2001) 'Social Capital and Political Fantasy: Robert Putnam's "Bowling Alone"', *Theory and Society*, 30, 2: 281–97

Boltanski, Luc and Eve Chiapello (2005) *The New Spirit of Capitalism*, London: Verso

Bourdieu, Pierre and Loïc Wacquant (1992) *An Invitation to Reflexive Sociology*, University of Chicago Press

Broadman, Harry G. (2008) 'China and India Go to Africa – New Deals in the Developing World', *Foreign Affairs*, 87: 95–109

Bull, Hedley (2002), *The Anarchical Society*, Basingstoke: Palgrave Macmillan

Burchell, Graham (1991) 'Peculiar Interests: Civil Society and Governing "the System of Natural Liberty"', in Graham Burchell, Colin Gordon and Peter Miller (eds.), *The Foucault Effect: Studies in Governmentality*, University of Chicago Press: 119–50

(1996) 'Liberal Government and Techniques of the Self', in Andrew Barry, Thomas Osborne and Nikolas Rose (eds.), *Foucault and Political Reason*, London: UCL Press: 19–36

Cammack, Paul (2004) 'What the World Bank Means by Poverty Reduction, and Why It Matters', *New Political Economy*, 9, 2: 189–211

(2009) 'Poverty Reduction and Universal Competitiveness', *Labor, Capital, and Society*, 42, 1–2: 35–54

CASE Collective (2006) 'Critical Approaches to Security in Europe: A Networked Manifesto', *Security Dialogue*, 37, 1: 443–87

Castells, Manuel (1989) *The Information City*, Oxford: Blackwell

(1997) *The Power of Identity*, Oxford: Blackwell

(2005) *End of Millennium*, Oxford: Blackwell

(2006) 'The Network Society: From Knowledge to Policy', in Castells and Gustavo Cardoso (eds.), *The Network Society: From Knowledge to Policy*, Washington, DC: Center for Transatlantic Relations: 3–21

(2009) *The Rise of the Network Society*, Oxford: Blackwell

Castells, Manuel and Gustavo Cardoso (eds.) (2006) *The Network Society: From Knowledge to Policy*, Washington, DC: Center for Transatlantic Relations

Chandler, David (2005) *Constructing Global Civil Society: Morality and Power in International Relations*, Basingstoke: Palgrave Macmillan

(2006) *Empire in Denial*, London: Pluto

Cheru, Fantu (2006) 'Building and Supporting PRSPs in Africa: What Has Worked Well So Far? What Needs Changing?', *Third World Quarterly*, 27, 2: 355–76

Chhotray, Vasudha and Gerry Stoker (2009) *Governance Theory and Practice: A Cross-Disciplinary-Approach*, Basingstoke: Palgrave Macmillan

Christiansen, Thomas, Andreas Føllesdal and Simona Piattoni (2003) 'Informal Governance in the European Union: An Introduction', in

Thomas Christiansen and Simona Piattoni (eds.), *Informal Governance in the European Union*, Cheltenham: Edward Elgar: 1–21

Coker, Christopher (2002) *Globalisation and Insecurity in the Twenty-First Century: NATO and the Management of Risk*, Adelphi Paper 345, London: International Institute of Strategic Studies and Oxford University Press

Coleman, James S. (2000) 'Social Capital and the Creation of Human Capital', in Partha Dasgupta and Ismail Serageldin (eds.), *Social Capital: A Multifaceted Perspective*, Washington, DC: World Bank: 13–39

Commission on Global Governance (1995) *Our Global Neighbourhood*, New York: Oxford University Press

Coole, Diana (2009) 'Repairing Civil Society and Experimenting with Power: A Genealogy of Social Capital', *Political Studies*, 57, 2: 374–96

Cox, Robert (1987) *Production, Power, and World Order*, New York: Columbia University Press

(with Timothy Sinclair) (1996) *Approaches to World Order*, Cambridge University Press

(ed.) (1997) *The New Realism: Perspectives on Multilateralism and World Order* (Basingstoke: Palgrave Macmillan)

Craig, David and Doug Porter (2003) 'Poverty Reduction Strategy Papers: A New Convergence', *World Development*, 31, 1: 53–69

Davis, Mike (2006) *Planet of Slums*, London: Verso

Dean, Mitchell (1999) *Governmentality: Power and Rule in Modern Society*, London: Sage

(2002) 'Liberal Government and Authoritarianism', *Economy and Society*, 31, 1: 37–61

(2007) *Governing Societies: Political Perspectives on Domestic and International Rule*, Maidenhead: Open University Press

Death, Carl (2011) 'Foucault and Africa: Governmentality, IR theory and the Limits of Advanced Liberalism'. Paper prepared for British International Studies Association (BISA) annual conference, 27–29 April, Manchester, UK

Deb, Debal (2009) *Beyond Developmentality: Constructing Inclusive Freedom and Sustainability*, London: Earthscan

Defort, Daniel (1991) 'Popular Life and Insurance Technology', in Graham Burchell, Colin Gordon and Peter Miller (eds.), *The Foucault Effect: Studies in Governmentality*, University of Chicago Press: 211–33

Diehl, Paul F. (ed.) (1997) *The Politics of Global Governance: International Organizations in an Interdependent World*, Boulder, CO: Lynne Rienner

Dillon, Michael (2007) 'Governing through Contingency: The Security of Biopolitical Governance', *Political Geography* 26, 1; 41–7

Dillon, Michael and Julian Reid (2000) 'Global Governance, Liberal Peace, and Complex Emergency', *Alternatives: Global, Local, Political*, 25, 1: 117–43

(2001) 'Biopolitics, Security and War', *Millennium*, 30, 1: 41–66

Donzelot, Jacques (1988) 'The Promotion of the Social', *Economy and Society* 17, 3: 106–37

Duffield, Mark (2001) *Global Governance and the New Wars: The Merging of Development and Security*, London: Zed Books

(2002) 'Social Reconstruction and the Radicalization of Development: Aid as a Relation of Global Liberal Governance', *Development and Change* 33, 5: 1049–71

Durkheim, Emile (1964) *The Division of Labor in Society*, New York: Free Press

Escobar, Arturo (1995) *Encountering Development: The Making and Unmaking of the Third World*, Princeton University Press

European Commission (1993) *Growth, Competitiveness, Employment – The Challenges and Ways Forward into the 21st Century*, (White Paper) Luxembourg: Office for Official Publications of the European Communities

(1996) *Living and Working in the Information Society: People First* (Green Paper), Brussels: European Commission

(1997) *Partnership for a New Organisation of Work* (Green Paper), Brussels: European Commission

(2001) *European Governance: A White Paper*, Brussels: European Commission

(2003) *Report from the Commission on European Governance*, Brussels: European Commission

(2004a) *Facing the Challenge: The Lisbon Strategy for Growth and Employment*, Luxembourg: Office for Official Publications of the European Communities

(2004b) *Information Society, Work and the Generation of New Forms of Social Exclusion SOWING: Final Report*, Luxembourg: Office for Official Publications of the European Communities

(2006) *Global Europe: Competing in the World. A Contribution to the EU's Growth and Jobs Strategy*, Brussels: European Commission

(2007) *Taking European Knowledge Society Seriously: Report of the Expert Group on Science and Governance to the Science, Economy and Society Directorate, Directorate-General for Research*, Brussels: European Commission

(2008a) *Renewed Social Agenda: Opportunities, Access and Solidarity in 21st Century Europe*, Brussels: European Commission

(2008b) *Report on the EU Contribution to the Promotion of Decent Work in the World*, Brussels: European Commission

(2008c) *A Renewed Commitment to Social Europe: Reinforcing the Open Method of Coordination for Social Protection and Social Inclusion*, Brussels: European Commission

(2009) *Third Strategic Review of Better Regulation in the European Union*, Brussels: European Commission

(2010a) *Lisbon Strategy Evaluation Document*, Brussels: European Commission

(2010b) *Europe 2020: A Strategy for Smart, Sustainable and Inclusive Growth*, Brussels: European Commission

European Council (2000) 'Presidency Conclusions, Lisbon European Council 23 and 24 March 2000', www.bologna-berlin2003.de/pdf/PRESIDENCY_CONCLUSIONS_Lissabon.pdf (accessed 12 January 2012)

(2004) *The Hague Programme: Strengthening Freedom, Security and Justice in the European Union*, Brussels: European Council

(2009) *The Stockholm Programme – An Open and Secure Europe Serving and Protecting the Citizens*, Brussels: European Council

Ewald, François (1991) 'Insurance and Risk', in Graham Burchell, Colin Gordon and Peter Miller (eds.), *The Foucault Effect: Studies in Governmentality*, University of Chicago Press: 197–210

Falk, Richard (1995) *On Humane Governance: Toward a New Global Politics*, Cambridge: Polity

Featherstone, Mike and Scott Lash (1995) 'Globalization, Modernity, and the Spatialization of Social Theory', in Mike Featherstone, Scott Lash and Roland Robertson (eds.), *Global Modernities*, London: Sage: 1–24

Ferguson, James and Akhil Gupta (2002) 'Spatializing States: Towards an Ethnography of Neoliberal Governmentality', *American Ethnologist* 29, 4: 981–1002

Ferrera, Maurizio (2006) 'Friends not Foes: European Integration and National Welfare States', in Anthony Giddens, Patrick Diamond and Roger Liddle (eds.), *Global Europe, Social Europe*, Cambridge: Polity: 257–78

Field, John (2003) *Social Capital*, London and New York: Routledge

Fine, Ben (2001) *Social Theory versus Social Capital: Political Economy and Social Science at the Turn of the Millennium*, London and New York: Routledge

(2003) 'Neither the Washington nor the Post-Washington Consensus: An Introduction', in Ben Fine, Costas Lapavitsas and Jonathan Pincus (eds.), *Development Policy in the Twenty-First Century: Beyond the Post-Washington Consensus*, London: Routledge

(2010) *Theories of Social Capital: Researchers Behaving Badly*, Pluto: London

Fontana, Alesandro and Mauro Bertani (2004) 'Situating the Lectures', in Michel Foucault, *Society Must Be Defended*, Harmondsworth: Penguin Books: 273–93

Foucault, Michel (1974) *The Order of Things: Archaeology of the Human Sciences*, London: Tavistock

(1979) *Discipline and Punish*, Harmondsworth: Penguin Books

(1980) *Power/Knowledge: Selected Interviews and Other Writings 1972–1977*, ed. Colin Gordon, New York: Pantheon Books

(1981) *The History of Sexuality Volume 1: An Introduction*, Harmondsworth: Penguin Books

(1989) *The Archaeology of Knowledge*, London: Routledge

(1991) 'Politics and the Study of Discourse', in Graham Burchell, Colin Gordon, and Peter Miller (eds.), *The Foucault Effect: Studies in Governmentality*, University of Chicago Press: 53–72

(1994) *Dits et écrits IV*, Paris: Gallimard

(2001a) 'Governmentality', in *Michel Foucault: Power*, ed. J. D. Faubion, Harmondsworth: Penguin Books: 200–22

(2001b) 'Truth and Power', in *Michel Foucault: Power*, ed. J. D. Faubion, Harmondsworth: Penguin Books: 111–33

(2001c) 'The Subject and Power', in *Michel Foucault: Power*, ed. J. D. Faubion, Harmondsworth: Penguin Books: 326–48

(2004) *Society Must Be Defended*, Harmondsworth: Penguin Books

(2005) *The Hermeneutics of the Subject*, New York: Picador

(2007) *Security, Territory, Population*, Basingstoke: Palgrave Macmillan

(2008) *The Birth of Biopolitics*, Basingstoke: Palgrave Macmillan

(2010) *The Government of Self and Others*, Basingstoke: Palgrave Macmillan

Fougner, Tore (2008a) 'Neoliberal Governance of States: The Role of Competitiveness Indexing and Country Benchmarking', *Millennium*, 37, 2: 303–26

(2008b) 'Corporate Power in World Politics: The Case of the World Economic Forum', *Journal of International Trade and Diplomacy*, 2, 2: 97–134

Fox, Jonathan (1997) 'The World Bank and Social Capital: Contesting the Concept in Practice', *Journal of International Development*, 9, 7: 963–71

Fraser, Alastair (2005) 'Poverty Reduction Strategy Papers: Now Who Calls the Shots?', *Review of African Political Economy*, 104/5: 317–40

Fraser, Nancy (2003) 'From Discipline to Flexibilization? Rereading Foucault in the Shadow of Globalization', *Constellations* 10, 2: 160–71

Fukuyama, Francis (2001) 'Social Capital, Civil Society and Development', *Third World Quarterly*, 22, 1: 7– 20

Giddens, Anthony (1979) *Central Problems in Social Theory*, Berkeley, CA: University of California Press

(1990) *The Consequences of Modernity*, Cambridge: Polity

(1991) *Modernity and Self-Identity. Self and Society in the Late Modern Age,* Cambridge: Polity Press

(1998) 'Risk Society: The Context of British Politics', in Jane Franklin (ed.), *The Politics of the Risk Society*, Cambridge: Polity: 23–34

(2006) 'A Social Model for Europe?', in Anthony Giddens, Patrick Diamond and Roger Liddle (eds.), *Global Europe, Social Europe*, Cambridge: Polity: 14–36

(2007) *Europe in the Global Age*, Cambridge: Polity

Giddens, Anthony, Patrick Diamond and Roger Liddle (eds.) (2006) *Global Europe, Social Europe*, Cambridge: Polity

Gill, Stephen (2003) *Power and Resistance in the New World Order*, Basingstoke: Palgrave Macmillan

Gilpin, Robert (1981) *War and Change in World Politics*, Cambridge University Press

Gordon, Colin (1980) 'Afterword', in Michel Foucault, *Power/Knowledge: Selected Interviews and Other Writings 1972–1977*, ed. Colin Gordon, New York: Pantheon Books: 229–59

(1991) 'Governmental Rationality: An Introduction', in Graham Burchell, Colin Gordon, and Peter Miller (eds.), *The Foucault Effect: Studies in Governmentality*, University of Chicago Press: 1–51

Gowen, Peter (2010) *A Calculus of Power*, London: Verso

Gramsci, Antonio (1971) *Selections from the Prison Notebooks*, London: Lawrence and Wishart

Grootaert, Christian (1998) *Social Capital: The Missing Link?*, Social Capital Initiative Working Paper 3, Washington, DC: World Bank

Grootaert, Christian and Thierry van Bastelaer (2002) 'Social Capital: From Definition to Measurement', in Grootaert and van Bastelaer, *Understanding and Measuring Social Capital: A Multidisciplinary Tool for Social Practitioners*, Washington, DC: World Bank: 1–16

Gruffydd Jones, Branwen (2006) *Explaining Global Poverty: A Critical Realist Approach*, London: Routledge

Haahr, Jens Henrik (2004) 'Open Co-ordination as Advanced Liberal Government', *Journal of European Public Policy*, 11, 2: 209–30

Hass, Ernst B. (1983) 'Words Can Hurt You; or, Who Said What to Whom about Regimes', in Stephen D. Krasner (ed.), *International Regimes*, Ithaca, NY: Cornell University Press: 23–59

Hajer, Maarten and Wytske Versteeg (2005) 'Performing Governance through Networks', *European Political Science*, 4: 340–7

Harrison, Graham (2001) 'Post-Conditionality Politics and Administrative Reform: Reflections on the Case of Uganda and Tanzania', *Development and Change* 32, 4: 658–79

(2004) *The World Bank and Africa: The Construction of Governance States*, London and New York: Routledge

Harriss, John and Paolo de Renzio (1997) '"Missing Link" or Analytically Missing? The Concept of Social Capital: An Introductory Essay', *Journal of International Development*, 9, 7: 919–37

Harvey, David (1999) *The Limits to Capital*, London: Verso

(2001) *Spaces of Capital*, Edinburgh University Press

(2005) *A Brief History of Neoliberalism*, Oxford University Press

Hay, Colin (1998) 'The Tangled Webs We Weave: The Discourse, Strategy and Practice of Networking', in David Marsh (ed.), *Comparing Policy Networks*, Buckingham: Open University Press: 33–51

Hay, Colin and David Marsh (2000) *Demystifying Globalization*, Basingstoke: Palgrave Macmillan

Hay, Colin, Martin O'Brien and Sue Penna (1997) 'Giddens, Modernity and Self-Identity: The Hollowing Out of Social Theory', in Christopher G. A. Bryant and David Jarry (eds.), *Anthony Giddens: Critical Assessments*, vol. IV, London and New York: Routledge: 85–112

Hay, Colin and Ben Rosamond (2002) 'Globalization, European Integration and the Discursive Construction of Economic Imperatives', *Journal of European Public Policy*, 9, 2: 147–67

Hearn, Julie (2000) 'Aiding Democracy? Donors and Civil Society in South Africa', *Third World Quarterly*, 21, 5: 815–30

(2001) '"Uses and Abuses" of Civil Society in Africa', *Review of African Political Economy*, 28, 87: 43–53

Held, David (2004) *Global Covenant: The Social Democratic Alternative to the Washington Consensus*, Cambridge: Polity

(2005) 'Democratic Accountability and Political Effectiveness from a Cosmopolitan Perspective', in David Held and Mathias Koenig-Archibugi (eds.), *Global Governance and Public Accountability*, Oxford: Blackwell: 240–67

Held, David and Anthony McGrew (2003) 'The Great Globalisation Debate: An Introduction', in David Held and Anthony McGrew (eds.), *The Global Transformations Reader*, Cambridge: Polity: 1–50

Held, David and Anthony McGrew (eds.) (2003) *The Global Transformations Reader*, Cambridge: Polity

Held, David and Mathias Koenig-Archibugi (eds.) (2005) *Global Governance and Public Accountability*, Oxford: Blackwell

Held, David, Anthony McGrew, David Goldblatt and Jonathan Perraton (1999) *Global Transformations*, Cambridge: Polity

Hemerijk, Anton (2006) 'Social Change and Welfare Reform', in Anthony Giddens, Patrick Diamond and Roger Liddle (eds.), *Global Europe, Social Europe*, Cambridge: Polity: 106–23

Herbert, Ross (2007) *Governance and APRM Programme. Influencing APRM: A Checklist for Civil Society*, Johannesburg: South African Institute of International Affairs, www.saiia.org.za/images/upload/aprm_cso_guidebook_20070620_en.pdf (accessed 12 January 2012)

Herbert, Ross and Steven Gruzd (2008) *The African Peer Review Mechanism: Lessons from the Pioneers*, Johannesburg: South African Institute of International Affairs

Hewson, Martin and Timothy J. Sinclair (1999) 'The Emergence of Global Governance Theory', in Martin Hewson and Timothy J. Sinclair (eds.), *Approaches to Governance Theory*, Albany: State University of New York Press: 1–22

Higgott, Richard (2000), 'Contested Globalization: The Changing Context and Normative Challenges', *Review of International Studies*, 26: 131–53

Higgins, Winton (2006) 'How We Are Governed Now: Globalisation, Neo-liberal Governmentality and the Nullification of Substantive Policy', *Journal of Australian Political Economy*, 57: 5–29

Hindess, Barry (2005a) 'Politics as Government: Michel Foucault's Analysis of Political Reason', *Alternatives* 30: 389–413

(2005b) 'Liberalism – What's in a Name?', in Wendy Larner and William Walters (eds.), *Global Governmentality: Governing International Spaces*, London and New York: Routledge: 24–9

Hirst, Paul (2000) 'Democracy and Governance', in Jon Pierre (ed.), *Debating Governance: Authority, Steering and Democracy*, Oxford University Press: 13–35

Hirst, Paul and Graham Thompson (1999) *Globalization in Question*, Cambridge: Polity

Hooghe, Liesbet and Gary Marks (2001) *Multi-Level Governance and European Integration*, Lanham: Rowman and Littlefield

Hoogvelt, Ankie (1997) *Globalisation in the Postcolonial World: The New Political Economy of Development*, Basingstoke: Palgrave Macmillan

Howell, Jude and Jenny Pearce (2001) *Civil Society and Development: A Critical Exploration*, Boulder, CO: Lynne Rienner

Ilcan, Susan and Lynne Phillips (2008) 'Governing through Global Networks: Knowledge Mobilities and Participatory Development', *Current Sociology*, 56, 5: 711–34

IMF (1997) *World Economic Outlook*, Washington, DC: International Monetary Fund

(2001) 'Strengthening Country Ownership of Fund-Supported Programmes', www.imf.org/external/np/pdr/cond/2001/eng/strength/120501.pdf (accessed 12 January 2012)

Jessop, Bob (1990) *State Theory: Putting Capitalist States in their Place*, Cambridge: Polity

(2002) 'Capitalism, the Regulation Approach and Critical Realism', in Andrew Brown, Steve Fleetwood and John Michael Roberts (eds.), *Critical Realism and Marxism*, London: Routledge: 88–115

(2007) *State Power*, Cambridge: Polity

Jessop, Bob and Ngai-Ling Sum (2006) *Beyond the Regulation Approach: Putting Capitalist Economies in their Place*, Cheltenham: Edward Elgar

Joseph, Jonathan (2004) 'Foucault and Reality', *Capital and Class* 82: 141–63

(2007) 'Philosophy in International Relations: A Scientific Realist Approach', *Millennium*, 35, 2: 345–59

(2010) 'The International as Emergent: Challenging Old and New Orthodoxies in International Relations Theory', in Joseph and Colin Wight (eds.), *Scientific Realism and International Relations*, Basingstoke: Palgrave Macmillan: 51–68

Kaldor, Mary (2003) *Global Civil Society: An Answer to War*, Cambridge: Polity

Keane, John (2003) *Global Civil Society?*, Cambridge University Press

Keck, Margaret E. and Kathryn Sikkink (1998) *Activists beyond Borders: Advocacy Networks in International Politics*, Ithaca, NY: Cornell University Press

Keohane, Robert O. (1983) 'The Demand for International Regimes', in Stephen D. Krasner (ed.), *International Regimes*, Ithaca, NY: Cornell University Press: 141–71

(1984) *After Hegemony: Cooperation and Discord in the World Political Economy*, Princeton University Press

(2006) 'International Institutions: Two Approaches', in Friedrich Kratochwil and Edward D. Mansfield (eds.), *International Organization and Global Governance: A Reader*, New York: Pearson: 56–72

Keohane, Robert O. and Joseph S. Nye (1989) *Power and Interdependence*, 2nd edn, New York: HarperCollins

Kiely, Ray (1995) *Sociology and Development: The Impasse and Beyond*, London: UCL Press

(2005) *The Clash of Globalisations: Neo-Liberalism, the Third Way and Anti-Globalisation*, Leiden and Boston: Brill

(2007a) *The New Political Economy of Economic Development: Globalization, Imperialism, Hegemony*, Basingstoke: Palgrave Macmillan

(2007b) 'Poverty Reduction through Liberalisation? Neoliberalism and the Myth of Global Convergence', *Review of International Studies* 33, 3: 415–34

Kindleberger, Charles P. (1973) *The World in Depression 1929–1939*, London: Penguin Books

King, Roger (2007) *The Regulatory State in an Age of Governance: Soft Words and Big Sticks*, Basingstoke: Palgrave Macmillan

Klijn, Erik-Hans (2005) 'Designing and Managing Networks: Possibilities and Limitations for Network Management', *European Political Science*, 4: 328–39

Klugman, Jeni (2002) 'Overview', in *A Sourcebook for Poverty Reduction Strategies*, vol. I, *Core Techniques and Cross-Cutting Issues*, Washington, DC: World Bank

Koivisto, Marjo (2010) 'State Theory in International Relations: Why Realism Matters', in Jonathan Joseph and Colin Wight (eds.), *Scientific Realism and International Relations*, Basingstoke: Palgrave Macmillan: 69–87

Kozal, Valerie, Pierre Fallavier and Reena Badiani (2008) *Risk and Vulnerability Analysis in World Bank Analytic Work: FY2000–FY2007*, SP Discussion Paper, Washington, DC: World Bank

Krasner, Stephen D. (1983) 'Structural Causes and Regime Consequences: Regimes as Intervening Variables', in Stephen D. Krasner (ed.), *International Regimes*, Ithaca, NY: Cornell University Press: 1–21

Kratochwil, Friedrich and Edward D. Mansfield (eds.) (2006) *International Organization and Global Governance: A Reader*, New York: Pearson

Kurki, Milja (2008) *Causation in International Relations: Reclaiming Causal Analysis*, Cambridge University Press

Larner, Wendy and William Walters (2002) 'The Political Rationality of the "New Regionalism": Toward a Genealogy of the Region', *Theory and Society* 31, 3: 391–432

(2004) 'Globalization as Governmentality', *Alternatives*, 29: 495–514

(2005) 'Global Governmentality: Governing International Spaces', in Wendy Larner and William Walters (eds.), *Global Governmentality: Governing International Spaces*, London and New York: Routledge: 1–20

Lash, Scott (2002) *Critique of Information*, Sage: London

Lash, Scott and John Urry (1987) *The End of Organized Capitalism*, Madison: University of Wisconsin Press

(1994) *Economies of Signs and Space*, London: Sage

Lazarus, Joel (2008) 'Participation in Poverty Reduction Strategy Papers: Reviewing the Past, Assessing the Present and Predicting the Future', *Third World Quarterly*, 29, 6: 1205–21

Leander, Anna and Rens van Munster (2007) 'Private Security Contractors in the Debate about Darfur: Reflecting and Reinforcing Neo-Liberal Governmentality', *International Relations*, 21, 2: 201–16

Lemke, Thomas (2003) 'Comment on Nancy Fraser: Rereading Foucault in the Shadow of Globalization', *Constellations*, 10, 2: 172–9

(2007) 'An Indigestible Meal? Foucault, Governmentality and State Theory', www.thomaslemkeweb.de/publikationen/IndigestibleMealfinal5.pdf (accessed 12 January 2012)

Lentzos, Filippa and Nikolas Rose (2009) 'Governing Insecurity: Contingency Planning, Protection, Resilience', *Economy and Society*, 38, 2: 230–54

Lin, Nan (2001) *Social Capital: A Theory of Social Structure and Action*, Cambridge University Press

Lipietz, Alain (1986) 'New Tendencies in the International Division of Labor', in Alan J. Scott and Michael Storper (eds.), *Production, Work, Territory*, London: Allen and Unwin: 16–39

(1987) *Mirages and Miracles: The Crises of Global Fordism*, London: Verso

Lipschutz, Ronnie (with James K. Rowe) (2005) *Regulation for the Rest of Us? Globalization, Governmentality, and Global Politics*, London and New York: Routledge

Luke, Timothy (1995) 'New World Order or Neo-World Orders: Power, Politics and Ideology in Informationalizing Glocalities', in Mike Featherstone, Scott Lash and Roland Robertson (eds.), *Global Modernities*, London: Sage: 91–107

(1996) 'Governmentality and Contragovernmentality: Rethinking Sovereignty and Territoriality after the Cold War', *Political Geography* 15, 6/7: 491–507

Lyakurwa, William (2005) 'Sub-Saharan African Countries' Development Strategies: The Role of the Bretton Woods Institutions', in Jan Joost Teunissen and Age Akkerman (eds.), *Helping the Poor: The IMF and Low-Income Countries*, The Hague: Fondad 132–80

Manners, Ian (2002) 'Normative Power Europe: A Contradiction in Terms?', *Journal of Common Market Studies*, 40, 2: 235–58

Marcussen, Henrik Secher (1996) 'NGOs, the State and Civil Society', *Review of African Political Economy*, 23, 69: 405–23

Marsden, Richard (1999) *The Nature of Capital: Marx after Foucault*, London and New York: Routledge

Martin, Matthew and Hannah Bargawi (2005) 'Protecting Africa against "Shocks"', in Jan Joost Teunissen and Age Akkerman (eds.), *Protecting the Poor: Global Financial Institutions and the Vulnerability of Low-Income Countries*, The Hague: Fondad: 42–71

Marx, Karl (1956) *The Poverty of Philosophy*, Moscow: Foreign Languages Publishing House

(1973) *Grundrisse*, Harmondsworth: Penguin Books

(1976) *Capital*, vol. I, Harmondsworth: Penguin Books

(1992) 'On the Jewish Question', in Marx, *Early Writings*, trans. Rodney Livingstone and Gregor Benson, Harmondsworth: Penguin Books: 211–42

Marx, Karl and Friedrich Engels (1976) *The German Ideology*, Collected Works 5, Moscow: Progress Publishers

Mathoho, Malachia (2008) 'An African Peer Review Mechanism: A Panacea for Africa's Governance Challenges?', Policy Briefing 29, Centre for Policy Studies, South Africa, www.cps.org.za/cps%20pdf/polbrief29.pdf (accessed 12 January 2012)

May, Christopher (2002) *The Information Society: A Skeptical View*, Cambridge: Polity

Mercer, Claire (2004) 'Engineering Civil Society: ICT in Tanzania', *Review of African Political Economy*, 99: 49–64

Merlingen, Michael (2003) 'Governmentality: Towards a Foucauldian Framework for the Study of NGOs', *Cooperation and Conflict*, 38, 4: 361–84

(with Rasa Ostrauskaitė) (2006) *European Union Peacebuilding and Policing*, London: Routledge

Mészáros, István (2000) *Beyond Capital: Toward a Theory of Transition*, London: Merlin

Milchman, Alan and Alan Rosenberg (2002) 'Marxism and Governmentality Studies: Toward a Critical Encounter', *Rethinking Marxism*, 14, 1: 132–42

Miller, Peter and Nikolas Rose (2008) *Governing the Present: Administering Economic, Social and Personal Life*, Cambridge: Polity

Nadesan, Majia Holmer (2008) *Governmentality, Biopower and Everyday Life*, Abingdon: Routledge

Neal, Andrew (2004) 'Cutting off the King's Head: Foucault's *Society Must Be Defended* and the Problem of Sovereignty', *Alternatives*, 29: 373–98

Nelson, Paul (2001) 'Information, Location and Legitimacy: The Changing Bases of Civil Society Involvement in International Economic Policy', in Michael Edwards and John Gaventa (eds.), *Global Citizen Action*, Boulder, CO: Lynne Rienner: 59–72

Neocleous, Mark (2008) *Critique of Security*, Edinburgh University Press
NEPAD (2001) *The New Partnership for Africa's Development*, Johannesburg: NEPAD
Neumann, Iver and Ole Jacob Sending (2010) *Governing the Global Polity: Practice, Mentality, Rationality*, Ann Arbor: University of Michigan Press
Norrlof, Carla (2010) *America's Global Advantage: US Hegemony and International Cooperation*, Cambridge University Press
OAU (2002) '38th Ordinary Session of the Assembly of Heads of State and Government of the OAU: African Peer Review Mechanism', 8 July 2002, Durban, South Africa, www.au2002.gov.za/docs/summit_council/aprm.htm (accessed 12 January 2012)
O'Brien, Robert, Anne Marie Goetz, Jan Aart Scholte and Marc Williams (2000) *Contesting Global Governance: Multilateral Economic Institutions and Global Social Movements*, Cambridge University Press
OECD (2001) *The New Economy: Beyond the Hype. Final Report on the OECD Growth Project*, Executive Summary, www.oecd.org/dataoecd/2/26/2380634.pdf (accessed 12 January 2012)
(2003) *Information and Communications Technologies. ICT and Economic Growth: Evidence from OECD Countries, Industries and Firms*, Paris: OECD
O'Malley, Pat (2002) 'Imagining Insurance. Risk, Thrift and Insurance in Britain', in Tom Baker and Jonathan Simon (eds.), *Embracing Risk*, University of Chicago Press: 97–115
(2004) *Risk, Uncertainty and Government*, London: Glasshouse Press
Onuf, Nicholas (1989) *World of Our Making: Rules and Rule in Social Theory and International Relations*, Columbia: University of South Carolina Press
(1998) 'Constructivism: A User's Manual', in Vendulka Kubálková, Nicholas Onuf and Paul Kowert (eds.), *International Relations in a Constructed World*, Armonk, NY: M. E. Sharpe: 58–78
Ostrom, Elinor (2000) 'Social Capital: A Fad or a Fundamental Concept?', in Partha Dasgupta and Ismail Serageldin (eds.), *Social Capital: A Multifaceted Perspective*, Washington, DC: World Bank: 172–214
Panitch, Leo and Martijn Konings (2008) 'The Politics of Imperial Finance', in Leo Panitch and Martijn Konings (eds.), *American Empire and the Political Economy of Global Finance*, Basingstoke: Palgrave Macmillan: 225–52
Pearce, Frank and Steve Tombs (1998) 'Foucault, Governmentality, Marxism', *Social and Legal Studies*, 7, 4: 567–75
Performance and Innovation Unit (2002) 'Social Capital: A Discussion Paper', London: Cabinet Office, www.cabinetoffice.gov.uk/media/

cabinetoffice/strategy/assets/socialcapital.pdf (accessed 12 January 2012)

Perry, Richard Warren and Bill Maurer (eds.) (2003) *Globalization under Construction: Governmentality, Law, and Identity*, Minneapolis: University of Minnesota Press

Phillips, Lynne and Suzan Ilcan (2007) 'Responsible Expertise: Governing the Uncertain Subjects of Biotechnology', *Critique of Anthropology*, 27, 1: 103–26

Pierre, Jon and B. Guy Peters (2000) *Governance, Politics and the State*, Basingstoke: Macmillan

Porpora, Douglas (1998) 'Four Concepts of Structure', in Margaret Archer, Roy Bhaskar, Andrew Collier, Tony Lawson and Alan Norrie (eds.), *Critical Realism: Essential Readings*, London: Routledge: 339–55

Portes, Alejandro and Patricia Landolt (2000) 'Social Capital: Promise and Pitfalls of Its Role in Development', *Journal of Latin American Studies*, 32: 529–47

Poulantzas, Nicos (1978) *State, Power, Socialism*, London: New Left Books

Power, Michael (1997) *The Audit Society*, Oxford University Press

(2007) *Organized Uncertainty*, Oxford University Press

Prodi, Romano (2000) 'Shaping the New Europe', speech to the European Parliament in Strasbourg, 15 February, http://europa.eu/rapid/pressReleasesAction.do?reference=SPEECH/00/41&format=HTML&aged=1&language=EN&guiLanguage=en (accessed 12 January 2012)

Puchala, Donald J. and Raymond F. Hopkins (1983) 'International Regimes: Lessons from Inductive Analysis', in Stephen D Krasner (ed.), *International Regimes*, Ithaca, NY: Cornell University Press: 61–91

Putnam, Robert (2000) *Bowling Alone: The Collapse and Revival of American Community*, New York: Simon & Schuster

Putnam, Robert D., Robert Leonardi and Raffaella Y. Nanetti (1993) *Making Democracy Work*, Princeton University Press

Rai, Shirin M. (2005) 'Networking across Borders: South Asian Research Networks (SARN) on Gender, Law and Governance', in Diane Stone and Simon Maxwell (eds.), *Global Knowledge Networks and International Development*, Abingdon: Routledge: 123–38

Reinicke, Wolfgang, Francis Deng, Jan Martin Witte and Thorsten Benner (2000) *Critical Choices: The UN, Networks and the Future of Global Governance*, Ottawa: International Development Research Centre, http://web.idrc.ca/en/ev-9312-201-1-DO_TOPIC.html#begining (accessed 12 January 2012)

Rhodes, R. A. W. (1997) *Understanding Governance: Policy Networks, Governance, Reflexivity and Accountability*, Buckingham: Open University Press

Riles, Annelise (2001) *The Network Inside Out*, Ann Arbor: University of Michigan Press

Roach, Steven C. (2010) *Critical Theory of International Politics: Complementarity, Justice and Governance*, Abingdon: Routledge

Roberts, David (2010) *Global Governance and Biopolitics: Regulating Human Security*, London and New York: Zed Books

Roberts, John Michael (2004) 'What's "Social" about "Social Capital"?', *British Journal of Politics and International Relations*, 6: 471–93

Roberts, John Michael and Fiona Devine (2003) 'Hollowing Out of the Welfare State and Social Capital', *Social Policy and Society*, 2, 4: 1–10

Robertson, Roland (1992) *Globalization: Social Theory and Global Culture*, London: Sage

Robinson, William (2004) *A Theory of Global Capitalism, Production, Class and State in a Transnational World*, Baltimore: Johns Hopkins University Press

Rodrigues, Maria João (2003) *European Policies for a Knowledge Economy*, Cheltenham: Edward Elgar

Rojas, Cristina (2005) 'Governing through the Social: Representations of Poverty and Global Governmentality', in Wendy Larner and William Walters (eds.), *Global Governmentality: Governing International Spaces*, London and New York: Routledge: 97–115

Room, Graham (2005) *The European Challenge: Innovation, Policy Learning and Social Cohesion in the New Knowledge Economy*, Bristol: Policy Press

Rose, Nikolas (1996) 'Governing "Advanced" Liberal Democracies', in Barry, Osborne and Rose (eds.), *Foucault and Political Reason*, London: UCL Press

(1999) *Powers of Freedom: Reframing Political Thought*, Cambridge University Press

Rosenau, James (2006) *The Study of World Politics*, vol. II, *Globalization and Governance*, London and New York: Routledge

Rosenau, James and Ernst-Otto Czempiel (eds.) (1992) *Governance without Government: Order and Change in World Politics*, Cambridge University Press

Rosenberg, Justin (2000) *The Follies of Globalisation Theory*, London: Verso

(2005) 'Globalisation Theory: A Post-Mortem', *International Politics*, 42, 1: 2–74

(2006) 'Why Is There No International Historical Sociology?', *European Journal of International Relations*, 12; 307–40

(2007a) 'The "Higher Bullshit": A Reply to the Globalization Theory Debate', *International Politics*, 44: 450–82

(2007b) 'And the Definition of Globalization Is …? A Reply to "In at the Death?" by Barrie Axford', *Globalizations*, 4, 3: 417–21

Ruckert, Arne (2009) 'A Decade of Poverty Reduction Strategies in Latin America: Empowering or Disciplining the Poor?', *Labour, Capital and Society*, 42, 1–2: 56–81

Ruggie, John Gerrard (1998) *Constructing the World Polity: Essays on International Institutionalization*, London and New York: Routledge

Rupert, Mark (2005) 'Class Powers and the Politics of Global Governance', in Michael Barnett and Raymond Duvall (eds.), *Power in Global Governance*, Cambridge University Press: 205–28

Sbragia, Alberta (2000) 'The European Union as Coxswain: Governance by Steering', in Jon Pierre (ed.), *Debating Governance: Authority, Steering and Democracy*, Oxford University Press: 219–40

Scholte, Jan Aart (2000) *Globalization: A Critical Introduction*, Basingstoke: Palgrave Macmillan

(2001) 'The IMF and Civil Society: An Interim Progress Report', in Michael Edwards and John Gaventa (eds.), *Global Citizen Action*, London: Earthscan: 87–103

(2002) 'Civil Society and Governance in the Global Polity', in Morten Ougaard and Richard Higgott (eds.), *Towards a Global Polity*, London and New York: Routledge: 145–65

(2005) 'Civil Society and Democratically Accountable Global Governance', in David Held and Mathias Koenig-Archibugi (eds.), *Global Governance and Public Accountability*, Oxford: Blackwell: 87–109

Senarclens, Pierre de and Ali Kazancil (2007) *Regulating Globalization: Critical Approaches to Global Governance*, Tokyo: United Nations University Press

Sending, Ole Jacob and Ivor B. Neumann (2006) 'Governance to Governmentality: Analyzing NGOs, States, and Power', *International Studies Quarterly*, 50: 651–72

(2007) '"The International" as Governmentality', *Millennium*, 35, 3: 677–701

Simai, Miha'ly (1994) *The Future of Global Governance: Managing Risk and Change in the International System*, Washington, DC: USIP

Sinclair, Timothy J. (1999) 'Synchronic Global Governance and the International Political Economy of the Commonplace', in Martin Hewson and Timothy J. Sinclair (eds.), *Approaches to Governance Theory*, Albany: State University of New York Press: 157–71

Soete, Luc (2006) 'Innovation, Technology and Productivity: Why Europe Lags behind the United States and Why Various European Economies Differ in Innovation and Productivity', in Manuel Castells and Gustavo

Cardoso (eds.), *The Network Society: From Knowledge to Policy*, Washington, DC: Johns Hopkins Center for Transatlantic Relations, 125–46

Sørensen, Eva (2006) 'Meta-governance: The Changing Role of Politicians in Processes of Democratic Governance', *American Review of Public Administration*, 36, 1: 98–114

Sørensen, Eva and Jacob Torfing (2007) 'Theoretical Approaches to Metagovernance', in Eva Sørensen and Jacob Torfing (eds.), *Theories of Democratic Network Governance*, Basingstoke: Palgrave Macmillan: 169–82

Stiglitz, Joseph (2001) 'An Agenda for Development for the Twenty-First Century', in Anthony Giddens (ed.), *The Global Third Way Debate*, Polity, Cambridge: 340–52

Stoker, Gerry (2002) 'Governance as Theory: Five Propositions', *International Social Science Journal*, 50, 155: 17–28

Stone, Diane (2005) 'Knowledge Networks and Global Policy', in Diane Stone and Simon Maxwell (eds.), *Global Knowledge Networks and International Development*, Abingdon: Routledge: 89–105

Strange, Susan (1983) '*Cave! Hic Dragones*: Critique of Regime Analysis', in Stephen D. Krasner (ed.), *International Regimes*, Ithaca, NY: Cornell University Press: 337–54

Sum, Ngai-Ling (2004) 'From "Integral State" to "Integral World Economic Order": Towards a Neo-Gramscian Cultural International Political Economy', Cultural Political Economy Working Paper 7, Lancaster: Institute for Advanced Studies in Social and Management Sciences, University of Lancaster

Telò, Mario (2002) 'Governance and Government in the European Union: The Open Method of Coordination', in Maria João Rodrigues (ed.), *The New Knowledge Economy in Europe: A Strategy for International Competitiveness and Social Cohesion*, Cheltenham: Edward Elgar: 242–71

Teschke, Benno and Christian Heine (2002) 'The Dialectic of Globalisation', in Mark Rupert and Hazel Smith (eds.), *Historical Materialism and Globalization*, London and New York: Routledge: 165–87

Thompson, Graham (2003) *Between Hierarchies and Markets: The Logic and Limits of Network Forms of Organization*, Oxford University Press

Tickell, Adam and Jamie Peck (2003) 'Making Global Rules: Globalisation or Neoliberalisation', in Jamie Peck and Henry Wai-chung Yeung (eds.), *Remaking the Global Economy*, London: Sage: 163–82

Tömmel, Ingeborg (1998) 'Transformation of Governance: The European Commission's Strategy for Creating a "Europe of the Regions"', *Regional and Federal Studies*, 8, 2: 52–80

Triantafillou, Peter (2004) 'Addressing Network Governance through the Concepts of Governmentality and Normalization', *Administrative Theory and Praxis*, 26, 4: 489–508

Tussie, Diana and Maria Fernanda Tuozzo (2001) 'Opportunities and Constraints for Civil Society Participation in Multilateral Lending Operations: Lessons from Latin America', in Michael Edwards and John Gaventa (eds.), *Global Citizen Action*, London: Earthscan: 105–17

United Nations (2005) *In Larger Freedom: Towards Development, Security and Human Rights for All*, New York: United Nations

(2006) *World Economic and Social Survey 2006: Diverging Growth and Development*, New York: United Nations

UNDP (2004) *Reducing Disaster Risk: A Challenge for Development*, New York: UNDP

(2005) *Innovation in Development: A Practical Plan*, New York: UNDP

(2008) *Roots of Resilience: Growing the Wealth of the Poor*, World Resources 2008, Washington, DC: World Resources Institute

Urry, John (2003) *Global Complexity*, Cambridge: Polity

Van der Pijl, Kees (1998) *Transnational Classes and International Relations*, London and New York: Routledge.

Van Dijk, Jan (1999) *The Network Society: Social Aspects of New Media*, London: Sage

Vrasti, Wanda (2011) 'Universal but Not "Truly Global": Governmentality, Economic Liberalism and the International', *Review of International Studies*, DOI:10.1017/S0260210511000568 (FirstView)

Wade, Robert (2004) 'The World Bank and the Environment', in Martin Bøas and Desmond McNeil (eds.), *Global Institutions and Development: Framing the World*, London and New York: Routledge: 72–94

Walker, Rob (2006) 'Lines of Insecurity: International, Imperial, Exceptional', *Security Dialogue*, 37, 1: 65–82

Walters, William (2002) 'Social Capital and Political Sociology: Re-imagining Politics?', *Sociology*, 36: 377–97

(2005) 'Political Rationality of European Integration', in Wendy Larner and William Walters (eds.), *Global Governmentality: Governing International Spaces*, London and New York: Routledge: 155–73

Walters, William and Jens Henrik Haahr (2005) *Governing Europe: Discourse, Governmentality and European Integration*, London and New York: Routledge

Waltz, Kenneth (1979) *Theory of International Politics*, New York: McGraw-Hill

Waters, Malcolm (2001) *Globalization*, London: Routledge

Wendt, Alexander (1987) 'The Agent-Structure Problem in International Relations Theory', *International Organization*, 41: 335–70

(1999) *Social Theory of International Politics*, Cambridge University Press

(2004) 'The State as Person in International Theory', *Review of International Studies*, 30, 2: 269–80

Whitman, Jim (2005) *The Limits of Global Governance*, Abingdon: Routledge

Wight, Colin (2004) 'State Agency: Social Action without Human Activity?', *Review of International Studies*, 30, 2: 289–16

Wilhelm, Vera and Philipp Krause (eds.) (2008) *Minding the Gaps: Integrating Poverty Reduction Strategies and Budgets for Domestic Accountability*, Washington, DC: The International Bank for Reconstruction and Development / World Bank

Wood, Ellen Meiksins (1997) 'Modernity, Postmodernity or Capitalism?', *Review of International Political Economy*, 4, 3: 539–56

(2002) 'Global Capital, National States', in Mark Rupert and Hazel Smith (eds.), *Historical Materialism and Globalization*, London: Routledge: 17–39

World Bank (1994) *Adjustment in Africa: Reforms, Results and the Road Ahead*, World Bank Policy Research Report, New York: Oxford University Press

(1997) *World Development Report: The State in a Changing World*, New York: Oxford University Press

(1999) *World Development Report: Entering the 21st Century*, New York: Oxford University Press

(2000) *Consultations with Civil Society: General Guidelines for World Bank Staff*, Washington, DC: World Bank

(2001) *World Development Report: Attacking Poverty*, New York: Oxford University Press

(2002) *World Bank Development Report 2002: Building Institutions for Markets*, Oxford University Press and the World Bank

(2005a) *World Development Report 2006: Equity and Development*, Oxford University Press and the World Bank

(2005b) *Enabling Country Capacity to Achieve Results*, vol. I, *Overview 2005 CDF Progress Report*, Washington, DC: World Bank

(2006) *Civil Society Engagement: Review of Fiscal Years 2005 and 2006*, Washington, DC: World Bank

(2007) *Results-Based National Development Strategies: Assessments and Challenges Ahead*, Washington, DC: World Bank

Young, Oran (1986) 'International Regimes: Toward a New Theory of Institutions', *World Politics*, 39, 1: 104–22

Zanotti, Laura (2005) 'Governmentalizing the Post-Cold War International Regime: The UN Debate on Democratization and Good Governance', *Alternatives*, 30: 461–87

Index

Cambridge Studies in International Relations

109 Rodney Bruce Hall
Central banking as global governance
Constructing financial credibility

108 Milja Kurki
Causation in international relations
Reclaiming causal analysis

107 Richard M. Price
Moral limit and possibility in world politics

106 Emma Haddad
The refugee in international society
Between sovereigns

105 Ken Booth
Theory of world security

104 Benjamin Miller
States, nations and the great powers
The sources of regional war and peace

103 Beate Jahn (ed.)
Classical theory in international relations

102 Andrew Linklater and Hidemi Suganami
The English School of international relations
A contemporary reassessment

101 Colin Wight
Agents, structures and international relations
Politics as ontology

100 Michael C. Williams
The realist tradition and the limits of international relations

99 Ivan Arreguín-Toft
How the weak win wars
A theory of asymmetric conflict

98 Michael Barnett and Raymond Duvall
Power in global governance

97 Yale H. Ferguson and Richard W. Mansbach
Remapping global politics
History's revenge and future shock

96 Christian Reus-Smit
The politics of international law

95 Barry Buzan
From international to world society?
English School theory and the social structure of globalisation

94 K. J. Holsti
Taming the sovereigns
Institutional change in international politics

93 Bruce Cronin
Institutions for the common good
International protection regimes in international security

92 Paul Keal
European conquest and the rights of indigenous peoples
The moral backwardness of international society

91 Barry Buzan and Ole Wæver
Regions and powers
The structure of international security

90 A. Claire Cutler
Private power and global authority
Transnational merchant law in the global political economy

89 Patrick M. Morgan
Deterrence now

88 Susan Sell
Private power, public law
The globalization of intellectual property rights

87 Nina Tannenwald
The nuclear taboo
The United States and the non-use of nuclear weapons since 1945

86 Linda Weiss
States in the global economy
Bringing domestic institutions back in

85 Rodney Bruce Hall and Thomas J. Biersteker (eds.)
The emergence of private authority in global governance

84 Heather Rae
State identities and the homogenisation of peoples

83 Maja Zehfuss
Constructivism in international relations
The politics of reality

82 Paul K. Ruth and Todd Allee
The democratic peace and territorial conflict in the twentieth century

81 Neta C. Crawford
Argument and change in world politics
Ethics, decolonization and humanitarian intervention

80 Douglas Lemke
Regions of war and peace

79 Richard Shapcott
Justice, community and dialogue in international relations

78 Phil Steinberg
The social construction of the ocean

77 Christine Sylvester
Feminist international relations
An unfinished journey

76 Kenneth A. Schultz
Democracy and coercive diplomacy

75 David Houghton
US foreign policy and the Iran hostage crisis

74 Cecilia Albin
Justice and fairness in international negotiation

73 Martin Shaw
Theory of the global state
Globality as an unfinished revolution

72 Frank C. Zagare and D. Marc Kilgour
Perfect deterrence

71 Robert O'Brien, Anne Marie Goetz, Jan Aart Scholte and Marc Williams
Contesting global governance
Multilateral economic institutions and global social movements

70 Roland Bleiker
Popular dissent, human agency and global politics

69 Bill McSweeney
Security, identity and interests
A sociology of international relations

68 Molly Cochran
Normative theory in international relations
A pragmatic approach

67 Alexander Wendt
Social theory of international politics

66 Thomas Risse, Stephen C. Ropp and Kathryn Sikkink (eds.)
The power of human rights
International norms and domestic change

65 Daniel W. Drezner
The sanctions paradox
Economic statecraft and international relations

64 Viva Ona Bartkus
The dynamic of secession

63 John A. Vasquez
The power of power politics
From classical realism to neotraditionalism

62 Emanuel Adler and Michael Barnett (eds.)
Security communities

61 Charles Jones
E. H. Carr and international relations
A duty to lie

60 Jeffrey W. Knopf
Domestic society and international cooperation
The impact of protest on US arms control policy

59 Nicholas Greenwood Onuf
The republican legacy in international thought

58 Daniel S. Geller and J. David Singer
Nations at war
A scientific study of international conflict

57 Randall D. Germain
The international organization of credit
States and global finance in the world economy

56 N. Piers Ludlow
Dealing with Britain
The Six and the first UK application to the EEC

55 Andreas Hasenclever, Peter Mayer and Volker Rittberger
Theories of international regimes

54 Miranda A. Schreurs and Elizabeth C. Economy (eds.)
The internationalization of environmental protection

53 James N. Rosenau
Along the domestic-foreign frontier
Exploring governance in a turbulent world

52 John M. Hobson
The wealth of states
A comparative sociology of international economic and political change

51 Kalevi J. Holsti
The state, war, and the state of war

50 Christopher Clapham
Africa and the international system
The politics of state survival

49 Susan Strange
The retreat of the state
The diffusion of power in the world economy

48 William I. Robinson
Promoting polyarchy
Globalization, US intervention, and hegemony

47 Roger Spegele
Political realism in international theory

46 Thomas J. Biersteker and Cynthia Weber (eds.)
State sovereignty as social construct

45 Mervyn Frost
Ethics in international relations
A constitutive theory

44 Mark W. Zacher with Brent A. Sutton
Governing global networks
International regimes for transportation and communications

43 Mark Neufeld
The restructuring of international relations theory

42 Thomas Risse-Kappen (ed.)
Bringing transnational relations back in
Non-state actors, domestic structures and international institutions

41 Hayward R. Alker
Rediscoveries and reformulations
Humanistic methodologies for international studies

40 Robert W. Cox with Timothy J. Sinclair
Approaches to world order

39 Jens Bartelson
A genealogy of sovereignty

38 Mark Rupert
Producing hegemony
The politics of mass production and American global power

37 Cynthia Weber
Simulating sovereignty
Intervention, the state and symbolic exchange

36 Gary Goertz
Contexts of international politics

35 James L. Richardson
Crisis diplomacy
The Great Powers since the mid-nineteenth century

34 Bradley S. Klein
Strategic studies and world order
The global politics of deterrence

33 T. V. Paul
Asymmetric conflicts: war initiation by weaker powers

32 Christine Sylvester
Feminist theory and international relations in a postmodern era

31 Peter J. Schraeder
US foreign policy toward Africa
Incrementalism, crisis and change

30 Graham Spinardi
From Polaris to Trident: the development of US Fleet Ballistic Missile technology

29 David A. Welch
Justice and the genesis of war

28 Russell J. Leng
Interstate crisis behavior, 1816–1980: realism versus reciprocity

27 John A. Vasquez
The war puzzle

26 Stephen Gill (ed.)
Gramsci, historical materialism and international relations

25 Mike Bowker and Robin Brown (eds.)
From cold war to collapse: theory and world politics in the 1980s

24 R. B. J. Walker
Inside/outside: international relations as political theory

23 Edward Reiss
The strategic defense initiative

22 Keith Krause
Arms and the state: patterns of military production and trade

21 Roger Buckley
US-Japan alliance diplomacy 1945–1990

20 James N. Rosenau and Ernst-Otto Czempiel (eds.)
Governance without government: order and change in world politics

19 Michael Nicholson
Rationality and the analysis of international conflict

18 John Stopford and Susan Strange
Rival states, rival firms
Competition for world market shares

17 Terry Nardin and David R. Mapel (eds.)
Traditions of international ethics

16 Charles F. Doran
Systems in crisis
New imperatives of high politics at century's end

15 Deon Geldenhuys
Isolated states: a comparative analysis

14 Kalevi J. Holsti
Peace and war: armed conflicts and international order 1648–1989

13 Saki Dockrill
Britain's policy for West German rearmament 1950–1955

12 Robert H. Jackson
Quasi-states: sovereignty, international relations and the third world

11 James Barber and John Barratt
South Africa's foreign policy
The search for status and security 1945–1988

10 James Mayall
Nationalism and international society

9 William Bloom
Personal identity, national identity and international relations

8 Zeev Maoz
National choices and international processes

7 Ian Clark
The hierarchy of states
Reform and resistance in the international order

6 Hidemi Suganami
The domestic analogy and world order proposals

5 Stephen Gill
American hegemony and the Trilateral Commission

4 Michael C. Pugh
The ANZUS crisis, nuclear visiting and deterrence

3 Michael Nicholson
Formal theories in international relations

2 Friedrich V. Kratochwil
Rules, norms, and decisions
On the conditions of practical and legal reasoning in international relations and domestic affairs

1 Myles L. C. Robertson
Soviet policy towards Japan
An analysis of trends in the 1970s and 1980s

Made in the USA
Las Vegas, NV
08 February 2021

17355189R00177